The Blantyre Project

A Journey in time

Volume 4

By Paul D Veverka

Cover Watercolour "*Auchentibber Inn, Sydes Brae, Blantyre*" by Mr Rob Thorpe

DEDICATION

The fourth Volume in this series of books is dedicated to my history enthusiast friends and colleagues, for their passion of all things relating to history, for their knowledge and interest in local history and for keeping me motivated, inspired, (correct) and busy. In no particular order, this is a noted dedication to my esteemed contemporaries, namely Gordon Cook, Alex Rochead, Robert Stewart, Chris Ladds, Jim Brown and Garry Lee.

Paul Veverka, November 2018

CONTENTS

ACKNOWLEDGEMENTS

As a future historical reference aid, it is important that 'The Blantyre Project' is accurate and clearly separates actual or fabled events. As well as my own research, I called upon permissions and actively sought or was offered assistance. Many people showed me a great deal of kindness, patience and involvement. In recognition of this, and in no particular order, it is necessary to say a hearty thanks to the following people and businesses who have been instrumental in helping me create the fourth exciting volume in this series of books –

The staff at Blantyre library, Glasgow Road (for their interest and permitting presentations)
The staff at Hamilton Reference library (for putting up with me and supporting my books)
The staff at The Haven (Part of the proceeds of this book are going to The Haven charity)
Mr Alex Bowie (long lost relative – for providing several high resolution photos of Blantyre)
Mr Jim Brown (Photographer – for use of some excellent photographs and kindly walking me through historical sites and woodland in Blantyre. Please check out his photos on Flickr Website)
Mr Jim Cochrane (for his knowledge and photos relating to Calderside and Auchentibber history)
Mr Gordon Cook (fellow history enthusiast for sharing his inspirational Blantyre research & photos.)
Mr Jack Daniels (for providing detail about Joanna Baillie, poetress)
Miss Alice Fookes (for her amazing Calderglen Collection so kindly gifted to me)
Mr Neil Gordon (dec. The late Community Historian – for the invaluable archives and inspiration)
Mrs Leona Greenan (Reporter – for promoting The Blantyre Project story in local newspapers)
The Hamilton Advertiser (Scottish & Universal Newspaper Group)
The National Library of Scotland (for permitting & assisting me with archiving Blantyre's history)
Mrs Marion Robertson (for access to copies of the Blantyre Gazette)
Mr Alex Rochead (for his interest, ancestry, census and valuation roll information and kindly providing several captivating photos)
Mrs Margaret Stewart (for providing a rare photo of Blantyre Ambulance at Milheugh)
Mrs Norma Marr (for her insight and photos of Calderside Row)
Mr Robert Stewart – (for sharing his photos from various decades and for all his valuable local knowledge, especially in relation to cemetery, interment and council matters)
Mr Rob Thorpe (for a further professional and excellent water-colour cover painting. The originals from all 4 books are now framed in my hall with further paintings commissioned in readiness for future!)
Mr Steve Timoney & Alison Reid Timoney
Mr Sandy Wilkie (for his photo of his father horse and comments about Bardykes)
Mrs Helen Williams (for her comments on her mining family heritage)
Mr George Young (for his photo of Blantyre Muir Turbines)
To the "Friends of the Calder" & "Blantyre Heritage" groups.

Also to all the countless other individuals who have emailed me on a daily basis throughout the writing of this book between 2015 and 2018 with stories and photos taking an interest. Finally, a thanks to the wonderful 13,456 people who currently freely subscribe to The Blantyre Project Facebook page whose lively discussion and comments have enabled much of this history to be pieced together. This deluge of social media comments on each article was essential in completing many of the stories in this book and provides an added layer of interesting social history and community related detail, which no newspaper could ever hope to produce.

INTRODUCTION

Has it really been three full years since I started this book? Whilst that may be 'the norm' for most people producing a publication, it is somewhat protracted for me and I reflect back upon several 'distractions' to my writing in recent years. Having completed working on the new Queensferry Crossing Bridge in 2016, my construction job then took me to Aberdeen to build the new bypass road and inevitably, I was again living away from home during Mondays to Fridays with time on my hands in the evenings. To those who know me, it will come as no surprise that I continued investigating Blantyre's history each evening, with all my files securely with me on a mobile keying hard-drive. So it was, when my working day was done, I would boot up my laptop, plug in my research and write further historical articles, updating my Blantyre Project website each evening. So how come this book, with articles already researched took so long? As I update this introduction now in November 2018, I have to admit, quite simply, day-to-day life got in the way of writing, something I'm rather pleased it did, for it gave me a good work-life balance. Three years on, I'm now staring at the drafted manuscript, proud as punch and looking forward to the excitement of pressing, "publish".

Here's my number one rule when writing any book. Always immerse yourself to make it the best it can possibly be. For this task, I sorted through all my unpublished research to pick the "*best of the best*" stories and photos, for inclusion in this Volume 4, which in my opinion is the most exciting and fascinating book in this established series. Before I tell you more about the book, let me do the right thing and introduce myself, for it is wholly my intention that this book should be a standalone and not rely in any way upon reading previous Volumes 1 to 3 first. You will be able to pick up this book, understand it and enjoy it without having to refer to anything in other volumes.

Making Time

My name is Paul Veverka, a forty-seven year old Commercial Manager in the UK construction industry. I live in High Blantyre, just off Main Street, married to a Professional Photographer with a young daughter at nursery school. Born in 1971, I was brought up in Stonefield Crescent and with siblings nearby, feel that Blantyre is very much my foundation and home. Home certainly is where the heart is. Speaking of heart, beating strong is my enthusiasm for a particular project, a small online and offline newspaper called "*Blantyre Telegraph*". This non-profit making venture is entirely charity based with all proceeds going to monthly good causes within Blantyre. In addition, I host a history website called "*The Blantyre Project*" which is now also the name of my small publishing company, and indeed is the subject of this book. My goal is nothing less than being able to archive and protect as much diverse history about Blantyre as possible. It's all there in a free, growing daily archive online, currently representing the largest, factual, single source of Blantyre historical data on the web with over 5,000 articles and 12,000 old Blantyre photos and now also in this growing series of books. I'm also Secretary of Blantyre Community Committee and very proud of the charitable work that our little group does to ensure Blantyre has an annual Summer Gala and a memorable Christmas Lights Switch on event for all to enjoy.

I've said this before. Fitting many external community pursuits into a busy life can often be difficult, but I like to think I have good time management skills and know when it's time to put the computer away and ensure quality, family time, especially spending time with my wife and daughter. There is nothing more important than being with family. After all, that's what life is about.

Setting Goals

"The Blantyre Project, A Journey in Time Volume 4" is the fourth amazing book in this popular series. It features 228 pages, 84,200 words and 208 new illustrations and is one of the largest books I've ever written about Blantyre. This book has been a true labour of love, the articles deeply researched and wherever possible, I have added to any provided detail, with further comments and conclusions. Readers will be pleased to see that the narrative is fresh and laid out in a fun and informative manner and that importantly all the illustrations and photos are entirely new, unseen from any of my previous publications. Photographs are of a high quality and in a sufficiently high resolution to compliment the quality of this publication in general. Sources of each story have been double-checked and where required, permissions sought. It's my intention, as always that this book can be picked up by children and adults alike, understood and enjoyed. It is intended both as an educational tool and for its entertainment value.

New in this book

In this latest book, I've adjusted the font size making it slightly smaller to enable more stories, more photos and content to be included, yet maintain a respectable number of pages, importantly being able to hold the affordable price. This was especially important to me, and I trust will be well received. In short, you're getting more for your money! The size, cover fonts and format are deliberately similar in style, as this book is after all, part of a series, which I hope is becoming recognisable. As with each of my "Journey in Time" books, the beautiful, brand new hand painting on the cover was commissioned especially.

Chapters are set out exploring each individual hamlet or area in Blantyre and for the first time are expanded upon, with brand new sections for more familiar areas. The penultimate chapter, as with other volumes, includes the popular and well-received *"Anecdotes"* section, a collection of witty, amusing stories and comments from people throughout the world with Blantyre connections and memories. I guarantee you'll laugh out loud. I've also been fortunate enough to have received many brand new previously unseen old photos released for publication, making this book very pictorial. We all love a picture or two!

Articles are structured in a simple, fun and informative manner and always short enough, so that if a story is of lesser interest, the next entirely different story starts very soon after. A deliberate format straying away from chronological order and a format proven to feed the reader's desire, for *"what's coming next?"*

More apparent than simply relating newspaper articles, is the quantum leap of proper research, finding out what happened to people and buildings and piecing them together in an exclusive and detailed manner. The book therefore sees a further move towards research of my own, calling upon ancestry databases, census, valuation rolls, newspaper archives and verbal recollections, gathered wherever I've had time to meet people in and around Blantyre. However, I've still included many news articles, to give a real interesting mix of recorded historical stories and newly recorded research. On occasion, where myths or incorrect information circulates in the public domain, on other websites or in books by others, I've been bold enough to correct that, now having confidence to do so. Great care is taken on each article, for history books have a habit of relying upon and repeating previously published historical information, time and time again. One person's simple mistake or opinion has a habit of lasting generations, another reason I often start from scratch on important topics.

Let's not forget the kind assistance given to me on several articles. Not just the occasional correction or nudge in a particular direction, but proper *"on tap"* local knowledge available to me each day, an email away from two or three particular individuals (who are thanked graciously in the acknowledgements section).

Wishing also to ensure content is exclusive to Blantyre Project, I found that I sometimes needed to use contemporary photos. Whilst people offered modern photos of their own, I made the decision to incorporate many of my own current, modern photographs. Of course, where photos taken by others have been used, full permission was sought first and credit has been noted in each context. Some photos may not seem remarkable just now, but Blantyre is going through rapid development (just look at Clydeview Shopping Centre as an example) and as such today's photos will certainly be interesting tomorrow and in future generations.

I'm by no means a perfectionist, but every effort has been made to ensure the information in this book is factual and correct. I therefore extend an open invitation for anybody to contact me privately if anything is believed to the contrary. However, please remember, Construction managers are never known to use perfect grammar!

The Present & The Future

It would be amiss of me not to mention what's happening now and in future with Blantyre Project, taking this opportunity here at time of writing in November 2018. I continue to publish multiple daily updates to The Blantyre Project website, for there is not one day goes by, when somebody has not emailed a request, or shared a photo, or wants to tell me a story. I mean that sincerely. Even the smallest Blantyre detail, is recorded and archived there.

There is much still to write about. To that end, my brain has been bursting with new enthusiasm and passion to get those words down in as many different formats as possible. Whilst work has been slow on this particular book, I haven't been idle in 2015 to 2018 and you may have noticed smaller books like *"Annals of Blantyre"*, *"Blantyre Statistics"*, *"Blantyre Images"* and of course my epic *"Glasgow Road South – The Real Story"*, the single largest book about Blantyre ever written.

The fact that Blantyre Project books have been shipped to 17 difference countries worldwide, is perhaps testament to the popularity and interest of Blantyre's history, not just from its residents, but from ex pats all over the world. I'm surprised, gracious and extremely proud of that, as the proceeds of these books will continue to be donated to local charities, as has always been the case.

Blantyre is changing rapidly. Development and arrival of major businesses like Crossbasket Castle, the rebuilt Carrigans and housing estates like Greenhall Village springing up makes it as important as ever that our proud heritage is shared if Blantyre is to grow and prosper. With the Boundary Commission also chopping and changing Blantyre Ward 15 boundaries, we as a town are in danger of losing some of our Heritage to Hamilton wards. A frightening thought!

Before we get started, I would add, if YOU would like your Blantyre photos of family and friends, or your stories archived in a permanent collection, to be made available not just to Blantyre's Library, but to the National Library of Scotland, please get in contact with me. For now though, it is with my utmost pleasure and sincere hope for your enjoyment, I present to you *"The Blantyre Project – A Journey in Time – Volume 4"*

CHAPTER 1
HIGH BLANTYRE

The area to the south and elevated above much of the rest of Blantyre in South Lanarkshire, Scotland is called High Blantyre. It spans from Barnhill through Hunthill to the old area of Kirkton and eastwards towards Auchinraith. A prominent street is Main Street, one of the more notable 'retail areas' in the town. High Blantyre had several coal mining pits, with Dixons being the Coalmasters of that particular area. The above photo shows some of the blacksmiths employed by Dixons standing at one of High Blantyre's collieries, the last of which closed in the late 1950's.

BEADLE OF BLANTYRE

Figure 1 The Beadle

At a time before 1856 and the circulation of the then newly formed Hamilton Advertiser newspaper, the Beadle of Blantyre was known to let people know what was going on by *"crying the news"* at the Church door on Sundays. The Church at the time was at Kirkton within the current cemetery and kirk-yard. The Beadle would stand at the gates and not only reiterate the good impressions produced in the minister's sermon, but also add in the news of the week, some of which certainly proved very strange indeed. The Annals of Blantyre 1885 book commented some of these news readings, shouted at the top of his voice in the early 1800's, included haystacks or fields of beans to be sold. On other occasions it was the hindquarter of a cow to be disposed of, or what Lord Blantyre's factor was up to, to ensure the gathering of rents. One such strange news event was cried out exactly to the people as: *"This is to give notice that there was found on the Sides (Sydes Brae) an empty sack, with a cheese at the bottom of it. Whoever has lost the same, by applying to me will get it back!"*

LINT BUTTS

Lint Butts was a small, detached tenement, which formerly stood on the south side of Main Street, directly across from Cemetery Road. With address 267 Main Street, the property had a slate roof and was made of stone, with a large rectangular yard at the back. Bill Graham who was brought up in Blantyre, added, *"Hi my grandfather owned a building in Main Street, High Blantyre. It was called Lintbutts. I was brought up there in the late 50's and early 1960's. It was opposite the old Post Office and Ian Hobson's butchers."*

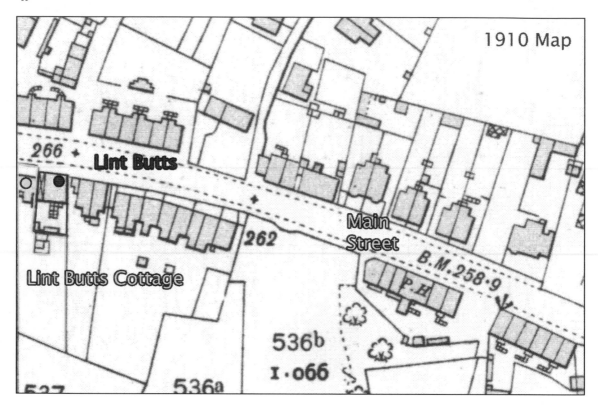

Figure 2 Lint Butts, formerly on Main Street, High Blantyre as per this 1910 map

What Bill remembers though would have only been part of the building. Lint Butts was originally built prior to 1859, named initially as 'Lint Butts Cottage', in a more westerly position to what Bill remembers. There is a good reason for that, as will be explained below. It was directly across the road from Cemetery Road. In 1891, it was divided into two shops. Seventy three year old Mr Thomas Peden ran a tailors business there and also that year, 59-year old William Thomson, a joiner and glazier, lived there with his wife Margaret and two of their children.

The two businesses had an extensive yard at the back. William Thomson died on 4th November 1898 after a short illness. He had been a well-known beekeeper in the area, keeping bees in hives at the rear of Lint Butts. Mr Thomson had spent his whole life with the hobby of bee keeping and according to his obituary in the Glasgow Herald, had even brought out some inventions in relation to the efficient preparation of making honey. He enjoyed great popularity in that respect. His half of the property passed to Matthew Kae, whom in 1901 was 62 years old and running a hardware business from the store. In the other half of the property by 1901, Mr Peden had passed away and the new owners were John McLachlan and his family, who were coal miners. The property was to hugely be extended when land adjacent to it was sold in 1905. The extended property was initially immediately adjacent to the property described above on its westward side, hence why a close was needed to access the yard at the back. The extended property also called Lint Butts, owned by the Graham family had a small yard and the back.

During WW1, on 19th April 1915, a lady named Morrison died there leaving behind two daughters Meg and Mary. In 1918 this family were on the move and an advert appeared in the paper selling their poultry, hens, wire cages and fences in the back yard. This, I believe paved the way for the Graham family around the time Hugh Graham and his wife Effie bought the property.

By 1936, the adjacent 'Lint Butts Cottage' older property had been demolished leaving the close redundant and only the more modern extended Lint Butts part of the building standing, i.e. the part that Bill remembers and used only ever as residential homes. Mr Graham lived upstairs and let out the homes below. 20th Century maps would suggest that Lint Butts back yard was initially very small, but after the subsequent demolition of the next-door property, the whole yard was owned and used by the Grahams. The double close on the right hand eastward side, which at one time was wide enough to let a car through, became redundant. However, during World War 2, it was partly (half) bricked up and a wall was built at the back, possibly of use as a sort of air raid shelter.

The late Blantyre historian, Neil Gordon's book of 2004, suggested that the Apothecary Hall and the chemist was located in this property, but I think that was a slight error. The Chemist, known as 'Patersons' in the 1960's was actually located in a small semi-detached building to the *east* of Lint Butts, i.e. adjacent to it. That small building was divided between the Chemist and McMillan's Haulage. Mr McMillan lived at that address and had a yard at the back.

After Lint Butts was demolished in the 1970's, the property was remembered by a new street in honour of the name near Burnbrae Road. The new 'Lint Butts' is now several modern homes in the middle of Blantyre.

JOHNSTONE'S LAUN

Mr William Johnstone was a baker, during the 1850's and 1860's at High Blantyre. He is recorded as often providing the meals for the local curlers or the ploughing societies and had premises on the north side of High Blantyre's Main Street. This consisted of a double tenement near Kirkton, and included a bake-house, the Post Office, two shops (one of which was to become a public house) and several houses. These were known as 'Johnstone's Laun' or Land.

These buildings were once located to the immediate west of the site of the current Masonic Hall and old Apollo Bar location on Main Street, although Mr Johnstone's buildings were well before the masonic halls. William died in 1861. It is unknown who took over the property upon William's death, but it is known that Mr James B Struthers took over the buildings in 1873. Mr Struthers had a relative named James Struthers who was a shoemaker and lived nearby. James B Struthers set about building the concert hall and stabling on vacant land advertising it as ready for functions by 1879. This is the building we now know today as the Masonic Halls and derelict Apollo Bar which now has planning to be turned into shops). There is no trace left of Mr Johnstone's former buildings on Main Street. The map on the next page shows Johnstone's Laun in 1859.

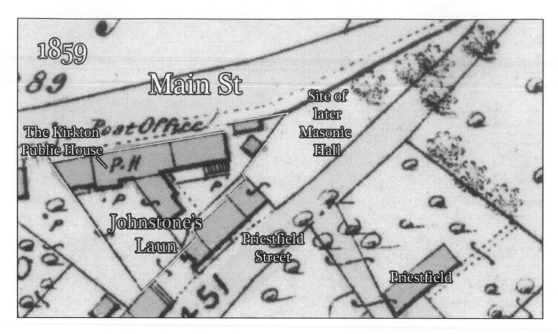

Figure 3 Johnstone's Laun, a long forgotten part of Main Street

CALDERVIEW & CAPTAIN BARR

"Calderview", was a building, which once stood on Hunthill Road at the corner of Stonefield Crescent. It had the address of 55, 56, 58, 60 and 62 Hunthill Road. There are no entries for Calderview on the 1905 Valuation roll, but the building is on the 1898 map, indicating that it may have been called a different name prior to 1905. On the 1898 map, the building is shown as 2 large semi-detached properties with 2 homes upstairs, 2 downstairs, but by 1910, the homes are shown as 4 downstairs and 4 upstairs, but with the same footprint, confirming like many buildings in Blantyre, they were subdivided to accommodate more people to maximise rents. It was aptly named looking across to the Calder fields, long before any nearby housing estates were built.

Calderview sat on the western side of Hunthill Road. It was there well before Stonefield Crescent was built and was immediately next to the busy railway junctions at Hunthill with a small signal box overlooking the houses. The likely constructors of this stone tenement building were the Aitkenhead builders of High Blantyre in the 1890's, for prior to WW1; several members of their family lived there. Alexander Aitkenhead owned a house and shop there during 1915 but it was let out to spirit dealer Patrick Conway at a rent of £16 per year. On 30th November 1915, Joan Paterson, the 2nd daughter of Paton Aitkenhead passed away at Calderview. A stable was also noted at the end of the building. The building was clearly home to several families, so I decided to look into that a little more.

In 1915, the occupiers were Patrick Conway, James Brownlie (a roadsman), Hugh Daly (a miner), Archibald Hamilton (a miner), James Brownlie Junior (who would go on to be the famous footballer), widows Jane Button and Mary Douglas, Jessie Aitkenhead and Donald McLean.

Figure 4 Pictured looking south on Hunthill Road around 1915

During the 1920's, a Captain Barr lived in one of the homes in this small tenement. The Captain was at the time, a county councillor for the district and well known within the local area. He served on duty during the First World War and became a prominent citizen in local affairs. He was a member of the High Blantyre Ratepayers Association and also stood for election on the Parish County Council. By 1929, he had become established as a notable architect.

It is thought Calderview was demolished in the 1960's, many tenants rehoused in sprawling new modern housing estates of that decade. In the 1970's a new, detached large home was built on the site, causing a stir in Blantyre at the time when rumours circulated that Sydney Devine was building it (which proved untrue). It is said that either Felix McLaughlin or his son Brian built it. At that time they had sold their undertakers business and had moved into haulage.

BELLSFIELD FARM MILK DELIVERIES

Dating from around the 1910's, this next previously unseen photo shows Blantyre milk deliveries taking place. Pictured are Alexander Craig and two employee milkmaids at the former farm at Bellsfield, High Blantyre. The maids stand holding milk jugs for delivering smaller quantities from the milk churns.

The cart is clearly labelled with Mr Craig's business although the exact location in unknown as rural areas like this could very well be built upon by today. This is a photo from the David Ritchie collection, an early photographer from High Blantyre's Main Street. We'll see more great photos of David's exclusively in this book later on.

Figure 5 Bellsfield Farm, Milk Deliveries pictured around 1910

COUNCILLORS IMPRISONED

Feelings ran high in Blantyre during summer 1934 about the level of unemployment. This came to a head when on 29th June 1934 seventeen people were charged and found guilty with inciting a riot in High Blantyre after besieging the offices of the Blantyre Council. Can you imagine such a thing today? This occurred after the council decided not to let a body representing the unemployed into the chambers at Cemetery Road. Charges against three other men were dropped.

Backtracking a little, during an earlier meeting on 19th April 1934, the councillors themselves got caught up in a heated exchange and when police were called, found themselves amongst the arrested! This included James Beecroft, a member of the council who was sentenced to 40 days imprisonment, McNaught for 30 days and Hughes for 20 days.

The story of the unemployed was completely overshadowed by the scandal of councillors being imprisoned and fined. The Sheriff said he took a severe view of their conduct, noting *"They make a serious mistake if they suppose they advance the interests of people by resorting to methods of violence. Violence will not be tolerated in this country."*

The accused were: James Beecroft, 240 Main Street, High Blantyre (a member of the District Council); Matthew McNaught, 10 Cemetery Road, High Blantyre: James McSorley, 80 Logan Street, Blantyre; Daniel Kelly, 152 Glasgow Road, Blantyre; Allan Hughes, 27 Douglas Park Rows, Bellshill; John McLaughlin, c/o Gillan, 13 Windsor Street, Burnbank; William Dobson, 67 Auchinraith Road. Blantyre: Robert Currie, 16 Viewpark Avenue, Blantyre; John Fleming, 45 Dixon Street Blantyre; Alexander Robertson, 59 Welsh Drive, High Blantyre; Patrick Kelly, 293 Glasgow Road, Blantyre;

David Park, 165 Glasgow Road, Blantyre; Joseph Gough, 15 Nursery Place, High Blantyre; Edward Kelly, Hall Street, Blantyre; Frank Smith, 65 Auchinraith Road, Blantyre: John Donnelly, 5 Morgan Street, Hamilton; John McInally, 61 Auchinraith Road, Blantyre; John Paterson, Logan Street, Blantyre: John Oouph, 55 Victoria Street, Blantyre; Elizabeth Robertson or Gillespie, 1 Welsh Drive, High Blantyre; Mary McAnulty or Hainev, 88 Forrest Street. Blantyre; Agnes McBeth or Sneddon. 11 Nursery Place, High Blantyre; Eliza Fulston or Baird, 16 Main Street, High Blantyre; Arthur Donnelly, 25 Logan Street, Blantyre.

As a member of Blantyre Community Committee, the story made me somewhat thankful that controversial items like employment are now dealt with by central local authority offices, and not by devolved branches of them within the town itself. Local man David Downie told me in 2015 that his grandfather Joseph Gough was amongst those accused. Former local Councillor John McNamee of Blantyre Ward 15 told me back in 2015, *"I'm glad this story is not a contemporary one!"*

BLANTYRE WAR MEMORIAL

Pictured next around 1920 is the High Blantyre War Memorial commemorating those who were killed during World War One. The memorial, in the shape of a cross, is decorated with wreaths and union flags. The dates '1914' and '1918' are just visible as is the tribute 'OUR GLORIOUS DEAD'.

The memorial is situated at the entrance to High Blantyre Cemetery in South Lanarkshire. You can clearly see how fresh this was in the minds of Blantyre people. Many, many wreaths of flowers lay at the memorial base, compared to today.

Blantyre men, Gordon Cook and the late Charlie Neilson once described The Great War – or World War One as being *"fought between the Central Powers (Germany, the Austro-Hungary Empire, the Ottoman Empire and Bulgaria) and the Allied Powers (who included Britain, France and Belgium). War broke out in 1914. A truce was declared with the signing of an Armistice in 1918. A formal state of war between the two sides continued until the signing of the Treaty of Versailles in June 1919. During the conflict, about 6 million Allied soldiers were killed and about 4 million soldiers from the Central Powers."*

Figure 3 War Memorial 1920

During October 2018, South Lanarkshire Council replaced the bench seating in the Cemetery with beautiful remembrance benches. The design matched the new bins and all the railings were freshly painted in advance of 11th November to commemorate 100 years since the end of WW1. The same week the council finally cut down the overgrown conifer trees surrounding the Dixon's Pit Disaster memorial close by, much to the delight of many people.

NEW ICON

I love Blantyre humour, and this is definitely witty playfulness at its best! In November 2014, the controversial "Big H" metal sculpture at High Blantyre roundabout was dismantled and removed. Quite right too, it represented HAMILTON Technology Park, firmly sited within Blantyre! A discussion arose locally about what sculpture would be fitting there instead. Blantyre residents spoke out on snowy 20th January 2015. I would like to shake the hand to the witty and wonderful person who took the time to put up this "new sculpture!" in the middle of the roundabout.

Figure 7 The "new" temporary icon at the High Blantyre Roundabout

Made from 2 spare car tyres, balancing on each other and the word "tyre" written in the snow, there is a real wit going on here that put a smile on the faces of a lot of drivers that month. As I saw this photo, I couldn't help but wonder if it would turn into a more lasting icon, just like the traffic cone on the Duke of Wellington's head in Glasgow. If it had, the instigator of this monument (whom I believe to be a certain well know photographer in High Blantyre) would have surely gone down in Blantyre legend and myth. However, the council had other plans and in August 2018, they planted several fast growing, fairly mature fir trees in the centre. This busy, little roundabout at the end of Douglas Street is always well kept with colourful heathers and neatly cut grass.

PRIESTFIELD SENIOR CITIZENS HALL

The Council owned Priestfield Senior Citizens Hall is situated on the Main Street in High Blantyre, next to the old Cooperative tenement buildings. South Lanarkshire Council's website incorrectly has the Priestfield Hall opening in November 1982, but this book seeks to correct that, by pointing out that it was opened in 1980, a full 2 years earlier. The event was well documented in local newspapers. The plaque commemorating the building being opened and coming into active use, was unveiled on 8th November 1980. Provost James Swinburne had the honour of doing that and many senior citizens who were to benefit from the hall opening attended.

The building had been commissioned just 6 weeks earlier in late September 1980 and one person delighted that the construction time had been so short, was the late Chairman of the Council's Leisure & Recreation Committee, Councillor D Murray Tremble. Murray welcomed a large representative group to the opening ceremony and went round the crowd personally chatting to everybody about the benefits of the project. However, the requirement for a hall had been discussed much earlier, back in 1979. Hamilton District Council had set aside £60,000 for the project, but in July 1979, members of the Leisure and Recreation Committee learned that the revised costings would be £114,700. The hall had almost doubled in price, even before a brick was laid! This didn't even include the cost of furnishings and fittings. Murray Tremble said to fellow Councillors at the time, *"I'm not surprised to see the expressions of astonishment on your faces. These are estimated costs and the most up to date we have."* Provost Charles Brownlie challenged the proposed expenditure adding that the original £60,000 must surely just have been a figure "plucked out of thin air." In July 1979, there still was no proposed starting date, but this was to change in late summer 1980 with building work commencing.

Upon it's opening, the hall had cost £115,000 and three quarters of that was funded by a Government grant under the Urban Aid scheme. When the building opened, there was no carpark adjacent, but instead it looked out upon an open expanse of grass at Priestfield, offering a nice rural panorama for senior citizens inside. Another environmental plus point was retaining large mature trees at either end of the building, giving it a ready made and settled look.

At the opening ceremony, officials touched upon a sad note. On the platform speeches were made about the likely Government spending cuts and perhaps an end to the building of such properties for clubs and organisations for some time to come. Councillor Mrs Senga Dallas gave the vote of thanks to all for coming. The hall now faces out on to a well-used council car park and has a direct view across to the Masonic building, the former Apollo Bar. The hall was originally provided for the senior citizens in the area and is managed by a local senior citizens committee. It comprises a main hall, two meeting rooms, kitchen and toilet. The main hall is 128sqm and can accommodate up to 100 people in concert style seating or 90 people for catered functions. The two meeting rooms can accommodate up to 20 people. This hall is increasingly used by community groups like Friends of the Calder and Blantyre Community Council but can occasionally be booked for other suitable activities. This facility can be used for a variety of community, social and commercial activities including but not restricted to Courses and Classes, Arts and Crafts, Sports Activities, Community Meetings, Birthday Parties, Engagement Parties, Discos, Wedding Receptions, Slimming Clubs, Martial Arts etc. During the day, each weekday, an inexpensive volunteer cafe is open (which is highly recommend). In the 1980's, there were children's discos on a Friday evening. A committee ran the business of the hall, amongst them long-standing member Andy Gilmour, a member on that committee for over 20 years. The hall is now nicely decorated with various painted Blantyre scenes.

STORY OF THE 1877 PIT EXPLOSION

High Blantyre minister Rev. Stewart Wright penned the following words in 1885 within his book, "The Annals of Blantyre." Who better to tell the story than an actual observer.

The annals of our parish would certainly not be complete without some allusion to that catastrophe which so recently brought death out if its obscurity into a sad prominence before the whole world, we mean the Pit Explosion, which took place on the morning of 22nd October 1877. Up till then Scotland had been peculiarly fortunate in being exempted from those terrible Colliery accidents, which were too often experienced by the mining communities of England and Wales. But now its turn had come; and the records was to be made in a page of its history, of one of the most devastating explosions as had happened in any land. By it, "in a moment, in the twinkling of an eye," 218, if not more, men and boys were killed, leaving behind them, to the mercy of God and man, 106 widows, 300 fatherless children, and about 50 other relatives, such as aged parents, who were more or less dependent upon the dead.

Figure 8 Nursing the injured at the pithead

What a gloomy morning that October Monday was. How indelibly it is engraved on our memory. We were dressing at the time. The window of our room looked over against the pits. A sudden flash darted up from the most distant shaft, accompanied by debris, and a report not very loud; then forthwith there arose from the shaft nearest to us a dense volume of smoke, "the blackness of darkness," which spread itself, a terrible funeral pall, over the surrounding plain. We were soon at the scene of the disaster, whither hundreds of eager and terrified creatures were hurrying, and there for hours we remained, a stricken shepherd amongst a stricken flock.

The one shaft was blocked up with ruins, but the other was partially clear; again and again did gallant men descend to rescue, if possible, their buried comrades, but all in vain; the merely succeeded in bringing up a few dead bodies, when they themselves were overpowered by the choke damp and had to be brought up to the surface. Some of them were more dead than alive, and it was with difficulty we succeeded in restoring them. Still, no matter the danger, there were no lack of volunteers, many of them wildly demanding to be lowered down, until at last, when the short winters day was drawing to a close, imperative orders were issued that no more lives were to be risked. Then hope fled; and the agonised crowd were left in the darkness and pitiless rain to face the terribleness of its magnitude that not one of the 200 miners and more that were entombed beneath us would ever see the light. Nor did they. Day after day for three weeks following, and after laborious exertions, were the bodies found and brought up for internment.

With the exception of the Roman Catholics, and there were not many of them, and a few others, all the dead were laid side by side in two long trenches that had been dug in the newly made cemetery. The report of the funerals in one evening, as given in the Herald, was characteristic of them all: – *"the scene in the parish burying ground, where the bodies where interred, was very impressive, and by the time that Mr Wright got as far in the service at 'Earth to Earth, Ashes to Ashes, dust to dust,' many of the onlookers were in tears. Few of them will soon forget the sight – the cold grey twilight, the dark overcast sky, the long deep trench, the silent uncovered multitude, and the solemn tones of the preacher's voice"*

Gradually the dead were buried; but the living remained, bereft of their breadwinners. No time was to be lost; starvation must be averted; so on the morning after the disaster, surrounded by widows and orphans, we issued, through the kind reporters, the following appeal: – *"We, the undersigned, appeal to the sympathies of the nation on behalf of the mothers, wives, and orphans, who have, in very many cases, been rendered perfectly destitute by the terrible Colliery explosion which has occurred in this district. 218 men and boys have been killed, all the male members of several families had been swept away, and widespread desolation prevails. There is lamentation and bitter weeping. Contributions are earnestly solicited to meet the destitution of the afflicted families"*

And what a response came to that appeal! The rich man's thousand and the widow's mite; the noble lady's gift of a hundred mourning dresses, and the orphan girls gift of a few pair of warm, knitted stockings. Here is still before us the pile of letters, which we keep with a kind of reverential feeling, for they tell of the noble sympathy and brotherly kindness of whole nation, from our beloved Queen (Victoria) to some of the poorest in her realm. The citizens of Glasgow were not slow to take up the cause of the bereaved. A meeting was called together by the Lord Provost, when an influential committee was appointed to collect subscriptions, and frame rules for the distribution of relief. Through their exertions, the contributions speedily reached magnificent total of £48,246; and under their unwearied superintendence the remaining widows and orphans still receive their allowances. They have never known moments want, and never will, as long as they continue on this fund. What a blessing it has been; and how earnestly we wish that such a fund was in existence and the wide basis, to meet the destitution arising from accident, serious and fatal, that are continually happening in our mining districts.

Before closing this short record of the explosion, we must not fail to pay a just tribute of praise to the gallant conduct of the miners, as we ourselves witnessed on that calamitous day, and for many days afterwards. Better than any words of ours could do, were they thus spoken of by the reporter of the Daily Telegraph: – "the British miner can fight with as much strength and majesty as the British soldier. If one falls in the imminent deadly breach, another coolly takes his place, and carries on the assault with a sublime unconsciousness of any odds that can be against him. So it was at High Blantyre. When a disabled hero was brought to bank in carefully covered with earth to free him from the influence of the poisonous gas, 10 more were eager to descend into the depths and risk a similar fate, or worse. We are glad to think that there are thousands upon thousands of men in these islands who know that they themselves would have done same had they been present. Yet few are able to realise the circumstances amid which the noble Scotchmen proved their bravery and devotion. A battlefield is ghastly enough, and its horrors might well appal those who look upon them. The soldier, however, had all the excitement of personal conflict, and sometimes a burning thirst for revenge, to sustain him; whereas, in the High Blantyre mine, the rescuers struggled against an invisible foe, whose distinctiveness was evidenced on every side in the most horrible forms. The other day we paid a tribute of admiration to Welshman; now it is Scotchmen who claim a like reward. In due time, when the 200 bodies shall have been brought up, and consigned by loving hands to their last resting place, the cause of the disaster will receive attention, a jury will return a verdict, and a government inspector will make his report. But all this has been done often before, and we seem as far off as ever from the ability to protect our miners against the dangers that surround their calling."

IDENTIFYING THE DEAD

I simply cannot imagine the horror the families faced on the days following 22nd October 1877, to identify the bodies of their loved ones. Pictured here, the bodies were slowly brought up and placed in a temporary mortuary, which became known as "The Death House".

Figure 9 Identifying the Bodies in "The Death House" following the Pit Disaster

One report in the Hamilton Advertiser describes, *"The bodies conveyed to the morgue were washed and dressed as decently as the circumstances would permit and then handed over to the care of the families and friends. It is to be noted that the bodies recovered almost all had the marks of injuries by burning. Some were contorted in the most dreadful manner, with the faces as black as the coal they had been shovelling. Others were torn and bruised; with dark crimson streams of blood trickling through their mud covered and dust begrimed clothes. A few had shreds of their pit clothes torn away and were battered and bruised in a shocking manner. The small number who had apparently succumbed to the choke-damp, wore a peaceful expression as if in sleep and those, when found, were discovered lying on their faces in the levels, as if they had been making haste to the pit bottom, when overtaken by the deadly, suffocating gas."*

FUNERALS OF THE DEAD MINERS

With so many men and boys losing their lives in the Dixon's Pit Disaster in High Blantyre on 22nd October 1877, the only way the authorities could deal with such funeral arrangements, was by a mass burial. This took place at High Blantyre Cemetery, where all non-Catholics were buried, with Catholic men and boys taken to Dalbeath.

At High Blantyre, nine days after the explosion, thousands of Blantyre residents (keeping in mind there were only about 10,000 people in the town at the time) lined the streets and crammed themselves on to the pavements at Cemetery Road. People jostled with each other to gain the most advantageous view. The crowd was extended hugely more, by visitors who poured off trains to come and see the spectacle, including many reporters from all across Britain. Amongst them, a number of opportunists, intending to make the best of the empty houses. It is alleged, when caught, several of these people were left in the hands of the miners, rather than police. Blantyre's muddy and grimy streets failed to cope with such an influx of people into the town and with the weather being particularly wet that week, the roads struggled and people are known to have been stuck knee deep in mud.

At the North East side of High Blantyre Cemetery the authorities dug a huge trench of 50 yards x 3 yards and 2 yards deep. The lengthy procedure of lowering the coffins carefully into the ground began, observed closely by the families of the deceased. For many though, this was still a period where their loved ones hadn't yet been recovered from the pit, and nine days on, hope of them being rescued would have been diminishing rapidly, especially as they witnessed the sight of their colleagues being buried. The coffins were covered over on land known today as the "Common Ground". Dixons, the colliery owners would later go on to place an Obelisk monument to all the people lost that October day and indeed in other disasters they incurred.

The final numbers of the dead vary greatly from report to report. From 215 to 240 and I've even seen a report that suggested there were 262 miners dead (although I think that one included the survivors or was the subject of sensationalist reporting.) Blantyre lady Ann Crossar told me, *"My 2nd great grand uncle died in Dixon's disaster – William Primrose age 17 – he was interred in a double family lair at High Blantyre Old Cemetery – section D lair 323/324 on 6/11/1877."*

SCARY BLANTYRE SANTA

Figure 4 Santa!

This photo is kindly shared by Elizabeth Cardoo (Nee Anderson) and features a Christmas Masonic party in High Blantyre during the early 1950's. Elizabeth is pictured as a little girl aged 6 years or so and will likely look back on this photo fondly with memories of Blantyre before she emigrated.

The children look happy and enjoying Santa's company. However, regardless of the festive smiles and frolics, I have to admit on seeing this photo, I have to say, that is indeed one pretty scary looking Santa! He looks positively terrifying by comparison to today's jolly fat man traditional Santa.

This took me back to my own childhood to Christmas parties in High Blantyre Old Parish Church Halls for the Sunday school. I recall happy family occasions in the 1970's and a great deal of fun on the lead up to them too, as we children busied ourselves with making festive paper chains and decorations from anything lying around our home. I have photos with Santa from that decade too, but by then, thankfully in the 1970s, there was no need to blacken faces to disguise which parent or elder was dressed up.

I will never forget as a 6 or 7 year old walking up those cold stone steps in the old Church Hall to the upper concert hall with its wooden floorboards and small stage for parties and Sunday school. It was there I befriended a lass or two, who would still catch my eye, even as a teenager later!

ORRS VISIT BLANTYRE

In 1948, an American couple returned home to Blantyre for a holiday. Mr and Mrs James Orr arrived in mid July 1948 from their home in Pawtucket, Rhode Island, USA with the intention of spending a six-week holiday in Blantyre. They holiday residence was with Mrs Orr's sister Mrs George Preston, at 5 Muir Street, High Blantyre.

Mr Orr was an elder brother of "Wull" Orr, former Blantyre Vics centre-half. He was originally a native of Blantyre and after 25 years of employment in Blantyre coalmines, including Auchinraith Colliery had decided in 1922 to try his luck in the United States.

Jimmy Orr gave up his home at Merry's Rows and with his wife and eight children, five sons and three daughters, and accompanied by his brother and his wife and family, had set out for the USA. Now with himself and sons all in good USA jobs, and with immediate family happily married, he had no reason to regret the day he left Blantyre. Mr Orr himself was employed as a ring groover with the Pawtucket Spinning Ring Company.

Asked whilst on holiday by a Blantyre Gazette reporter if he had made a name for himself in football like his brother Bill, Mr Orr jocularly replied that he had considered he was just too light for the game and his only achievements were with a *"tanner baw"*. But if he didn't hit the headlines in football he had certainly some very notable success on the bowling greens. He was attached to the Smithfield Avenue bowling club and in 1934 was included in the rink, which won the New England Championship. This was one of the largest bowling competitions in the US, with over sixty clubs taking part.

In 1939 when the Scotland International Football team were touring Canada and the United States, Mr and Mrs Orr brought Blantyre lad Jimmy Carabine, a member of the team, to their US home and entertained him in very hospitable fashion. He was reared beside the Orr family in Merry's Rows and as Mr Orr put it, *"he was only a wee laddie kicking a rubber ball around when I left Blantyre."* Mr and Mrs Orr enjoyed their Blantyre 1948 holiday visiting many friends.

BEGG'S BUILDING

Begg's Building was a small single storey tenement building, which originally stood on the south side of Main Street not far from a location across from the entrance to Cemetery Road. Some confusion exists around this building, where a previous Blantyre history book suggested this small tenement was known as Lint Butts, but I can confirm this is incorrect as Lint Butts was slightly more westwards, although immediately next door to Beggs.

Begg's building was likely named after Mr. H Begg, a High Blantyre Blacksmith whom in 1879, owned a business called H Begg & Son. Built between 1860 and 1879, the small building was single storey, subdivided, semi-detached and was once known as the Apothecary Hall, after the chemists at the east side. Indeed, a chemist existed there for quite some time and is remembered even up until the 1960's, known as 'Patersons'. Next door, was McMillan's Haulage located in the same semi-detached property. Mr McMillan lived at that address and had a yard at the back.

Figure 11 High Blantyre Main Street looking eastwards around 1910

Sometime in the 20th Century, the small building may have had an upper level or rooms added. Pictured in 1910 on the right hand side of Main Street is the Apothecary Hall in Begg's Building. The site in a modern context was directly across the road from the current bus stop near Family Shopper store.

ENGLISH MINERS ARRIVE

Figure 5 Dixons Miners in the 1890's

The 1877 October Pit Disaster does not seem to have put off men coming into Blantyre in the following months, seeking employment.

The Hamilton Advertiser told on 5th January 1878, *"A considerable number of English miners have lately arrived in this district, and, as a few of them are still in search of employment. Letters addressed to the care of Mr D. McNaughton, Livingstone Tavern, Stonefield, will be taken charge of until called for. "*

Perhaps this influx of families was connected to the many English names we now see in Blantyre. Helen Williams added, *"I know 'Cook' to originate from England, but my Grandfather moved from Dunbar to work in the mines in Blantyre. His name was James and I believe he lived in no. 5 Watson Street. His wife was Lizzy Burgoyne. (From France) that's as much as I know. When I look back at my childhood, I remember friends and neighbours from, Ireland, Poland, England and Germany. I never thought about it back then but we really were a mixed bunch but a strong community. I would have loved the opportunity to have asked them their stories now."*

REDCROFT

In High Blantyre land came up for sale in 1863 near the Old Parish Church, called 'Redcroft'. The advert went thus: "To be sold by Public Roup, in the Faculty Hall, Saint George's Place, Glasgow, on Wednesday, 18 February, 1863, at Two o'clock, afternoon, unless previously disposed of by private bargain. An enclosed FIELD, called the REDCROFT, part of the lands of Priestfield, lying near to the Parish Church, and containing about Two Scotch Acres of excellent Land, pleasantly situated, and well adapted for the Erection of Villas. To insure a sale, the Upset Price will be only £250. For further particulars, apply to Archibald Brownlie, Writer, Barrhead, at No. 5 Dundas Street, Glasgow, who has the Title Deeds and Articles of Roup."

The name Redcroft is all but forgotten in High Blantyre and there are only a handful of historical references to give us a clue as to where this field was. William Scott won a prize in the dairy section of the Cambuslang, Blantyre and Rutherglen Agricultural Show in 1869 and is noted as being at Redcroft Farm High Blantyre. Redcroft Farm, from the description of the advert sounds like it may have been an original name of the 'Back Priestfield Farm'.

Picking apart more clues, "an enclosed field", suggests it was not open to a roadway, but enclosed by other fields or perhaps enclosed by a wall? "Red" is interesting and suggests iron or ironstone connections, such as Redburn.

The advert in 1863 suggests the field was "lying near the Parish Church", but that may be a simplified description in the same way Kirkton Cross is "near the Church". On the subject of that church, at the time of the advert, the construction of the current Old Parish Church must have been underway, the church masonry rising out the ground, some 4 or 5 months before opening. 1865 Valuation Book: Mr. Thomas Scott owned land called Redcroft at High Blantyre (there is no mention of Redcroft in 1855 valuation roll). Mr. William Scott was the occupier (surely farming it?) There is nothing in 1875 valuation roll and beyond it, so it would appear the name Redcroft was short lived. In the Glasgow Herald on 23rd May 1868, William won 1st prize for a bull he put into a competition. On 22nd May 1869, William Scott won 4th prize in a contest for the butter he entered. These mentions of Redcroft are both beside long lists of other farmers and notably their farm names.

With an earliest reference being 1863 and the latest reference being 1869 for farming this land, question has to be what happened after 1870 that caused the name to vanish from future reference? Perhaps it vanished due to the arrival of Dixons (coalmasters), known in the early 1870s. Looking at the 1859 map, the closest map to the first mention of the name, there are a few enclosed fields nearby to Priestfield. Another consideration is that location could have been in one of the several little fields between near to Bellsfield.

1871 Census: There is a William Scott in Blantyre in 1871; aged 30 years old with a son William aged 3. In that year, William and his brother Thomas aged 17, lived at Priestfield Farm House with their uncle Thomas Scott, aged 69, the head of the household and farmer of 77 arable acres. Thomas Scott employed 2 men and 2 women. One of the employees was nephew William, who was the ploughman. (Presumably of Redcroft field) With the family were also Thomas Scott's sisters, Mary 65, Ann 63 and Lillias 50, all spinsters. Thomas Scott appears not to have married. The census describes their home (where these people all lived together) as the 5 roomed, "Priestfield 1 storey farmhouse". There is a line drawn under it saying in bold, "End of Kirkton", the next entries towards Causeystones and Bellsfield.

1881 Census: Reveals more. William is still at Priestfield with his brother. William is now 40 and still a ploughman. Old Thomas Scott is now 79, and incredibly he has 4 sisters, all spinsters living with him, the 3 mentioned above plus Janet aged 81. The sisters were housekeepers and elderly dairymaids. Importantly though, there is a distinction made on the location this time. They all lived at Priestfield Farm. The next entry beside it is for Andrew Hunter, born in Linlithgow who was head of Back Priestfield Farm, noted as closer to Kirkton. (Back Priestfield was the farm beside the later masonic hall) and that the Farm on Main Street (where Priestfield halls are now) was actually Priestfield Farm where the Scotts lived. Of note on the 1881 census, old Thomas Scott owned 75 arable acres, 2 short of his total 10 years earlier, i.e. He had sold Redcroft's 2 acres and we now see the first mention of Back Priestfield.

We are left to conclude here, although not for certain (and rarely for me, speculation in my humble opinion), that Redcroft was a previous and former name for Back Priestfield farm, near Kirkton Cross.

1928 CANDIDATES WITHDRAW

A particularly unusual occurrence took place in early December 1928 in the County and Parish Council Elections for Blantyre. Four candidates whose names appeared on the ballot papers and after month's of separate campaigning, suddenly issued a joint manifesto, just before the election asking for the people of Blantyre NOT to vote for them!

The Candidates Hugh McKerrell, James Stoddart, John Ross and John Sturton were the nominees for the "Unemployed Workers Committee and the Communist Party". However, since they started their campaign in summer 1928, considerable changes took place in the party due to the breakaway of over 400 workers at Auchinraith Colliery favouring the Lanarkshire County Miners Union. It's likely the candidates' thought that their votes would be hugely affected by losing 400 prospective voters and had either given up or knew they would not win. The workers had formed their own branch union. Of course the candidates names were still to appear on the ballot paper and it is interesting their excuse noted on the manifesto of the growing divide between communist attitudes:

"We, the undersigned repudiate the action of the Unemployed Workers' Committee, with whom all were associated at the outset of the local election campaign having now declared that they are not the representatives of the unemployed workers but are representatives of the communist party only. We therefore ask the electors to refrain from voting for us, as we have no desire to participate in the elections under such conditions, and as our names will appear on the ballot papers, we take this step to notify the electors."

Communist organisations in Blantyre were often miner led and fell way in popularity very sharply towards the end of the 1930s.

OLDEST BLANTYRE STREET PHOTO

The following photo was taken in 1869 and shows Main Street looking eastwards. To give you an indication of how old this photo is, it is 8 years BEFORE the Blantyre Pit Disaster and even before the coal-mining era properly got underway in Blantyre!

The building on the left is 'Dales', a single storey building of several homes. These were knocked down and replaced by the current tenements of the same name. After Dales, there's a gap, but that's not Cemetery Road, it was the entrance to the High Blantyre Bethany Hall, which sat back off the street. Staying on the left, the wooden fence line would be removed a few years after this photo and the entrance to Cemetery Road would be formed at that location, before the Cemetery opened in 1875.

I suspect the photo was taken to celebrate the newly built row of tenement homes and shops on the left (no longer there), where now there is a grass field. On the right hand side, construction is actually underway of a property no longer there today. You'll see a large tree in the background, again not there today under which is the gable end and chimney of the former property called Lint Butts.

This is the boundary between Causeystanes and Auchinraith. Some of the people standing outside Dales may have lived there. I first noticed this name between 1875 and 1885. In 1905, Mr Robert Hamilton was the owner of this property. The name Dales should not be confused with Dales Cottages, which were on the former Hospital Road at the top of Victoria Street.

Figure 13 Main Street looking East in 1869, one of the oldest photos of Blantyre

In Summer 2018, this area of Blantyre was "beautified" when the environmental group, "Bonnie Blantyre" planted up flowers in some of the redundant concrete planters. Aided by TACT Healthy Park Garden, it ensured during the warm summer of 2018, there were beautiful displays of flowers, something that promises to be expanded upon in 2019.

GLEBE COTTAGE

Glebe Cottage was a former, substantial double villa dating from between 1875 and 1879 located on Craigmuir Road immediately adjacent to the High Blantyre Station. The land was owned by the church, in particular with Rev. Stewart Wright noted as being the owner in the Valuation 1875 roll, which indicated "Glebe Land" with no indication of the villa at that time. It is known even earlier in 1865, Mr William Downie and Mr Russell of Burnbrae owned parts of the Glebe Land.

It may have initially been one large detached home and perhaps good business sense to for the single property to be divided into smaller properties. Dr Grant still lived there in 1881 with his family, however by then, it was three separate terraced houses. Two were five apartments the other was a two apartment. Robert Pollock was a Contractor there in 1879 his wife Agnes still living there in 1885 who also owned one of the 3 homes at that time. R. C McCallum owned the other 2 homes, based at 69 Union Street Glasgow who was letting out his homes. Mr Walker, a sawmiller and Mr Ramsay a contractor were the occupants in 1885, likely working next door at the sawmill. It would appear to have had an outside toilet on the southern side.

By the early 1890's, the homes saw further subdivision and by 1895, it was 4 homes. John Young, Veterinary Surgeon, lived there in 1894 and John Hall, a clerk, Charles Reid (a brakesman) and Agnes Pollock were living there, 2 of the homes now in ownership of the trustees of R.C McCallum.

Figure 14 The Glebe Cottage shown on right at Craigmuir Road

By 1905 only John Hall and Robert Pollock were living there indicating that a couple of the homes may have been unfit or they have been pieced back to being larger, but fewer homes. In 1915, Robert and John Hall occupied the only 2 inhabited homes. On 9th March 1917, Isabella Fotheringham died at Glebe Cottage, the daughter of William and Ann Fotheringham. John Hall may have needed some help, when in July 1916 and in May 1918, adverts in the Hamilton Adveriser asked for a cleaner about aged 16 for "Hall" at Glebe Cottage, High Blantyre, noting the girl would be permitted to sleep "at home." By 1920 John Hall and Allan Jack were occupiers, who were still there in 1925.

Margaret McKenzie (the Minister's wife) in reminiscing about her days in Blantyre, remembered the 'Glebe Cottage' as being on the "Brickie" (Craigmuir Road), and it had a paper storage building right next to it (disused sawmill). The McKenzies lived there from 1934 till 1951, partly due to the deteriorated condition of the former Manse House nearby. The Glebe Cottage(s) were demolished sometime between 1951 and 1963. A modern detached house named "The Glebe" is now on this site built by the Weaver family. Today, it has white roughcast, solar panels and decking. It is best seen behind the church, through the trees on the slipway leading from the A725 Expressway on to Douglas Street.

INDUSTRIAL ESTATE

High Blantyre Industrial Estate was the third of seven massive Industrial Estates in Scotland opened in 1946, destined to overturn unemployment and bring post war prosperity back to Central Scotland. Blantyre's Industrial Estate was opened on Monday 25th March 1946 by Mr Tom Fraser, joint Under Secretary for Scotland. Spread over a massive 42 acres and using some land bought by compulsory purchase order, the buildings were created to employ up to 5,000 people, around a third of Blantyre at the time.

Unemployment was a problem. Just 2 decades earlier, there were 12 collieries in the area and in 1946 only one was still operating. At the time of opening, 2 companies had secured premises with firm enquiries for up to another 60,000 square feet. Mr Fraser spoke of the need to diversify industry in the area away from a declining coal mining operation. He added there were 12,000 unemployed in Lanarkshire at the time, 5,500 of whom were men. The estate is located just off Main Street and High Blantyre Road and separated into sequentially named streets.

Many prominent engineering companies rented premises including Rolls Royce, Honeywell and Reyolle Belmos. Indeed, there are simply too many businesses to mention occupying factory units throughout the years but Botterils featured prominently and many of the units are currently rented out by a company called Evan Storage.

The large unit named David Williams Business Centre facing out on the Main Street closed down in May 2016 after being liquidated, forcing many smaller businesses to relocate. It has since become renovated and bought over again. Perhaps the most prominent former businesses were Simplicity Patterns the clothing manufacturers and the E.K Jig and Tool Company. An expansion to the estate in the form of adjoining Priestfield Industrial Estate has seen the area continue to flourish. There is no doubt that the estate brought employment and jobs to Blantyre at a time when mining was seriously in decline. The estate still is successful today with 2 different cafes open too. However, the ageing estate is starting to show signs of age and several of the buildings are now in need of attention and repair.

HIGH BLANTYRE BETHANY HALL

When we talk of the Bethany Hall in Blantyre nowadays, we tend to think of the existing hall at Glasgow Road, now used as a children's nursery. However, it may come as a surprise (as it did to me!), that there was another Bethany Hall in Blantyre in the 20th Century, at the opposite side in High Blantyre.

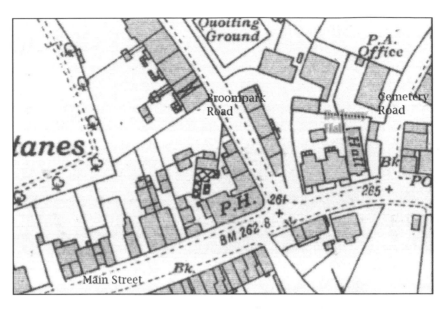

Figure 15 Bethany Hall shown on 1936 map

It is certainly known there was a Bethany Hall in High Blantyre as early as 1898, which was still there in the 1930's. This Bethany Hall was a green hut at the corner of Cemetery Road and Main Street, High Blantyre, and was a great centre for evangelistic meetings with many visiting speakers. Meetings were advertised in the local press, with invited speakers of faith.

The building occupied part of the land originally known as Dales and looks to have replaced a former building on the long, narrow, north-south plot. There are differences when comparing to 1896 map and the 1910 map, which by then is clearly marked hall.

It is still shown as existing on the 1936 map as single storey, although by then it is tightly situated next to the current double storey tenements known as "Dales" which still exist today.

The High Blantyre Bethany Hall, looks to have been demolished between 1936 and World War Two years, for aerial photos of December 1945, show the site cleared and vacant. I'm inclined to think the hall was demolished before WW2. The Christian Brethren saved the fate of a Glasgow Road building, but putting it back on track as a religious establishment and in 1936 renamed it "The Bethany Hall", in other words, I think they simply moved to better premises in Blantyre. It remained in their hands for 50 years until 16th December 1996, when they sold the Glasgow Road Church building to the World of Life Christian Fellowship. It is now Cosmic Cherubs Nursery.

Let's get back to High Blantyre! In post WW2 years, the land was used as a small Masonry, Gravestone and Memorial business called "Kirkland Memorials". Today, there is no sign of the hall or former business, the corner site now modern 2 storey brick flats. The Bethany movement has no visible presence in Blantyre at the moment.

1904 HIGH BLANTYRE CEMETERY

This photo is extracted from a beautifully illustrated promotional book from 1904, by Gilmour's of Glasgow Road. Pictured here (and I've zoomed in), is the High Blantyre Cemetery. The cemetery had opened just 29 years earlier in 1875 and by this time is looking quite established. However, what struck me immediately is the absolute care and attention the cemetery has been given. The paths well kept, the gravestones all standing, none dared to be toppled. The flowers on almost every grave, many carefully protected from weather by glass bowls, people remembered, their resting places and they were cared for often.

To the right of the photo is the DIxon's monument obelisk commemorating the 1877 pit disaster. Behind the wall at the back of the Cemetery at this time, where now Burnbrae Housing Estate is located, ran the former railway connecting to High Blantyre Station.

Figure 16 High Blantyre Cemetery in 1904

When the cemetery opened in 1875, little did High Blantyre minister know that just a couple of days later, his first funeral and internment would be his own baby son. It was a heartache that must have drawn much support from friends and family. This Cemetery is now all but full, with modern burials now taking place in Priestfield Cemetery, just off Hillhouse Road. As of 2018, a search is underway in Blantyre by the Council for a new, large Cemetery site, with a field in Sydes Brae in 2015, recently deemed unsuitable across from the Crematorium.

1908 LITTLE ROBERT RITCHIE

Pictured here in Broompark Avenue is little Robert Ritchie. Photographed by David Ritchie in 1908, Robert stands outside the door of his house in good clothes indicative of Sunday best, or perhaps part of a band or club. Robert's home looked out over to Broompark House, pictured in the background later the home of married doctors, The Jopes. The site of that large house later became the chapel in Broompark Road and is very built up today, nothing like the rural scene in the photo.

Figure 17 Robert Ritchie at Broompark Avenue in 1908

Broompark Avenue was then a cul de sac, dead end, just as it is today. More recently, there was an entrance into Kirkton Park, which would later be to the left of this photo, but the park at the time of David's photo, did not exist. The building to the left is part of the Broompark House property and may have been the doctor's surgery. The trees in the background, beyond the house are on the railway embankment, which ran from left to right immediately behind the house. Just out the picture the railway crossed Broompark Road. To the left in the picture were open fields all the way over to Old Mains Place. The houses in Broompark Avenue, where Robert lived are still there today.

1935 MASONIC HALL RAMMY

"The women who have given evidence have shown commendable pluck in the face of threats," said the fiscal, Mr D. W. Hiddleston, Hamilton J.P. Court when four High Blantyre men were up in the court for assault on 30th August 1935. In one of the cases, sentence of sixty days' imprisonment was imposed. The accused were Isaiah Beecroft, miner, 240 Main Street; Henry Rooney, labourer, 27 Maxwell Crescent; James Boyd, miner, and William Boyd, miner, both 78 Calder Street, all of High Blantyre. They were charged with assaulting Alexander Woods and Alexander Paton, two High Blantyre men at the Masonic Hall, Main Street, High Blantyre, and also with forcing their way into the hall and committing breach of the peace and brandishing chairs. A similar charge against Thomas Beecroft, brother of the first accused, was adjourned until October 3, the fiscal explaining that he was at present in prison on another charge.

Alexander Woods, the victim giving evidence, said he attended a dance at the Masonic Hall given by the Blantyre Quoiting Club as a benefit for local men in ill-health. Shortly before midnight Isaiah Beecroft began to argue with him, and he was warned he was going to get in trouble.

General Uproar. He and Paton sat down between the dances, and Rooney and another of the accused sat beside them. While William Boyd was dancing past him, said Woods, suddenly stopped, turned, and struck him. The remainer of the accused then attacked him, and he was kicked and struck. There were about 50 couples the hall, and a general uproar ensued. None of the men came to his assistance, but several women helped him to the other side of the hall, and kept the men from him. The Fiscal—Why did none of the men assist? —I would rather not answer. The Fiscal —Have you been threatened as to what would occur if you came as a witness? —Yes. The Fiscal—You know there is a great deal of terrorism in High Blantyre created by gangs?— Yes.

Wood said the accused left the hall, but returned ten minutes later. The brothers Boyd tried to get near him, but women kept them back. Then saw Paton being trailed into the centre of the floor and kicked and punched. Some women rescued him, and took him to the platform. Then he saw chairs brandished by men trying to reach Paton. The dance was abandoned.

Alexander Paton said that when entering the dance hall he was spoken to by Isaiah Beecroft, who asked, _ " What about the £10 fine? Are you going to help to collect the money at the corner?" Paton replied he had nothing to do with this, and this offended Beecroft. Paton spoke about being seriously assaulted inside the hall. Evidence was also given by Eleanor Orr, 213 Main Street; Elizabeth Paton, 505 Main Street; Mrs Baird, Muir Street; and David Baird, Muir Street, all of High Blantyre. The four accused denied having taken part in the disturbance, but all were found guilty. Isaiah Beecroft, who admitted previous convictions, was sent to prison for 60 days. Rooney, who had one previous conviction, was fined £3, with the option of 20 days' imprisonment; and James and William Boyd were each fined £2, with the option of days' imprisonment.

1955 ROLLS ROYCE INTAKE

This is the Rolls Royce Apprentice intake of 1955. Bill Duncan has kindly shared this photo and the following information. Bill is on the bottom left. My own Uncle John Duncan in the tall chap in the front middle.

Bill told me, "1955 was the year John and I started our working life. Successfully meeting Rolls Royce requirements by passing their Entrance Exam, we duly reported to Burnbank School of Engineering at 9.00am on Monday the 22nd of August to start a full time Pre-Apprentice training program prior to in plant training in the East Kilbride Plant in 1956. At Burnbank RR apprentices were consider the elite by virtue of the status the company had within 'Engineering' but it often led to conflict with apprentices from other local companies and they dubbed us with the collective nickname "Snowdrops" on account of the white overalls we had to wear. The white overalls were fine to us but horrors when we found out that the Training Department had chosen 'pink overalls' for our in plant training.

For the next four years it was the Chieftain bus up to Nerston, East Kilbride, over the General's Bridge via Stainymeadow. For the final year of my apprenticeship I was assigned to the High Blantyre Plant, handy for me as in 1957 I had moved from Stonefield Road to Waverley Terrace, which is within walking distance of the Plant."

Figure 18 The Rolls Royce Team in 1955

The large Rolls Royce factory closed down in 1977 and was then converted to house five separate industries; Newhouse Engineering, Gammas Electric, Hayhill Joinery, Machine Tool Engineering and CRS Haulage.

BY PAUL D VEVERKA

NEW UNIVERSITY AT HIGH BLANTYRE

The University of the West of Scotland has moved into Hamilton International Technology Park (HITP) and created a brand new, state-of-the-art, modern university campus in High Blantyre, the largest building to ever be built in this town.

Despite falling into Hamilton Ward, the building still sits on Blantyre land. The new Eco Campus located to a current greenfield site in High Blantyre, meant a move from their existing site (just over two miles away at Almada Street, Hamilton.) The new campus constructed on land behind the Technology Park at Sydes Brae now offers, from September 2018 a state-of-the-art teaching and learning facility with plans for student accommodation, Union, and specialist laboratory space.

It should see many, many jobs created for the Blantyre area and an immediate, adjacent further education facility for students from this area and beyond. Indeed the economic projection for this immediate local area as a result of this development is estimated to be as much as £25billion over the next 25 years.

It's already being called, "The Eco Campus" or "UWS Lanarkshire". No access was thankfully permitted to the campus from the rural area of Sydes Brae, with entrances being through the Technology Park itself.

Figure 6 The new UWS at the Technology Park

The arrival of Blantyre's very first University meant a rethink about public transport with a bespoke green travel plan already in place for public transport. It will now look to secure financial arrangements to ensure the best value with the aim of delivering an outstanding campus for its students, staff and the wider community.

Professor Craig Mahoney, Principal and Vice-Chancellor of UWS, said upon planning approval: "Today's decision is a major milestone in the development of an exciting new University campus for UWS, for Scotland and for Lanarkshire."

The stylish building constructed in glass and steel is enormous fitted with technologies which are sustainable and cost reducing. Convenient bus stops and established soft landscaping already beautify the surroundings and it surprisingly feels isolated, away from homes and shops.

Inside, a labyrinth of corridors leads to many classrooms over several floors with a large modern atrium at the entrance with mezzanine floors overlooking it. A large canteen and state of the art gym is available inside and parking is generally hidden underneath the structure in underground massive car parks. Already students from all over Lanarkshire are enrolled in classes of a variety of subjects, a major, handy further education outlet, right on our doorstep for many Blantyre future generations to enjoy. Now, if we can only educate the local authorities to recognise it's in Blantyre, rather than saying this is Hamilton, what a step that would be!

CHAPTER 2
GREENHALL, MILHEUGH & CALDER

The green, leafy areas of Greenhall, Crossbasket and Milheugh are located on the Western fringes of Blantyre near the Parish boundaries. For a long time they've been generally regarded as good walking areas, providing much needed outdoor space and woodland, and welcome retreat from the hussle and bussle of Blantyre's streets and buildings. The former estates of Milheugh and Greenhall are now council owned with environmental groups looking after and supporting the area through frequent litter picks and betterment projects. Pictured above in 2015 is one of the few isolated trees that stands on the green sloping field of Greenhall, captured on a foggy autumnal morning. This was in the 1960's and 70's the popular pitch n putt.

DYESHOLM OR DYSHOLM COTTAGE

Dyesholm Cottage – or Dysholm can be dated back to at least 1747, being shown on Roy's Military Map of that year, although it is likely to be even older. The cottage sat in an isolated position outwith Blantyre Parish in Cambuslang Parish, just over the boundary at the Rotten Calder River. Likely to have had a thatched roof, the cottage was made of stone and sat in an elevated position in the middle of a field, overlooking the river gorge not far from a bend in the river. The cottage was not on the river itself but overlooked a little beach area.

The Blantyre lands of Bardykes are across the river. A track once led down to Pattenholm Ford, a crossing point coming from Barnhill along a medieval track nicknamed, "The Path", which likely gave its name to nearby Pathfoot. The cottage was the home of the miller or dyer (person who dyes cloth) and it is thought the former mill was once situated nearby at the bend on the river as shown on 18th Century maps. Indeed the name Dyesholm is derived from 'the house of the dyer'. The nearby mill seems to have been gone by the 1850's.

Figure 20 The Ruins of Dysholm pictured in 2009 by Jim Brown

William Pettigrew, a master carter, married Jean Pollock 25 January 1800. Jane Pollock christened 11 July 1782, parents were Robert Pollock, the Blantyre blacksmith, and Jane Maxwell. William and Jane lived in the Dysholm (a corruption of Davisholm) Cottage .

The old Parish Register says, *"Out of the ruin of my life I see my great-great-great-grandfather William Pettigrew, aged 33, emerge from the door of his cottage Dysholm on a morning in January 1800 after his marriage to Jane Pollock, aged 17. William Pettigrew and his family moved up the hill from Dysholm to the family farm at Malcolmwood around 1860. Malcolmwood is a corruption of Milcolmwood, by Douglas Clark."* The 1841 and 1851 Censuses place the Pettigrews still at Dyesholm. The Pettigrews moved to nearby Malcolmwood farm perhaps prompted by the closure and demolition of the mill, which may have by then been very old. The cottage is noted as being "Dyesholm" on the 1859 map.

After 1860 when the Pettigrews moved out, the cottage was still habitable and the Pettigrews leased it out to sub-tenants in 1885. Margaret Miller or Bannatyne of Milheugh was the overall landowner and also owned Dyeholm outright, proving that the influence of Milheugh estate once spread into Cambuslang Parish. By then the land was twinned with Dicksholm. In 1895 Dyesholm and Dicksholm were back being occupied by a Pettigrew family member, this time John Pettigrew.

However, the old Dyesholm Cottage soon after became derelict and was eventually ceremonially burnt down in the winter of 1903/4. By 1905, John Pettigrew was farming the land of Dyesholm and Dicksholm and the house, gone had dropped off the valuation register. It is now an insignificant ruin, the earthworks and farming, long since covered up any trace. Beside it was Queen Mary's Well where Mary Queen of Scots allegedly and quite fancifully, watered her horse before the Battle of Langside. Pictured in this article is the ruin of Dyesholm Cottage in 2009, by Jim Brown. In the background is the current large and desirable modern house "Pattenholm" on Bardykes Road.

LETTER TO JOANNA, 1808

On August 23rd 1808, Miss Mary Berry an English aristocrat with a flair for writing, wrote from her visit to Bothwell Castle House, to her friend and fellow writer, Joanna Baillie. Joanna was born at the Manse in Bothwell but at the time of the following letter in 1808, was living in England. Mary took great delight in her visit to Bothwell and Blantyre areas.

Mary, far from home wrote to her friend, "Joanna -You and I have crossed over and figured in, in an odd way this last year. I wish there had been any setting and footing together in the course of our jigging about. I now In Scotland and you in England, I yesterday at Millheugh and you perhaps at Little Strawberry Hill.

Figure 7 Sketch of Milheugh House in 1799

What a pretty place Millheugh is! I walked all down the rocky bed of the river below the bridge and crossed over the stepping stones and back again, merely for the pleasure of doing it and then went all round the house at Millheugh and to the wooden bridge which looks at the little cascade then up the green walk at the side of the stream. We saw not a human creature either to welcome us or forbid us their premises, which being all open, we committed no trespass. I tried the echoes with some lines of Basil; but they were dumb and only muttered in return for your name, something about Muslin at Glasgow, a pattern of a handkerchief, and some stories of the poor in the village. Your heroic muse should have taught them better in such a romantic spot. I have been over too at my own dear little ravine at Blantyre Priory."

Mary's letter is telling in that Millheugh does not appear to be fenced off in that area, was still then being described with two "Ls", the falls described as a little cascade (lending weight that they may later have been made into something more impressive as they are today). The sketch attached was drawn in 1799 by Jean Claude Nattes.

WOMEN CREATE GREEHALL NATURE TRAIL

A first for Blantyre happened in springtime 1978, when the council created our very first public Nature Trail. The former Greenhall estate paths were upgraded in Greenhall Park, creating several new walks, with paths reinforced with timber and gravel. Signage set out the various walks in 6 different trails, located in and around the woodland on the banks of the River Calder. Work started on the 1.5 miles of nature trails in 1976 and by end of March 1978, it was nearly completed. The nature trails were part of a job creation project run by Hamilton District Council and Hamilton College of Education. Workers consisted entirely of female students of the college.

Figure 22 Greenhall Calder Nature Trail Paths pictured in 2015

Project Co-ordinator Ian Jamieson of the College Science department said just prior to opening, *"We hope to see the trail being opened at Easter (1978) just when the area should be at its most interesting. The project has been a great success and all the girls involved went on to have full time jobs."* Today, these paths are still maintained and well used.

In 2017, the conifer and pine trees at Greenhall, which were dangerously tall were felled, leaving quite a scar on the landscape. However, betterment was planned and the sale of the bark chippings was reinvested into improving the paths, making the park more accessible and allowing native vegetation and indigenous species of trees, like oaks, to flourish.

BLANTYRE AMBULANCE AT MILHEUGH

A privileged first! Previously unseen in any book or website is a rare photo of the WW1 Blantyre Ambulance in May 1915. Several postcards exist showing the ambulance at Calderglen and Caldergrove, but this photo was the first time seen at the former Milheugh House beside the Calder Falls. The ambulance was bought by funds raised by several well-known Blantyre ladies, following their dedication and hard work with many events collecting donations.

Figure 23 Miss Bannatyne beside the Blantyre Ambulance at Milheugh House 1915

Gordon Cook, who has written extensively about this subject matter, provides a short extract from his research: *"The motor ambulance arrived in Blantyre on Saturday, May 1st 1915. It was parked in Commercial Place, just off Stonefield Road, at three o'clock as had been intimated, and over two thousand people turned up to the dedication service. All the local ministers were there, and Rev Charles S. Turnbull told of how the idea for the fund had originated with the four young ladies mentioned earlier, the Misses Jackson, Cochrane, Moore and Bannatyne, and how, with the assistance of other well known local ladies they had "worked assiduously to make the scheme a success."* He also spoke encouragingly as to how the money was raised.

These ladies from Blantyre had raised an amazing £505 11s 4d in six months, and had delivered a Darracq motor ambulance, which cost £450 completely fitted out. The ambulance was fully equipped to accommodate patients on stretchers, with room also for eight sitting as well as a seat for an attendant.

The ambulance, with the single word 'Blantyre' painted in white just below the windscreen, was driven through Blantyre that afternoon, stopping here and there along the way to allow the public to inspect it. It was officially handed over to the Red Cross Society and as early as Wednesday morning it was in action, transporting wounded soldiers to Stobhill Hospital.

HUSBAND DISAGREES WITH POLICE

On Tuesday 21st August 1923, the Blantyre police completed their investigation in connection with a drowning the previous week, in a tributary of the Clyde. Mrs. O'Brien, the wife of a miner who lived at Watson Street had disappeared from home on the Friday night. Police were of the opinion that there was no foul play, and that the woman fell into the water.

On the other hand, the husband, Mr O'Brien did not believe police and stated there were marks of violence on the body. He said no one would convince him that it was anything else but foul play. Patrick O'Brien, the husband, stated that on the Friday evening his wife left the house as normal to go shopping. It was pay night, and she received £9 in wages from him and the family. She didn't return and alarm was raised all though the weekend.

On the Monday morning it was decided to drag the River Calder, and the woman's purse was found. A search of the bank showed about twenty shillings in silver scattered about, with an empty basket, a comb, and hairpins. Witnesses had come forward with strange stories. One miner stated that about ten o'clock on Friday night he saw a woman with her hair down her face, below a railway bridge, and a man in brown clothes beside her. Another pedestrian stated that, he saw the woman there in the company of two men, one of whom was adopting a menacing attitude towards her. When he approached and asked why they were ill-treating her one of the men said she was his wife and the pedestrian did not interfere further.

Patrick refused to believe it was an accident and took the death of his wife, hard. One evening a fortnight later, whilst under the influence of drink, he caused a breach of the peace at Blantyre Police Station demanding the return of his wife's clothing so he could look for further clues. The official conclusion to the investigation assumed that Mrs O Brien had fallen into the water.

MILHEUGH TROUT

On Thursday 28th August 1817, just over 200 years ago, a bizarre story appeared in the Perthshire Courier newspaper.

The story told that a brown trout had died at Milheugh, Blantyre in the well of James Miller. However, the strange thing was that the trout had been in the well for an astonishing 24 years and had become so tame, would take food out of James's hand. It had become a thing of legend.

The long living trout had nearly come to an end when about 6 years earlier in 1811; the fish had tried to eat a toad, which became stuck in the fish's mouth. Mr Miller removed the toad and saved the life of the fish. From that time the fish had become well known.

Incredibly, I was surprised to find out that some brown trout CAN live 2 decades. For a location for this story, there appears to be an open shallow well on the opposite side of the riverbank, not far from the falls, and certainly very close to the former Milheugh house. A circular feature marked in blue is marked on the Blantyre 1859 map, which may just have very well been the fish's final resting place!

THE FLAG BRIDGE

Whilst researching the history of the Calder, I recently found a description about Mid Letterick about third mile West of Milheugh, that mentioned it was the home of "The Flag Bridge". This name, being new to me and although just outside the Parish and no more, I decided to look at. This proved difficult and fellow history enthusiasts were equally stumped.

Looking at an 1859 map, I saw that the only crossing of the Cocks Burn (apart from the Dalton Road) was at Mid Letterick. Then, I remembered a visit to Mid Letterick I made in September 2014 and wondered if it could have been the little bridge I saw there, which at the time, I didn't think was too remarkable.

Figure 24 The Flag Bridge at Letterick as photographed in 2014

Looking back at photos of the day, I saw that the bridge DID have massive flagstones underneath it, supporting the weight of the structure on top. It is more than a glorified farming bridge and looking from this map, looks certain to be more than 150 years old. Worth another look, I'd say as the craftsmanship is actually quite good. Although I cannot be 100% certain, I'm fairly sure this is "The Flag Bridge". The whole area surrounding this is very scenic and best entered from Dalton junction near Stoneymeadow. Thanks to Jim Brown for guiding me around that day.

MOLE EARTH

Walking in Greenhall Park in August 2015, I noticed that large areas of the sloping field were covered in little mounds of earth. This was due to the burrowing night activity of moles. Creatures, which I suppose are not uncommon in Scotland of course, but it prompted a nice childhood memory, I thought I'd share here.

Figure 25 Mole Evidence at Greenhall Park photographed in 2015

It reminded me of my grandmother, Mary Duncan (nee Danskin) of Stonefield Crescent. During the 1970's, my gran, then in her 60's would pull a little shopping trolley (you know the kind you pulled behind you on a handle with 2 wheels) and head off to the Calder. She would collect that fine soil and wheel it all the way back to the garden at Stonefield Crescent. An avid gardener, this soil would then be mixed through the flower and vegetable patches, which were originally laden with clay and heavy soil.

The fine soil made the digging more manageable and changed the content of the soil to something much more suitable for maintaining and growing a thriving garden. The concept of buying a bag of topsoil in a shop would have been horrifying to her!

To this day, my sister now living at that house, (and probably unaware of the above), has a garden that has a fine soil, due to years of gran and her trolley trips to the Calder! It must have worked too. My childhood memories of gran's garden include seeing and tasting raspberries, gooseberries, peas, potatoes, carrots, onions and many more fruit and veg. Many a long summer was had popping pea pod shells and placing the peas into bowls. I convinced myself I liked peas at the time although looking back imaging their raw taste, that sentiment was probably misguided.

Who knows, maybe this is the magical secret formula that saw her live a long life!

GREENHALL RIFLE RANGE

Figure 26 The little known Greenhall Rifle Range, opened 1867

I once heard there was a rifle range at Greenhall (not to be confused by the well known range at Dechmont). It is a subject that took my fancy in 2018, so I've now pieced together the following.

On Saturday 1st June 1867, the 44th Rifle Volunteers in Blantyre took use of a custom made Rifle Range at Greenhall, High Blantyre. The range was to be exclusively used by this particular corps. The range was situated upon a flat part of the Greenhall Estate in High Blantyre, the lease of which had been taken by Captain Watkins with the proprietor's, Dr. Wardrop Moore's consent.

A substantial Butt (or earthworks mound) was erected and every provision made in conforming to the instructions of the Government Inspector, designed for shooting in third and second-class ranges. It was summer upon opening and with the weather being unusually fine, there was a large turnout of spectators. In addition to the officers of the company, there were several battalion officers present too, amongst whom were Colonel Simpson, Captain Gill the Adjutant, Captain Austine and Lieutenant Simpson. Also present were other friends of the movement, Sir Hugh Maxwell, Baronet of Calderwood and Hugh Maxwell. Esq.

Previous to the opening of the range, Captain Watkins had addressed the corps, and in the course his remarks referred to the obligations, which the members had to be mindful of towards Dr. Moore, the proprietor the ground. Dr Moore had greatly assisted him in making the arrangements for procuring the range and regulations were likely around the upkeep and use of the land. The Captain also referred to the able assistance of Ensign Strathern who had superintended the erection of the butt. After impressing the members with their duties as volunteers, he requested the Colonel to open the range by firing the first shot. The Colonel having consented, his rifle was handed to him, and incredibly a "bull's eye" was duly recorded. The officers and friends thereafter each took a shot, and some good shooting was made.

Thereafter, a competition took place for money prizes, which was presented by the Captain and Ensign Strathern. The winners were: Wm. Maxwell: 2d, William Todd; 3d. John Ness; 4th, Matthew McSkimming; 5th, John Struthers; 6th, David Eglinton; 7th John Thomson. Recruit prizes were to 1st Hugh Allan, 2nd. Francis Riddle; 3rd, James Roberts. After the presentation the prizes Sergeant Ness briefly addressed the members and proposed a vote of thanks to the donors of the prizes, which was heartily responded to.

Finding the Location

The range was described as being a good one, and worthy of the attention of officers who propose erecting similar ranges for their own corps. I have ruled out the range being near the former Greenhall House. There's no way Dr Moore would have permitted a range right beside his home and in any case the land surrounding the house is all wooded and very steep. That leaves the land to the south of the current A725. Using Stan Paul's map he gave me showing Greenhall Estate Boundaries, I homed in on the furthest away fields, without any woodland or any obstruction and especially those that are long. Now, on the 1898 map near the Craigmuir right of way, there is a raised earthworks feature that was NOT there on the 1859 map. It is immediately adjacent to a former hollowed quarry. The earthworks are indeed strange and attract attention as the opening of the range described the men working on creating an earthwork "butt" from where they could fire.

The long field right in front of it is an excellent contender for the range. It is north facing, meaning volunteers wouldn't be firing west or east into the sun. It faces directly across to Dechmont to the other rifle range and importantly is away from all homes and people. It is easily accessed too, from nearby Craigmuir Road and Sydes Brae, with a well present on the site also.

I'm willing to bet anybody with a metal detector will make some finds in the yellow marked area, where the shots would have fallen, and where targets would have been set up. It's been some time since I've walked that 'right of way' but the raised area is there behind some trees and distinctively separate from the gorse covered quarry beside it.

I think this is the most probable area for Greenhall Firing Range that the Blantyre 44th Rifle Corps designed and used. It's also on the exact boundary with Calderwood lands, and its notable that Baronet Maxwell of Calderwood attended the opening day of the range on 1st June 1867. More research is clearly needed, after all this was 151 years ago and long forgotten by even the grandparents of people alive today. However, I'm excited about this and fairly confident that my theory is pointing in the right direction. Have I found the 44th Rifle Range?

Competitions & Distances

In September 1867, just 4 months after the Volunteer Corps Rifle Range opened; an article appeared in the Hamilton Advertiser describing a competition held there. It is transcribed here, the interesting part for me listing the target distances the competition aimed to fire at.

"Rifle Competition – In accordance with a notice which appeared in our issue of Saturday last, a rifle competition in connection with the 44th Blantyre LBV, took place on that day [Saturday 14th September 1867] on the company range on the lands of Greenhall.

It was confined entirely to those members who were then entitled to receive the Capitation Grant and had completed their 60 rounds of ball practice. Distances were 200 and 300 yards, five rounds each. For these there were 10 prizes and three additional ones offered to those who had been engaged in volley firing prior to the 17th August last; highest scores at 200 yards to be the gainers. There were 56 entered [that's 56 x 2 targets x 5 shots = 560 shots let off!] Shooting commenced at 12 o'clock and continued till half past 6 o'clock. The weather was very favourable, especially towards the afternoon, although a strong wind blew at the onset.

Everyone concerned manifested the very best feeling during the day. The meeting was a great success. At the close, Col- Sergeant Ness, who was in command of the squads announced the winners to be as follows: Private Joseph Barr who won a short Ingram Enfield Rifle, 2. Bugler D McKercher, 3. Private Donald McLachlan, 4. Sergeant Robert Harper, 5. Private John Thomson, 6. Private George Allan, 7. Private William Roberts, 8. Private James Maxwell, 9. Sergeant Abraham Henshaw, 10. Private Archibald Brownlie. Additional Prizes to those who had fired volleys (7 shots per minute): 1. Private James Lindsay, 2. Sergeant Robert Harper, 3. Private Robert Gray.

The first prize was a gift by the Captain of the Corps, the 2nd, 6th, 7th, 8th and 9th, presented by the female workers in the spinning and weaving departments of H. Monteith & Co's Works. Members of the Corps desire us to record their very hearty appreciation of the kindness manifested to the Corps in these gifts "

An interesting article, I'm sure you'll agree. Seeing the distances of 200 and 300 yards in writing, using the measuring tool on Google Earth, I marked out where the targets would have been and they all fit nicely within the confines of that large, existing field. Gordon Cook told me that the Corps could fire much longer distances, which of course would have been possible back then in the fields beyond, before the creation of the Expressway.

Figure 27 Marked up Map showing Shooting range distances

Before we leave the subject of the former Greenhall Firing Range, it's worth noting how it looks now. In particular, the raised platform where the men fired their rifles from is pictured. Situated just off the Craigmuir right of way, not far from the ruins of Craigmuir Cottage, the mound is still apparent, manmade and enclosed by a stonewall, built in early 1867. Some of the raised mound is now covered with gorse, but it's not hard to picture where the men once stood upon to take their aim.

This is a little important piece of Blantyre history, now very much not talked about and forgotten. This old range almost always overlooked by memories of the more modern range at Dechmont. I hope these posts put it back in the spotlight.

Figure 28 Raised Platform ruins at former Rifle Range as it looked in 2016

CHAPTER 3
AUCHENTIBBER, CRAIGNEITH & CALDERWOOD

Auchentibber is an interesting old area of Blantyre elevated on the south upper slopes of our town. Its open spaces and green, tranquil fields lined with hedged paths and roads, make it an ideal spot for walking. Farming is now predominant and the hamlet is nowhere now near the size of community it once was, still largely detached from the rest of Blantyre. Craigneith and Calderside are on the fringes, bordered by the River Calder, looking across to Calderwood. Early photographer, David Ritchie above in 1908, photographed 'The Auchentibber Inn', which was owned at the time by J.B.H. Struthers. This wonderful picture has been painted as the cover of this book.

AUCHENTIBBER – ORIGINS OF THE NAME

Auchentibber is a hamlet, one of the original fermetouns of Blantyre in the Parish of Blantyre, Middle ward of the county of Lanark; which in 1846 contained 73 inhabitants. It is situated in the south-western part of the Parish, on high ground above Sydes Brae, and on the west, the Rotten-Calder water forms the boundary, and separates the parish from that of Kilbride.

Auchentibber may have been derived from "Achaw, Achan....a species of pear" which connects to the suggestion that fruit was grown in this area. The name may also have been derived from Gaelic, meaning, "field of the healing waters". There is evidence of healing springs nearby and it is said Victorian tourists came to Auchentibber to take advantage of the healing properties of the spring (likely situated on Park Farm). The area however, most likely took its name from the nearby farm, "Auchentibber", as the surrounding area already had names such as "Parkneuk, Muirfoot, Sydes Brae", all marked on early maps. The small population was mainly employed on the numerous farms, which were well built and many still exist today.

By the late 1700's, however, attention turned to the deposits of iron ore, found all over the area, which ended up being mined heavily, transported to Glasgow where it would eventually become pig iron. Then, in the early 1800's, mining activity expanded with limestone also being quarried. These activities and eventually coal, kept the population gainfully employed until the early 1900's. In 1898, there were over 70 homes in the area, whereas today there is roughly a dozen. During the 1800's, Auchentibber thrived as a community with many homes, shops, a school and a few pubs to support this community. A large stone quarry also supported the employment of many people right into the 1950's. Lighting was at that time done by paraffin lamp and dry external toilets even post World War 2, meant Auchentibber had some catching up to do. A post war decision by the Lanark 5th District Council not to immediately provide electricity or gas supplies to the area, led to its demise, with many people moving away to seek employment or better accommodation. Many Auchentibber homes were demolished and it was not for some time until the hamlet finally received electricity and gas supplies.

MINERAL SPRING AT PARK

In the 1791 "Statistical Account of Blantyre" written by Rev Henry Stevenson, there's a comment about a 'Spring in Blantyre' that was even visited as a tourist destination! Where from the description below could this be? The account had me puzzled as no particular Spring is currently famed today in Blantyre. I've recently had pointed out that there is a Spring in Park, Auchentibber, which is a more likely explanation than the Springs at Broompark. Having witnessed the Spring for myself and been assured from Jim Brown who has witnessed it bubbling up to the surface, I am forced to conclude the 1791 account of the Spring is referring to Park, Auchentibber and not in Springfield. A reminder of the account is below.

"Mineral Springs – There is a mineral spring in this parish, the water of which is frequently and successfully used, for sore eyes, scorbutic disorders, and a variety of other complaints. The water is sulphurous; it is very strongly impregnated, and is accounted the best of the kind in this part of the country. About fifty years ago (1740), it was the common summer resort of many families from Glasgow: but from the changes of fashion, so frequent in relation to such objects of medical regimen, it is now almost totally deserted."

The above theory about Park is further supported when I dug a little deeper. In 1885 within the Ordnance Gazetteer of Scotland, Francis H Groome wrote ad confirmed *"A mineral spring at Park, strongly impregnated with sulphur held in solution by hydrogen, was much frequented by Glasgow families toward the middle of last century, and still is famed in scrofulous and scorbutic cases."*

As well as the spring at Park Farm, there is a spring situated just off the old Park Road on the left hand side of the track from Auchentibber monument to the old Limekiln. The track is on the left hand side of Sydes Brae, directly across from the War Memorial on the left hand side. Follow it along for a short time, then just after a change in direction at the fenceline, on the left is a tree stump that rises up out of the spring itself. You can't miss it! It's not much to look at, but is worth a visit, especially if it's been raining.

<u>CALDERSIDE ROWS</u>

Calderside Row was a former single storey row of stone built, terraced homes, at Calderside, High Blantyre.

In July 1850, Mr. William Young, farmer and owner of Calderside Farm put his farm and all 177 acres of farmland up for sale. Within the advert of 19th July 1850 in the Glasgow Herald, it was noted that a valuable seam of Roman Cement runs through the whole lands, which was 'presently being wrought by the proprietor'. William McCreath, a mineral engineer had valued it as £1,000, a vast sum in 1850. The advert asked for the attention of dealers in cement noting that a seam so valuable was a rare event. Timber Woodland was valued at £770, which would later be sold in 1854.

The advert appears to have attracted the attention of Mr. George Anderson of Springfield who bought part of the farmlands in the second half of 1850, with the purpose of setting up cement kilns and continuing extracting the minerals. To do this he needed workers, ideally nearby. It's noted that by November 1850, Calderside Farm at a reduced area of 160 acres was still up for sale, but importantly, by that time no mention of the roman cement seam in the new advert. Those mineral rights and 17 acres of the 177 having been sold for the purposes of the kiln, extraction operations and its associated workers housing. George Anderson would go on in 1851 to negotiate a further sale for all of the remaining Calderside Farm.

Calderside Row Conditions

Figure 29 Calderside Row Pictured in 1930, courtesy of Norma Marr

Calderside Row was constructed in 1851 to accommodate the workers of the nearby new 'Calderside Cement Works', also built that year. [Source Caledonian Mercury Newspaper 2nd

September 1856]. As noted, Blantyre and Kilbride at that time shared the mineral known as 'Roman Cement' and having modest homes so close to the kilns was ideal. The rateable value of the small row was around £10 per annum; the lucrative cement works over 30 times that!

The area the houses were to be built on was historically important to Blantyre, right beside the Bronze Age earthworks and stone mound of 'Campknowe', perhaps the oldest referenced antiquity in Blantyre. A site was chosen a couple of hundred yards north of Calderside Farm, directly opposite the Cement kilns at an oblique bend in the road. A track existed directly beside Calderside Row, beyond homes 1 and 2, which connected across fields to Parkneuk Road, some distance to the east.

The row consisted of a block of 6 single storey homes. Built of sandstone with a slated roof. There were single chimneys at either gable end and 2 double chimneys spaced out within the middle of the row. Addresses were numbered from 1 in the north, to 6 in the south. The houses were built on a slightly raised, a few feet higher than the nearby road, just a few metres away. Each home had a doorway and one single window facing out on to the road and across to the cement kilns. Wooden window shutters on the west side would have screened out the late afternoon and evening sunshine.

There were originally no toilet blocks or wash facilities around in or around the homes and within no running water in the houses, all water was fetched from a nearby pump, fed by a well in front of home number 3. Vertical Downpipes for roof drainage stopped at waist height allowing fresh water to easily be collected in pails. Slop may have initially been carried to the nearby stream, which fed into the Rotten Calder River. By the 1890's, an outside toilet block had been constructed to the south of number 6. Adjacent and adjoining to the block, to the north was a small, single storey stable, perhaps used for a couple of horses required for the works.

Even within the first decade of the cement kilns opening, a small tramway had been constructed connecting the riverside quarry to the kiln. The tramway appears to have been lifted and removed prior to 1896, likely in the 1870s or 1880s. The 1896 map marks the quarry as being 'old.' By the turn of the 20th Century, Calderside Row had become small family homes and not just for cement workers, the kilns themselves no longer used by 1910.

The location of Calderside Row would have offered easy access to the beautifully laid out paths, pools, grotto and woodland beyond Auchentibber at the rivers edge with commanding views across to Calderwood Castle. It would have been an attractive, exciting playground for adventures of any child! By the late 1930's there was little signs left of the quarry or indeed the kilns. A Water Tap or standpipe replaced the Water pump outside the houses.

Owners and Occupiers

Prior to 1875, George Anderson left his cement kilns and the 6 homes to son, William Carrick Anderson. Anderson & Co still owned the kiln works which by then had a rateable value of £147, a reflection of the extent of the mineral extraction and half the value it had been 20 years earlier.

In 1885, William Carrick Anderson, (also the owner of nearby Calderside Farm) still owned the cement works and homes, and it is perhaps notable that year that 3 of them were lying empty, a reduction in workforce, no less! The kilns stopped producing between 1885 and 1895. By 1895, William still owned Calderside Row and Farm, but was now living in Glasgow. He let out the farm to farmers Robert and Gavin Watt, and the homes at Calderside Row would be let to separate tenants too. Gavin Young, a grazier occupied one of the homes and the stable. John Thomson, a labourer occupied another as did John Downie, a joiner renting for £3 and 10 shillings per year, a modest rent for modest homes. Tenants were similar with the addition of Miss Agnes Banner by 1905. It is also telling that a few of the homes in Calderside Row remained unoccupied in the 1890's and first decade of the 1900's, likely in need of modernisation and remotely some distance away from employment opportunity.

By the start of WW1, after the passing of William Anderson, new tenant Francis MacFarlane, a miner was renting the home at the north side of the row, and also renting the stable. Trustees of William Anderson held the homes. This was the start of over 100 years of MacFarlane occupation, which still exists today.

The Calderside Farm and Row passed to George Carrick Anderson and by 1925 Francis MacFarlane was in merged homes 1 & 2. Number 3 lay empty, Agnes Lennox a widow in number 4 ,Miss Agnes Banner spinster in number 5 and George Cumming, joiner in number 6.

Figure 30 Tenants outside 1 Calderside Row in 1944

By 1930, according to the valuation roll, Mr. George Carrick Anderson still owned houses 3 to 6 and the house at 1 and 2, which had been merged to form one house. He also owned the nearby stable. Francis and May MacFarlane were still at number 1 &2 that year. In number 3 was John Duncan, in number 4 James Marshall. Number 5 was Hugh Murchie's rented house and number 6 Michael Murray. The MacFarlane family also lived at Calderside Road.

By the 1950's new, larger front windows had been put into the houses and the former doorway of House 2 blocked up. Proper drainage off each roof was also formed.

The Downies and MacFarlanes continued to live in this location well beyond WW2 until the demolition of the old rows in the late 1960's. Calderside Row had existed for nearly 120 years.

Today, there are two 1970's detached houses, one of which is a bungalow on the site of Calderside Row. The MacFarlanes still live at Calderside Cottage. Where the kilns once were, is now a modest sized scrapyard, "Calderside Auto Salvage". Otherwise, and with exception of 3 wind turbines, which were removed from the field beyond in 2018, the area is still primarily rural and quiet.

MUIRFOOT

In 1859 the area of Muirfoot at Auchentibber was described as, *"A couple of houses named from the Muir of Blantyre coming formerly to this place, which is still divided into small portions of land that were formerly given to the Heritors of the Parish to cut peat in. Those portions do not, in some cases, exceed a few perches. They (the division marks) are all defaced, and now exist only in the memories of the persons who hold their right to the original portions for cutting peat upon. These small portions are all cultivated, it could not be perceived in the fields they are in as separate properties".*

The name dropped away from maps after 1898 and is now largely forgotten. It is now the area located at the junction of Sydes Brae and Auchentibber Road. This area would flourish in later times with the arrival of JBH Struthers who took over the Inn and built his famous Italian Gardens around a bespoke quoiting green. Directly across from the word "Muirfoot" in a modern context is now the Auchentibber War Memorial, which was demolished and rebuilt in September and October 2018.

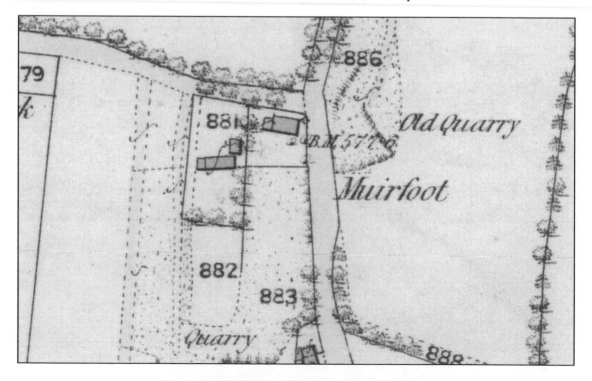

Figure 31 Muirfoot shown on the 1859 map

NEWHOUSEMILL DRUNKEN DEATH

About 9 o'clock on the morning of Sunday 13th October 1867, the body of man named Matthew Arneil was found laying face down in the Calder River under Newhousemill Bridge, on the boundary with East Kilbride Parish (back roads).

Figure 32 Newhousemill Bridge, the scene of this incident

Matthew was a miner residing at Newfield, Blantyre. When found quite dead, he appeared to have lain in the water for several hours. There a large cut between four and fire inches long on his head first prompting the suspicion of foul play.

However, upon investigation, it was found that Matthew was accustomed to drinking heavily, even during the day. It was learned that he had been drinking heavily for the previous eight days, and was seen in East Kilbride early the previous Sunday morning under the influence of liquor.

It is was therefore concluded that on his way home back to Blantyre, he had fallen over the bridge into the water, a height of somewhere between 20 and 30 feet, and sustained the injury when his head came into contact with rocks in the water. The body was removed to a relation's house at East Kilbride. Matthew Arneil was about 38 years of age, and unmarried.

Pictured is a modern photo of Newhousemill Bridge, the scene of the earlier fatality.

DIXON'S DYNAMITE MAGAZINE STORE

About halfway up Sydes Brae, before you reach Auchentibber, on the right hand side, sits in a field, a hidden little brick and stone building. Easily missed, it sits in a dip in the field, quite hidden and inconspicuous. It was situated as such for a very good reason. This was Dixon Collieries Dynamite Magazine Store, built and owned by Messrs of similar name, FC Dickson.

Built of brick and stone with a vaulted blast roof, the building had no windows and just one entrance in and out. The entrance was of course fortified with visible evidence of considerable blast doors still there today.

Dating likely back to the early 1880's the store most probably served Dixons 2 and 3 pits in High Blantyre, which were not a great distance away. The building must have been well built, not just to withstand any accident, but to prevent ingress from thieves and the elements. The top surface of the concrete was even scored with indentations, specifically so grass and vegetation would hold to it and hide it further. It's open to look inside.

Figure 33 Dixon's Dynamite Magazine Store 1980's

Gordon Cook sent me the photo above taken in the early 1980's. Even since then, nature is slowly reclaiming the building back. Most collieries in the vicinity had their own separate dynamite magazine for blasting operations. The store is still there today and worth a little visit next time you're in the vicinity.

CLYDE ROW

The Clyde Row was a row of eighteen one bedroomed small homes on the Sydes Brae near Auchentibber. They were located just above Dickson's old place, (where the present occupier sold plants till recently) on the opposite side of the road from the Auchentibber Memorial and down the hill a little. The homes belonged to ironstone miners of the area and their families and opened out on to the Sydes Brae itself. They were built of stone and divided into 3 equal blocks of 6 homes, each with a washhouse in the back garden. In the 1890's one of the nearby quarries was immediately beside these cottages, directly across the road from the nearby Auchentibber Inn.

This next rare photo shows the upper two sections of the three blocks of Clyde Rows, Auchentibber. The date is unknown, but estimated by the fashions as being in 1910's or 1920's. The photo shows a water tap outside one of the homes in the most southerly-elevated block.

The 1910 map shows the water pump served all 18 homes and is not shown on the 1898 map. The Gallagher family lived at number 18. The Browns at number 5, the McWalters at number 2.

Figure 34 Former Clyde Row during the 1920's

Sir Charles Cameron asked a health question in the House of Commons about this row on 14th August 1893. The water supply had become contaminated from some nearby sewage, and the Sanitary Authorities served eviction notices on the eighteen houses and had the people removed. Sir Charles also asked if a temporary standpipe could not have been fitted up rather than evicting people, but the Secretary of State for Scotland Sir George Trevelyan had no decent answer for him. The landlord threatened to sue the authorities for loss of rent. Enteric (typhoid) fever had broken. It is unknown if there were any deaths by it. There was a new reservoir due to open soon at Glengavel (likely, the one on the Strathaven Muirkirk Road) but it didn't come quick enough for these folk of that particular time.

Children living at Clyde Row would have had a short journey to school nearby at Auchentibber Road and would have delighted to be surrounded by so many fields to play in during evenings and weekends. We're sure many would have taken an interest in the nearby quoiting green and watching sports played there.

Today, the homes are no longer there. Clyde Row has a demolition date somewhere between April 1937 and summer 1939. Indeed there are no ruins remaining either. All that's left is a level grassed field, which has in 2018 been given planning permission for modern homes.

So many families had lived in this location and seeing just a field there today is somewhat sad. It's hoped this story will be remembered next time you drive by the location.

PRESENTATION TO HUGH WALLACE

Hugh Wallace was the son of Auchentibber's James Wallace. Hugh was a blacksmith to trade and by February 1900 he had been a member of the 2nd V.B.S Rifle Volunteers for 3 years. He had volunteered his services as a farrier in the Royal Horse Artillery.

On the first Wednesday in February 1900, just 1 month after saying goodbye to the 1890's, Hugh was ready to say goodbye again. This time he was leaving for Aldershot and expecting to sail out to South Africa the following week. At Auchentibber, the community rallied and he was presented with a powerful pair of field glasses, sportsman's knife, and a pipe and tobacco from a few friends who met to bid him farewell and to wish him good luck. Inspector Gracie of Blantyre made the presentation and spoke in the highest terms of Hugh's patriotic behaviour and of the volunteers in their country's hour of need.

He said 'Farrier' Wallace took an honoured name to the front and knew he would never do anything to dishonour it. Mr Wallace suitably replied and a pleasant hour was spent afterwards bidding farewell from close family and friends. War took place in South Africa from 1899 to 1902.

Hugh was the son of James Wallace b1845 and Helen Allan Russell b1842. Originally from Kirkintilloch James moved to Auchenitbber as a farrier. Wife Helen was working as a domestic servant in Hamilton on Kennedy's Farm. Hugh was born in 1879. This family had lived in Auchentibber throughout the 1870s, 1880s and 1890s.

Of course you should know how this ended. Hugh did survive the African conflict and was discharged from Army duty in 1902. Hugh Wallace married Lizzie Mckinlay on June 26, 1903, back in Blantyre, when he was 24 years old. His child James Jnr was born on November 23, 1903, in Motherwell, Lanarkshire. Another child Minnie would follow. Hugh, Lizzie and children visited America in 1906 but are thought to have returned to Blantyre.

His previous army experience made him a suitable candidate to return across the Atlantic to service when war broke out in 1914. He enrolled on 11th August 1914, listing Blantyre as his home. Hugh Wallace served in the military that year when he was 35 years old. He must have survived the war, for in 1920, following the war, he and wife Lizzie, are noted as living in the town of Eldorado Ward 3, Saline County, Illinois. The trail runs cold at about 42 years of age, but given he had his family with him there, I'm assuming there are American descendants living today that are familiar with this family story. His elder brother John lived a long life after emigrating to Australia.

CALLOUS AUCHENTIBBER FATHER

Life at the turn of the new Century in 1900 was not pleasant for Glasgow man John Thomson. The next few years would see him and his family in a downward spiral of bad luck, misfortune and tragedy.

In June 1901, his misfortune started when he became unemployed from his job as a Stickworker. The impact of losing his job was that he lost his ability to pay rent and to provide for his family almost straight away. So, it came to be that at the end of June 1901, Barnhiil Hospital and Poor House took in his wife and three children. This poorhouse although named Barnhill was unconnected to Blantyre and sited in Glasgow, opened in 1850. 'Paupers' who could not support themselves were sent here and were obliged to work at jobs such as bundling firewood, picking oakum (separating tarred rope fibres) and breaking rocks. The hours were long and the inmates worked unpaid under extremely poor conditions, with harsh discipline and dreadful food. In 1945 it was renamed Foresthall House and Hospital and was thereafter used as an old people's hospital and residential home. It was demolished in the late 1980s and a private housing development now stands on the site. But let's get back to the story.

In summer 1901, John, his wife and 3 children were living at this terrible place. The poorhouse may have been especially sympathetic to the families' plight for John's wife was heavily pregnant and in July, just 3 weeks later, went into labour in the poorhouse hospital. She gave birth to a daughter who died at the birthing table and sadly, his wife died at that table too. It's clear that left without a wife, John selfishly was not only able to cope with the children, but was thinking of himself, when he deserted the children by running from the poorhouse shortly after, perhaps affected by grief.

In October 1901, John was caught upon and the case brought before a Sherriff who sympathetically pointed John towards Auchentibber, Blantyre and job opportunities. John took his 3 children and in those days before any proper child welfare authorities, housed them in a one-roomed house at Clyde Row. He was able to rent as during that October he immediately got instant employment (I can't help but wonder if the Sheriff or authorities had arranged this?)

However during November and December 1901, he continued to struggle with being a father, and although in constant employment earning 22s per week, he failed to provide them with sufficient food, whereby they became dependent on neighbours. John left home at eight in the morning, and seldom returned before ten at night, leaving his three children for that length of time, aged 11, 5 and 3. He made little or no provision for them during his absence. No schooling. No food. No warmth in those harsh winter months.

Neighbours in the small row of miners cottages on Sydes Brae became more concerned when this had been going on for months, and despite giving the little ones some food on occasion, it was noticed how thin and poorly turned out they were becoming. The Society for the Prevention of Cruelty to Children was informed of the case in December and Dr Grant was called in. His report was read, and stated that the children were much emaciated, and the house deplorably dirty and unhealthy.

The children were taken away from John and taken to Hamilton poorhouse in Bothwell Road. However sadly, days after through ill health, the middle child, aged 5 died on Wednesday 6th January 1902. It was found that this had happened through the previous neglect. On 11th January 1902, single parent John Thomson appeared in court and before Sheriff Davidson, John pleaded guilty to his children's neglect throughout the autumn and winter of 1901. He openly admitted he had cruelly neglected all three of his children and had been unable to cope since the death of his wife. Feeling little sympathetic, the Sheriff imposed the highest penalty in his power—viz., six months' imprisonment, with hard labour.

Before I leave this sad story, I can't help but wonder what became of the surviving two Thomson children of Auchentibber. It's unlikely they would have returned to that small house. It is also perhaps unlikely they were ever returned to their father, once he left prison. Do you know more?

I'd love to find out what became of them.

HERMITAGE: HERMIT'S HUT

This photo dates from 1904, which featured in a brochure published by Gilmours of Glasgow Road. The brochure contained several excellent Blantyre related photos, which have been scanned now in high resolution.

Figure 35 The Hermit's hut in Calderwood Glen around 1904

Featured is the Hermitage, or Hermit's hut, which was located in Calderwood Glen, just beyond Auchentibber, on the Blantyre side of the River Calder. The little building dates from the period 1780-1850. Considering the re-development of Calderwood Glen by the 8th Baronet occurred, between 1840 and 1845, the Hermitage is likely to have originated closer to that date range. When this folly hermitage was entire, it would be best described as a rustic gazebo or summerhouse built of stone. The building stood approximately 12 feet tall including its pyramidal thatched roof, which took up about 5-6 feet of its entire height. The masonry consisted of about ten courses of rough dressed and pointed blocks of sandstone. In the southern face of the building was a window, vertically elongated, with a semi-circular top. The door was in the western face and was of identical design to the window. Some photographs suggest that another window may have been located on the northern side of the building.

This building was maintained during the SCWS ownership of Calderwood Estate, but by the end of World War I it had begun to fall into ruin, and by the mid 1920's was demolished. Now only two courses of rubble outlining the building remain.

The building was constructed on top of a large boulder in the middle of the Rotten Calder Water, with a spit of sand and river gravel and rocks tailing off to the north. The eastern side of the rock is a sheltered bay, above which the banks slope steeply up to the Blantyre farmlands. Water always flows on the western side, and at certain times of year flows on both sides, effectively cutting the location off as an islet in the river. The rock itself may have originated the name Grey Mare, as several references exist relating to river rocks and the title of Grey Mare. Thanks to Chris Ladds for his incredible knowledge on Calderwood and much of the information in this article.

VILLAGE IMPROVEMENT TRUST

The "Auchentibber Village Improvement Trust" was proposed and formed in early November 1915. This wartime organisation was to seek social and living standards improvement for the hamlet of Auchentibber and seek to bring it up to standard of Blantyre itself, particularly to address the problem of sewage in the area. A meeting was held in Auchentibber School on Monday 1st November 1915.

Mr. James. B.H Struthers presided and after briefly eluding to the benefits that such an organisation would bring called upon Parish Councillor McInulty to make the opening address. Mr. McInulty was listened to with great attention from an audience largely comprising of Auchentibber residents and he pointed out the amenities in the village and how they could be improved upon. His statistics about Auchentibber caused much reflection by people when compared by the statistics and standards expected in Blantyre.

MILITARY PRESENTATION

The Hamilton Advertiser reported when wounded WW1 soldiers were brought to Auchentibber and entertained, with local business owners presenting them with gifts and honours for their bravery. The report on Saturday 2nd September 1916 told:

"The military age portion of the village Auchentibber have done nobly in this war, as witness the Roll of Honour which has been placed in a most prominent position in the beautiful grounds of the Quoiting Club, situated in the heart of the place. The women folks, too have done their bit not less nobly by working hard night after night to provide comforts for the lads who have gone forth to serve their country in the highest calling one might well be asked to perform; and it was only what was expected to find the villagers anxious to show some gratitude to several of those soldiers who had been maimed in the fight by providing an afternoon's entertainment within the precincts of their well-known glorified paradise during the period of their convalescence.

This came off on Wednesday afternoon when a large party of wounded soldiers were motored from Hillpark Hospital, Bothwell. Led by two nurses, to the Auchentibber Quoiting Green, there to be the guests of the upland village. The arrangements for the reception of the soldiers were complete in every way. On arrival they were entertained a fine concert by Tom Colley, comedian, who is appearing at Blantyre Picture House this week, and Miss Lizzie and Master James Gibson, two juveniles who were successful in recent competitions at the Picture House. Mr Gideon Duncan ably played the accompaniments. The arrangements for this part the proceedings were the hands of Mr James Marchant, the Picture House manager, and he has every credit by the taste he displayed in his selection of entertainers. A feature of the afternoon's enjoyment was the presence of the Regimental Band and Pipers from Hamilton Barracks, under the leadership of Mr Louis Seymour, and needless to say, their musical selections provided an entertainment, which was heartily appreciated not only by the wounded Tommies, but the large audience surrounding.

About five o'clock an al fresco tea was served on the quoting green and here again the ladies of the place showed their interest by acting as table attendants, and with assistants galore there was "no waiting." The inner man having been satisfied, an abundant supply of cigarettes was served out, while at intervals thereafter the ladies went round and distributed sweets, fruit, etc. which were acceptably received the guests.

Figure 36 JBH Struthers pins medals to soldiers in 1916

One of the most interesting parts of the day's proceedings was the presentation of the Distinguished Conduct Medal to Corporal M'Anulty, Udston, of the Gordon Highlanders, which took place In the presence of the whole company. Corporal M'Anulty had the medal pinned to his tunic last week by Viscount French, but it was thought, to give the local touch to the high honour. No better opportunity could had that of Wednesday, to give the villagers a public opportunity of welcoming their own distinguished soldier, and right heartily joined in the ceremony. It fell to Mr James. B. H. Struthers the Auchentibber Inn landlord, to perform this pleasing duty, and addressing Corpl. M'Anulty, he said the villagers were proud of the high honour bestowed upon him the King. "It was men like Corpl. M'Anulty". said Mr Struthers "and those who were their guests that day, who were allowing them to enjoy sunny skies and peaceful homes, and they felt they could not do too much for the heroes who were fighting for them. Corpl. M'Anulty made a modest acknowledgment. The proceedings terminated about seven o'clock, all having spent a most delightful afternoon amidst delightful environment. The Auchentibber folks are to be heartily congratulated on their laudable efforts that day—efforts, which were spontaneous they were appreciative. Nevertheless one almost concluded that while the voice of Jacob was there so also was the hand of Esan—the 'hand" was that of Mr J. B. H. Struthers. Organiser-in-chief, that genial and large hearted soul who has done much to brighten the lives of the people of that secluded but pretty little upland hamlet."

Pictured is JB Struthers presenting the meal to Corporal McAnulty at the Auchentibber WW1 "Troops Entertainment" day.

BASKET HOSPITAL SITE

In early November 1928, authorities in this region were looking for a site for a new Maternity Hospital. Sites at Cambuslang, Larkhall and Bothwell Castle had been considered, but of interest to Blantyre residents at the time was the possible use of the fields around Basket Farm, High Blantyre and grounds of Calderwood Castle.

It was agreed that mining reports should be sought and sites at Bothwell, Blantyre and Calderwood were quickly dismissed by mining engineers as unsuitable. It is unknown to me where the eventual site was chosen, but I do know that it was neither at Hairmyres nor Bellshill at that particular time.

AUCHENTIBBER REMEMBRANCE

From November 1950. *"The folks of Auchentibber turned out well to a remembrance day service held at the War Memorial in the village last Sunday. A service appropriate to the occasion was conducted by Mr. William Liddle of the Baptist Church and a wreath was laid on the war memorial by Miss Margaret Boyle, Victoria Street, High Blantyre who had 2 nephews killed in the 1914 – 1918 war. At one point of the service the people assembled sung, "The Lord's Mr Shepherd" and a choral item was rendered by the children under the title of "God Bless the Boys in Khaki". The wreath placed on the War Memorial was the work of Mr. Robert Dickson of Auchentibber."* The War Memorial at Auchentibber has been neglected for some time and as such, was in dire need of repairs.

Blantyre Project in Autumn 2016 teamed up with various other stakeholders including SLC Cemeteries, Blantyre Community Council, local councillors, Blantyre Heritage Group, Auchentibber WI and residents, High Blantyre Baptist Church and other interested individuals, to form a plan for raising funds and saving the monument for future generations.

With funding secured, the Auchentibber War Memorial was recently demolished and rebuilt in September and October 2018, unveiled in the November in time for remembrance day.

AUCHENTIBBER GARDENS – LAST PICTURE

This photo is one of the last ever to be taken of the beautiful Italian Gardens surrounding the Auchentibber Quoiting Green. When J.B.H Struthers, owner of the nearby Auchentibber Inn died in January 1938, he was single and had no children. He died of illness and did not fall down a well, which you may have read on a website by 'ainother.

It is thought his Inn was demolished very shortly after his death, for it is not on the 1939 map. This beautiful photo dates from around that time and already you can see the effect of nature starting to take over the garden. In just the space of a couple of years without a gardener or person to maintain the area, the statues, steps and balustrades started to become overgrown and covered in ivy. Whilst the photo looks beautiful, some telltale signs of neglect are apparent.

Figure 37 Auchentibber Gardens in their final years. Pictured c1939

In time in the very late 1930's and early 1940's, the statues were removed by unknown individuals, along with many of the balustrades, presumably for reuse, leaving only the foundations we see today. The land was never rebuilt upon and fell completely into neglect and to nature. The timing co-incides with a downwardly spiral for population in Auchentibber, largely due to lack of working opportunity in that area.

However, additionally, I can't help but feel that Mr Struthers, whilst living had kept the area alive, much visited and talked about and that Auchentibber itself hugely suffered from the death of the well-known businessman.

THE SEA PLANE

In this context, a Seaplane was also known as a Screen Plane. From the 1960's until the late 1980's, some people may remember seeing the strangest thing in Auchentibber. A sea plane, sitting at the back of one of the old, derelict buildings (Brown's Land) on the left hand side of Sydes Brae at the start of Parkneuk Road. It sat there for years, wasting away, rusting, and never moving. ." It was behind the old Brown's land derelict building, out in the open and further up the hill, across the road from the Auchentibber War Memorial.

The seaplane sat in the back yard, out of sight from the road, but behind large fences. In January 1960, Kenneth MacDonald bought Browns Land and removed the upper level of the old tenement. The MacDonald family still own Brown's Land.

Figure 38 Illustration of Similar Plane

Linda MacDonald Stead added, *"My dad Kenneth MacDonald designed and built the plane known as a 'screen plane'. It started life as a boat (owned by my dad). I have the propeller I believe stored somewhere. The plane was built in our back garden in Larkhall before being taken to Strathaven air field for its maiden voyage (which was reported on radio) this would have been sometime between 1977-1979 as my husband was the pilot. It was stored in the open air on dad's land for some time unfortunately it was made of desirable material for selling making it a source of upset. Undesirables started stripping it for the parts."*

Another plane existed nearby at a similar time. Margaret Nimmo Lehmann added, *"When my oldest son, Glen was young, my dad (Robert Nimmo) told him a story about building an airplane with Robert Dickson in his Barn at Auchentibber Farm. I never knew about that until years later when my son told me. The plane was never finished. Dad and Robert Dickson were great friends."* Robert Dickson died in 1984 and it is unknown what became of his unfinished plane.

BLANTYRE MUIR TURBINES

In July 2007, Blantyre Muir Wind Energy Ltd submitted a full planning application to South Lanarkshire Council for planning consent to construct a 3-turbine wind farm within an area of agricultural land near Laigh Muirhouses Farm on the western side of Hamilton. In October 2011, planning consent was eventually granted (SLC planning reference HM/07/0563), with the 3 turbines each having a maximum blade tip height of 102m.

Additionally, on neighbouring land, 3 further turbines were proposed. These Blantyre Muir

Wind Farm 'Extension' turbines were also consented (SLC planning reference HM/10/0478) and have a maximum blade tip height of 115m, with a revisit to the original 3 constructed to increase the blade tip height to 115m. The 6 turbines have a 12.3MW capacity and can generate enough electricity to power 6,500 homes.

Figure 39 Blantyre Muir Turbines pictured by George Young

George Young shared this dramatic photo of 2 of Blantyre Muir wind turbines. George has a real talent for capturing colourful and beautiful moments. Whilst people know I'm no fan of turbines, I'm not opposed to them in general, only the turbines that are right beside people's homes.

It's a human right to choose where you live and the arrival of a turbine in your back yard, in my opinion is a step too far. I am however, all for them in places like moorland and offshore, and for lets face it energy is going to be a big topic this century.

CHAPTER 4
BARNHILL & BARDYKES

Barnhill and Bardykes are another two of Blantyre's hamlets, on the western fringes of Blantyre, bordered by the Calder woodlands. They generally stretch along Bardykes Road from the junction of Broompark Rd all the way to the West End. Prominent families in this area once included the Millars and The Jacksons. These communities housed weavers, farmers, nurserymen and miners.

In our cover photo above from the 1920's, Miss Aggie Bain walks along the crest of Broompark Road with the Calder in the background. The cottage pictured is now no longer there. Aggie's own cottage near the Barnhill Tavern, known more recently as Bardykes Cottage is the oldest house in Blantyre allegedly built in 1536 and as of October 2018, is up for sale.

HISTORY OF BARDYKES

Bardykes is likely taken from the word "Bar"- meaning 'low hills' and the Gaelic Dike, Dyk, as meaning "a wall of turf or stone". It is a fitting description for a lower part of Blantyre that would have stonewall farm fields.

Jacksons

The Jackson or Jacksone family were in possession of the lands of Bardykes, (or Bardykis as it was then known) officially from 25th October 1525 although other Blantyre historians have suggested it may be as far back as 1502. Incredibly, with the exception of the Miller family at

Milheugh, they are the longest surviving family owning land in one place in Blantyre, occupying and owning the land at Bardykes for the best part of 400 years.

Owning mineral rights on their lands, some wealth was accumulated from their nearby estates at Hallside and Spittalhill. However, their wealth was in later centuries derived from their vast tea plantations in Sri-Lanka (formerly Ceylon), conducting their business as merchants Messrs Jackson, Buchanan & Company in Glasgow. They went on to become one of the largest wholesale tea dealers in Scotland. The Jacksons were also known to own land and properties at Greencroft and nearby at Barnhill.

Heritors and Lord Blantyre

Being such a prominent family and as heritors of Blantyre, they owed a duty to Walter Stuart of Minto, the Commendator of Blantyre when he was given ownership of much of the Parish land on 18th January 1598. The land was noted as "Bairdisdykis" as well as other established areas. In 1606, when he became Lord Blantyre, as a gesture and a departure from paying taxes, the Jackson family presented an annual red rose to Lord Blantyre instead as a reddendo.

A John Jackson died in 1707; his will shows all belongings passing to his family of the same name. By mid Century the family were marrying into other large farms in the area, occupying other Blantyre farms like Park, Coatshill, Croftfoot and Old Place.

In 1745 when the highlanders of Bonnie Prince Charlie's army were returning north after the unsuccessful expedition into England to place the Prince on the British throne, many of the stragglers passed through Blantyre, just as they did when they marched south at the beginning of the ill fated journey. To prevent the highlanders from pillaging his house in search of food, the Laird of Bardykes ensured there was an ample supply of bannocks and whiskey at the gates of Bardykes House for the hungry soldiers.

In 1793 a John Jackson Junior lived at Bardykes. This gentleman died aged 98 in his home during October 1801.

On Monday 24th August 1847, crops and the entire equipment and stock at Bardykes were sold off, likely following another death of a Jackson family member. This may have signified the leasing of the farm to others. 20 Acres of Oats, 4 acres of beans, some barley, 3 acres of turnips, some potatoes, a quantity of rye grass, meadow hay, thrashing mill, gig and gig harnesses, 3 horses, 6 cows, some queys, carts, ploughs and farming utensils.

However, just 3 years later, in 1850, Bardykes was still owned by a Robert Jackson. By mid March 1853, Robert was letting his house out, placing an advert in the Glasgow Herald "To let The House at Bardykes consisting of 2 rooms and a kitchen, with Garret rooms and a good garden." He was again letting it out in 1856, this time unfurnished, a sign the previous tenancy had been short lived. Then again letting it in May 1857. It would appear people wishing to take tenancy certainly on this particular part of the farm at Bardykes were few and far between. This may have affected Robert's health for he died on 22nd September 1857 at Bardykes.

Robert's death prompted another sale of items at Bardykes Farm. On 14th November 1857, that winters day, the following items were auctioned off. 3 Horses and a foal, 12 cows and a calf, a number of young cattle, a great number of stacks wheat, oats, beans and hay. Turnips, carts, ploughs, harrows also sold off. It was noted that the crops and cattle were of a first class order. However, again we see no sale of property, the farm and outbuildings retained by the Jacksons. It didn't sell and was carried to a second more detailed auction on 14th December 1857, this time much more heavily advertised.

That same month, the Jackson estate put the farm up for lease for another 15 years. It amounted to 70 acres and it was noted that the farm had been well tended and the fields in excellent condition. At the time of the lease 12 acres had already been sown with wheat and a further 10 acres with rye grass.

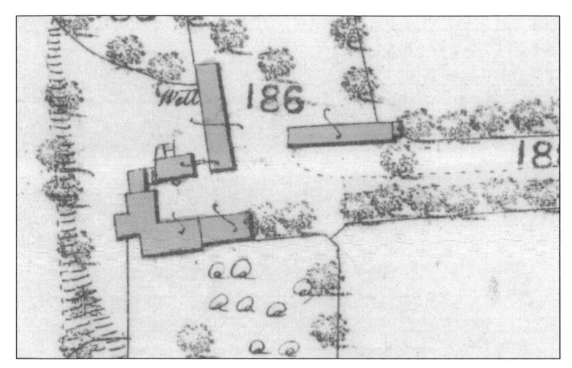

Figure 40 Bardykes Old Farm House pictured on 1859 Map

Whilst the name Bardykes relates to an area of Blantyre, it is now best associated with the large stone built detached house which is located off Callaghan Drive at Bardykes Road, not far from the west end of Glasgow Road.

Prior to the current house built, a good-sized farm steading was all that was on this land. The Valuation books for 1859 state, *"A good Farm Steading. The property of Mrs. Jackson."* Whilst Mrs Jackson was then the owner, a Robert Wilson was the occupier, likely the farmer, paying an annual rent to the Jacksons. Mrs Janet Jackson (nee Dick) died on 3rd January 1864.

Thomas and Robert Wilson who had been leasing the farm are known to have left sometime the next year. In December 1865, the land is known to have been 84 acres, showing that further fields had been farmed on and it was up for sale. The farm was to be shown by John Jackson of Spittalhill, the Jackson family living at that larger property nearby. The advert continued to January 1866, suggesting it was leased out in 1866, which I have found out was to a Mr. John Caldwell. A Mr Thomas Nelson also lived on a small building on the farm, according to 1865 valuation roll.

At that time, the original farm was one storey, set almost in a quadrangle with one side missing (U shaped). It was accessed off a track that led in exactly where the avenue leads in to the current house. Outside, were barns and buildings, which may have doubled as farmhand accommodation. As much as the Jacksons had accumulated a fortune, the farm buildings here may not have showed that to good effect, by comparison to the other large homes in Blantyre like Auchinraith, Milheugh, Crossbasket or Caldergrove.

As you came up the entrance, a low single storey long barn was on the right, as the road opened out on to the farm courtyard. Just off the courtyard to the right was another long single storey barn. The farmhouse was on the left, forming part of the courtyard itself. Opposite it was another building, which possibly could have been 2-storey, with steps at the side, and out the back of this was a well.

On 2nd February 1871, a dealer's quarrel took place on the farm when John Russell the farmer at Burnbrae was stopped by an officer of the law questioning why he was threshing wheat at Bardykes. Work was stopped as Russell explained he had bought it from Mr John Caldwell, the farmer at Bardykes. The case ended up in court and involved Allan Craig, portioner of Blantyre to resolve. Mr Caldwell was also subjected to a theft of £2 notes in Hamilton in 1872.

Around this time in 1871, Mr James Jackson was noted as the owner of Bardykes Farm. It is here we see the end of references to the old farm and new references to Bardykes House appear. Indeed in 1871 census 49-year-old James is living in "Bardykes Inatora House" along with his 3 brothers and sister Janet. 71-year old Janet Scott was the housekeeper of the new house.

As such, 1871 saw a fundamental change where Bardykes Farm was demolished in part and the building of a new property, becoming Bardykes House.

Bardykes House

With the Victorian fashion of extending or renovating homes to incorporate classical features, the Jackson family took the decision to build a new house entirely at Bardykes. This was to be a grander house, the one that we currently see today. This was most likely done by James Jackson.

Figure 41 Alexander 'Greek' Thomson

It was designed by a Glasgow Architect of the name "Alexander 'greek' Thomson. Born on 9th April 1817. Thomson developed his own highly idiosyncratic style from Greek, Egyptian and Levantine sources and freely adapted them to the needs of the modern city, particularly in Glasgow where he designed several churches. This style of columns on the facades of buildings earned him the nickname "Greek" which served also to distinguish his work from another architect of the same name in that era. He was a Pioneer of sustainable building, something not truly recognised until a hundred years later. From 1856 he concentrated on designing neo-greek or Italiane styled domestic homes. Similarities to Bardykes can be seen in his other works at Maria Villa, Langside or Alexander died on 22nd March 1875.

The Jackson family commissioned the design and were responsible for the construction of the house in 1871. It is alleged at this time that their wealth was such, that it permitted a duplicate copy of Bardykes out on their plantations in Ceylon. The timing of this construction fits well with other landowners in Blantyre extending their homes including the Clarks at Crossbasket, the Bannatynes at Milheugh. It may have been a decision of "keeping up with the Joneses" or simply that the old farm was in such, poor conditions having likely been there for a couple of hundred years beforehand, possibly longer! The new sandstone house was to be 2 storey, and accessed via a long tree lined avenue, that led off of Bardykes Road, the entrance located near the west end on Glasgow Road. A grand turning circle at the entrance and all former farm buildings demolished.

Figure 42 John P Jackson of Bardykes 1904

On 1875 valuation rolls, James Jackson is the owner of Bardykes House. In 1881 census John Jackson is noted as being a tea merchant. By 1888 James Jackson was living at Old Place and the owner of Bardykes House was still John Jackson. In 1889, James Campbell was a watchman at Bardykes House. In 1890 John Jackson was elected as county councillor for the Stonefield Division.

In October 1893, a young farm servant girl working for John Jackson was robbed whilst walking home on Blantyre Ferme Road.

In 1901 John P Jackson was living at Bardykes House, aged 48. His wife Alice was 38. They had 2 children Robert and little Alice, aged 12 and 11 respectively. 31-year old Kate Wales was a live in nanny. 34-year old Bella Duncan the cook and 30-year old Margaret Mcleod a table maid.

Jackson served on the Blantyre Parish Council and may have not been popular amongst certain spirit dealers after refusing licenses quite commonly in the early 1900's. Alice Jackson was particularly noteworthy for her fundraising efforts during the First World War, especially in relation to raising funds for a Blantyre ambulance.

In 1916, it was largely thanks to John Jackson that Station Road, then a quagmire of mud, was improved. Prior to that local reports of people missing their train, as they were stuck in mud, were common! It is likely around this time that some of the Jackson's estate was sold off the local authority, for improvement of roads in the Parish as a whole.

In 1918, John, by then a Councillor found himself in court for failing to comply with a standard set by Agricultural Committees. Whilst in court, he explained Bardykes had not been leased for some time. The matter revolved around John Jackson's unwillingness to break up any part of his land, wishing Bardykes to be kept as a whole for a long as possible. John may also have had dealings with the Bardykes road widening of 1923.

The last of the "Jackson Tea men" lived and died in Bardykes House on Tuesday 10th June

1930. His obituary read, *"The death occurred on Tuesday of Mr John Jackson, of Bardykes, Blantyre. A well-known figure in Lanarkshire. For over 400 years Mr Jackson's family have been proprietors of Bardykes. The property came into their possession in 1502, held on the yearly payment of red rose to Lord Blantyre. Jackson took an active part in local administration, and was for many years a member of Lanarkshire County Council and Justice of the Peace, in both which positions he gave good service. Yet another public with which served for a period was the Clyde Trust. At the time his death Mr Jackson was chairman of the Middle Ward of Lanarkshire Licensing Committee, a position he had held for number of years. He was re-elected to that office this year, but owing to failing health had not taken part in public affairs for last two years. Mr Jackson was head of the former firm Messrs Jackson. Buchanan and Co., tea merchants, Glasgow. He was years 77 age and is survived by his wife, one son and one daughter."*

His widow lived alone in Bardykes House until the late 1940's, and in her ailing years was tended by a District Nurse McCracken, who by a remarkable co-incidence would later become Mrs Wilkie herself to be part of the next family of owners. Whilst Mrs Jackson lived alone, assistance was few and far between otherwise. A farmhand would double as a gardener and an odd job man to take her out in her pony and trap, as well as a milkmaid. Sandy Wilkie, whose mother was that very nurse McCracken recalled, *"My mother was shown in via the servant's entrance, through the dreary kitchen with all the servants bells still on the wall, and on under the darkened ceilings and maroon cornicing, across the ebony like floorboards, passed the darkened skirting boards and wooden wall panels and up the almost blind staircase with its highly varnished and polished bannister and eventually, up to the gate, the one kept locked at the top of the stairs to keep pesky weans out, but more importantly, to keep senile old men and women, in! Mrs Jackson died rather mysteriously shortly after nurse McCracken started visiting her regularly and though she seemed to be making sound progress over the months, alas, it wasn't to be – she never fully recovered from her fever and passed away peacefully early into the winter. No-one local attended the funeral, in fact, sadly nobody ever heard about a funeral being held. Her maid moved back to her family in Strathaven and the Horseman sold the horses and then he too disappeared."*

The house in those post World War Two years, fell into considerable disrepair thereafter and was eventually bought by a Mr Loan from Helensburgh whom in 1954 planned to obtain a hotel licence then sell it to "The Brewers" for a handsome profit. However that never came to be, the application refused and perhaps seen as another attempt to get people drinking on a Sunday. After further deterioration, Mr Loan eventually sold Bardykes via Joe Daly and Jimmy Rusk (local council valuer and father of the famous hairdresser family of Bothwell Road), to Peter and Margaret Wilkie.

This transaction in 1957 proved rather fortunate, for the Wilkie family were almost homeless at that time, because the 2 nearby farms in High Blantyre known as Birdsfield and Bellsfield, (they milked the cows at the latter and farmed it on the former), were being "taken" by the 5th District Council via a "Compulsory Purchase Order", to build Council Houses. Indeed, demolition had actually started whilst the Wilkies were still living on the High Blantyre farm. Historic Scotland listed the building as a Category B protected building on 12th January 1971.

Wilkies Farm

People should not be confused by adverts for Wilkies, which started their business formation as being around 1904. Wilkie's Dairy was established then, but this is not to be confused with being established at Bardykes. It took until 5th April 1957 for the Wilkie Family to move in to Bardykes. Peter, Maragret and their 3 children, all at the time under 5 years of age flitted from High Blantyre to Bardykes for the first time, in the horse pulled milk float. With them was 'Dinky' the Alsatian dog and 'Minky' the cat.

Today, Blantyre residents still know the building most commonly known as Wilkie's Farm. It is officially known however as "Bardykes Farm" and today incorporates "Bardykes Farm Nursery School". The Wilkie family are still very well known and respected in this town. They are noted too for charitable work, being involved in the fundraising for many community campaigns, including hosting the fondly remembered Blantyre Highland Games from their fields from 1987, with their association with Blantyre Round Table.

And finally

There is much, much more to be written about Bardykes, the Jacksons and the Wilkies, and if Sandy Wilkie (whom in 2018 was given a Queen's Award) is reading this here or indeed if his sister Margo is reading too, I would love to take up Sandy's kind offer back in October 2015 of discovering and recording more about this wonderful house and heritage.

To end this article, I leave you with this beautiful verse taken from Revelations in the Bible chapter 14 verses 13, which served the Jackson family well. It's inscribed on the stone Obelisk memorial on their family graves, which can be witnessed in the Kirkton graveyard in High Blantyre.

"Blessed are the dead who die in the Lord. They rest from their labours and their works do follow them."

Simply put, it means have faith in the Lord, work hard and your efforts will be remembered. By the very fact that I'm writing about them, the motto has proved its worth. I think the statement is also very fitting for all the hard working farmers of Blantyre.

Figure 43 Bardykes House as it is now

ORIGINS OF BARNHILL

Barnhill was one of the original hamlets or fermetouns of the Barony of Blantyre. One of the oldest areas of Blantyre, it was originally known as Barnehill and can be traced in records, including the great seal of Scotland, as far back as 1598. However, it is known to be much older, one house still existing today claiming to have been built in 1536.

Walter Stewart of Minto was granted the lands of Barnehill, along with other hamlets of Blantyre in 1598, and would later go on to become Lord Blantyre in 1606.

Situated on the western fringes of the Blantyre, bordering on to the Calder woodland and river, it takes in an area currently known around Broompark Road and part of Bardykes Road from its junction at Hunthill Road.

Between the 1500s and 1700s, the main road from Glasgow came from Loanend, down past Malcolmwood Farm, but left at this point down through the fields known later for its site of Queen Mary's Well. It arrived at Pattonholm Ford and crossed the River Calder at a Shallow point, then up over a field at the Calder Braes known as "the Peth". This was likely a medieval road that came out halfway up the current Peth Brae (more locally known as Pech Brae, after a clergyman coined the phrase back in the 1860s).The lower half of the Peth Brae, at Niaroo, the bridge and Lindsay Hill leading up to Malcomwood most likely did not exist at that time and would have perhaps only been a small track. In time though, the medieval road became grown over and unused as horses, carts, vehicles and pedestrians favoured the modern road and bridge at the foot of the Peth Brae.

Families who owned land in Barnhill included the Miller family of Milheugh, the Jacksons of Bardykes, the Coates family and Pettigrews.

Barnhill was known for is thatched houses, even into the 20th Century. Thatched houses also sat at the top of the brae, next to a 10-foot high stone wall, which once encroached into where the modern carriageway at Bardykes is today, opposite the Barnhill Tavern. (Hoolets). Handloom weaving was the predominant business in the area, even prior to the construction of Dales Blantyre Works Village in 1785.

Against the Calder were thatched cottages, later a large tenement 2-storey building then more weavers single storey cottages, the end one belonging to Jock Stein, who bred pigs in the pigsty outside. The aforementioned tenement constructed in the 1870's was called Dixons Tenement but was only constructed after the demolition of the mid section of these smaller cottages. The building is also now gone, likely many original buildings in Barnhill and is now the site of a modern carpark across from the pub.

In 1864, Barnhill is a village, comprising of just twenty-four roofed buildings and two partially roofed building depicted on the 1st edition of the OS 6-inch map (Lanarkshire 1864, sheet xi).

People may know Aggie Bain's cottage or Brownlie Cottage/Bardykes Cottage which has a claim to be as old as 1536, being the oldest house in Blantyre. This is a distinct possibility. The present lane between Aggie Bain's Cottage and the Hoolets Pub, leading to Glenfruin road, was once the top of the only road down to the River Clyde from Blantyre Village. It ran alongside Wheatlandhead Farm and crossed a track, which is now Glasgow Road into the Dandy area and on to the Clyde.

Adjacent to the Hoolets Pub was "the back o the barns" and beside that "Barns End" next to an area of grassland, which even pre WW2, was being called "Dry Well Green", used for drying clothes. This may earlier have been the site of a sports ground at Barnhill in the mid to late 1800's, with sports such as quoiting and bowling. Nearby is the likely founding site of Blantyre Bowling Club in 1865 before they moved to Stonefield Road in 1872. This well was accessed by a path leading from Broompark Road, behind the farm, and is known to have flooded some of the ground where the current Hoolets Pub beer garden is. It was also prone to being polluted by sewage in the 1860's.

Figure 44 Bardykes Road at Barnhill looking South 1904

As can be seen from this photo looking south, the road had sharp changes in direction, which in 1929 were eventually smoothed out to allow traffic to pass by in a manner less dangerously. This road widening caused several buildings to have their gable ends cut away, including buildings at Barnhill Farm and Aggie Bain's Cottage itself.

Barnhill also had a nursery, with Brown's nursery being located at the corner of Broompark Road and Bardykes Road at the junction. Further up Broompark Road, was an old Smiddy. Now demolished and the site of a new modern house, it belonged in the Templeton family for many years. There were 2 farms. "The wee farm" and also Barnhill Farm, which was on Bardykes Road itself. The gate hinge holes of the farm gates can still be seen on the gable of the building adjacent to the Hoolets Pub. Today, Barnhill does still retain some character and charm and it is easy to envisage how peaceful and rural this area would have once been. Modern bungalows and houses adorn the junction area now, the thatched cottages all gone. The road is busy, especially in peak hours and still somewhat dangerously narrow close to the Hoolets, where there is no pavement.

BROWN'S NURSERY

Brown's Nursery may have also been known as Brown's Croft but should not be confused with Brown's Land, which was in Auchentibber.

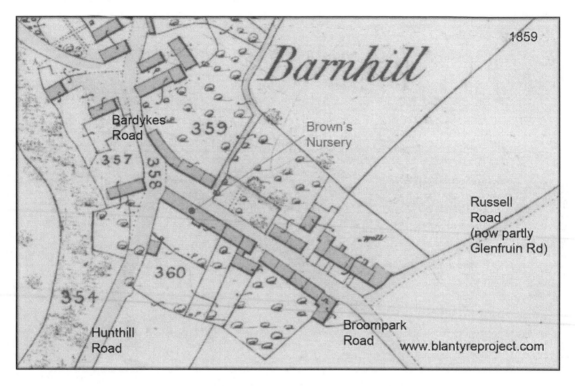

Figure 45 Barnhill 1859 map showing Brown's Nursery

Arthur Brown founded the former Barnhill Nursery (sometimes referred to as Brown's Nursery) in summer 1834. The nursery building was one storey, long and narrow and had a thatched roof sited at the southern corner of the junction of Broompark Road and Hunthill Road, where a modern bungalow is located today.

The nursery was once part of a whole row of terraced homes and businesses but by 1898, a gap had been created by one of the homes becoming ruined, between the row ending at the Barnhill smithy and the row comprising of the nursery and the Barnhill "wee" farm. The nursery building was made of stone, had a few doors opening out on to Broompark Road, and an apparent lack of windows on that side. At each gable were open fires, heating the building, smoke vented by a chimney on each side.

Arthur Brown's son, John Brown inherited the business and according to the 1851 census, John's wife was not there and it was John living at Barnhill with his 5 children, the youngest being 9 years old. In 1855, John is noted as being the tenant on 3 portions of land at Barnhill, owned by the Bannatyne family at Milheugh. At this time, George Brown at Orchardhead at Kirkton should not be confused with the Brown family at Barnhill. John Brown was 56 years old that year. His son James is noted as the farmer's son. The entry is interesting as it may suggest a tied connection to the adjacent "wee farm" at Barnhill. However, John is listed in 1862 directory as a freelance gardener. The 1861 census has John married to Janet Cross, each being 60 years old. Son, James is the farmer's servant.

By 1865, John is noted as occupying not just the land at Barnhill, but also an orchard at Greenhall, (some apple trees still exist there today near the riverside under the viaduct). It is his son James Brown, who that year is noted as occupying the house and stable at Barnhill, by then with fruit in production, the nursery appears to be trading. In 1875 John and James have land and a house at Barnhill. Around this same time, the Brown family from Orchardhead had established themselves at Boatland and they may have been relations of the Browns at Barnhill, being in the same business as fruit growers.

By 1885, younger James Brown is not present but elderly John Brown is still at the Barnhill address. Interestingly, he is noted as having a house and farm. The 1895 valuation roll returns a result for John Brown having a house at Barnhill and his younger son, Arthur Brown as tenant with the house and farm. By 1901, there are no records for John Brown, indicating he may have died between 1895 and 1901. By 1905, Arthur is noted as not only occupying the house and farm, but also a tomato house, greenhouse and sheds at Barnhill, as was the same right through to 1925 valuation roll.

Figure 46 Brown's Nursery, Broompark Road, 1920s

Then, according to the 1930 valuation roll, Arthur was not present there, indicating he may have passed away. Instead, his wife Eliza Brown was living there and the valuation roll notes the greenhouses, sheds and house had address 115 Broompark Road. Importantly by 1930, there is no mention of the farm being in ownership of the Brown family. By this time the nursery and land was still owned by the Miller-Bannatyne family of nearby Milheugh.

On Christmas day 1933, William Sommerville Ritchie, a farmhand at the nursery who had been made unemployed just before Christmas, broke into the barn and stole potatoes, was caught and fined. Sometime after 1958, according to the deeds of Milheugh Estate, the portions of land owned by them were sold off. It would appear that Mr. James Rochead acquired it outright, whose grandson Alex Rochead commented that James leased part of the building out as a business.

Most of the fresh produce the Brown family and their workers tended to, was sold locally to grocers and at times outwith Blantyre itself. Strawberries and Damsons were grown on the Calder braes on strips of land below the Cottage Hospital. Later, apples were added to the orchards. Some of these fruit trees are still there today near the medieval path leading down to Pattenholm. The winter months were known as "slack time", i.e. when the fruit business was poor. During "slack time" the Browns supplemented their income by growing willow trees, which were sold within the town for craftwork to the weavers. These bulrushes and willow can be found on the Calder braes.

Carved into the wall of Mr. Brown's house were 2 direction stones advising the way to Blantyre Kirk and Hamilton. These stones are still there today now built into the present garden wall at the corner of Broompark Road and Hunthill Road. The building was still occupied for a couple of generations beyond WW2 until it became ruined suddenly in 1970 or so, perhaps through neglect or abandonment. However, local man Gordon Cook has a more decisive suggestion, for he remembers seeing the whole building engulfed in flames in 1970, a fireman on the roof with an axe. If the building suffered such a catastrophic fire, the damage looks likely to have been so complete, that it had to be demolished shortly after.

JAMES BROWNLIE SENIOR

Mr. James Brownlie or Brownlee (Snr) was born Sunday 22nd June 1845 at Blantyre and lived to very old age. He was born in the old Hoolit's Nest Inn, which was then owned by his father, Mr. William Brownlie. Indeed the Brownlie family had already been resident in Blantyre above 300 years.

His first school was in a "but and ben" thatched one storey house directly across the road from where he was born. His teacher was Miss Elizabeth Lyon. When Miss Lyon died the school was closed down. The twenty odd scholars were transferred to the Kirkton Hall School, at School Lane, High Blantyre. Old James recalled at that time, there were many 'fine schools' in Blantyre, and all of them consisted of one classroom only. In fact, there was another school just fifty yards along School Lane with Mr. Money (pronounced Moonie) as Headmaster. As would be expected, a friendly rivalry existed between the two School Lane schools, and Mr. Brownlie tells us of a battle cry employed by the children of the Hall class as they barged passed the other scholars, *"Moonie's dugs keep up yer lugs, and let the Hall yins by ye."* His formal education ended in 1856, when, at just eleven years of age, he was sent to work for Henry Monteith & Co. in the village dye works.

Jimmy at the age of 15, in 1861 was a dye worker at Barnhill. Living at the house with the family were stepsisters Jean and Mary Inglis. Around 1871, he married Agnes Carmichael (b1840 – d1918) and they had 3 sons and 3 daughters. Between 1881 and 1891, they moved from Barnhill to McDougall's Property at Hunthill Road.

Later in life and certainly by 1934, he resided with his son in law Alex Wardrop and his daughter at 58 Hunthill Road, High Blantyre. The youngest of his 3 sons, James went on to become the famous player and later Manager of Dundee Football Club during the mid 1930's. Auld Jimmy worked until he was 82 years old, giving up his job in 1927 as a roadman for the county council.

On his 90th birthday in 1935, he was described as being known as "Old Jimmy", a popular and well-known character. He took his daily 1-mile walk and was hale and hearty.

Old Jimmy died on 16th November 1939. An article from the Dundee Courier on Friday 17th November 1939, stated, *"Mr. James Brownlie, father of Jimmy Brownlie, former manager of Dundee United, died yesterday morning at the residence of his widowed daughter, Mrs. Alex. Wardrope, Hunthill Road, High Blantyre. He was 94. Mr. Brownlie was born in the Auld " Hoolit's Nest Inn " in the Barnhill district of Blantyre. He had a vivid recollection of seeing Dr. David Livingstone when he paid a visit to his birthplace in Low Blantyre village on December 30, 1856."*

TAM TAYLOR'S INVENTION

Thomas Taylor was a man greatly in advance of his times. The Blantyre man was an inventor of one of the earliest reaping machines and Blantyre readers will be proud to know that he (attempted) to make one of the First Flying Machines, a full 43 years before the successful flight of the Wright Brothers in 1903!

Thomas also had another claim. He was the last tenant of Bardykes Mill which once stood hard against the Priory Bridge. However, even by 1880, the abandoned Mill was in ruins.

It is alleged in 1860, Thomas unveiled his great plans for a flying machine, which at the height of the industrial revolution, was to be powered by steam. Now Thomas (or Tam as he was known) had a great acquaintance in Mr Templeton, the blacksmith at Barnhill. The relationship was likely first a business one where Thomas commissioned parts for his inventions and Mr Templeton would make and supply them. So it was no surprise that the flying machine endeavour, involved them both working together. Mr Templeton did indeed make the machine parts and assisted Tam in constructing their flying machine, which was built in the barn at the old Barnhill Smiddy. The building was sold following the death of Bill Morrison in 2007, then demolished for a new house.

Figure 47 Previously unseen photo of Templeton's Blacksmiths in 1920's

When completed, the flying contraption was taken out into the adjacent Larkfield field (now where the High Blantyre Primary School is) and the engine was stoked, ready for an attempted flight. The local inhabitants of Larkfield and Barnhill although few at the time predating coal mines, would have been naturally curious upon the sight.

It is not recorded who piloted the flight, but it was likely Tam, given his investment and inventive nature. I've read incorrectly elsewhere that the Blantyre flight was successful as Tam waved to residents below. Fanciful and untrue I have to say. The proof and reality came about from an account written by Mr Templeton's son, almost 80 years later, which says word for word,

"The Smith's father made some of the parts of this machine over 80 years ago. The power unit was a steam engine. Tam and the Smith tried out the machine but just as it began to rise, the supply of steam gave out. The elements of success were there but the engine was not suitable. "I didna manage it", he said to the Smith, "but it will come yet whaever leeves tae see the day". A true prophet!" Pictured in 1891 is another invention of similar nature, an American contraption named Langley named after the man who mastered a better steam engine and managed a short flight.

Figure 48 The Experimental Flying Machine would have looked a strange sight

The principles of flight were known even in 1860, but the problem lay in steam engines not generating enough speed and therefore the lift needed for takeoff. It would take the petrol engine to be invented and used in a flying machine 43 years later for sustained, successful flight to be established. However, hopefully with the recording of this story, people will remember Tam Taylor, the Blantyre born inventor and his marvellous attempts.

I put it to you...before I leave this story, I will point out a little bit of a mystery. Tam Taylor was born in Blantyre in 1846. If the Smiths recollection is correct, Tam would only have been 14, and of course that doesn't seem likely. According to my research, in 1871, Tam was noted in the census as being in Bridgeton, which is entirely possible given the Bardykes Mill had closed by then.

Importantly, he's noted then, aged 24 as being a "Maker of Steam Boilers". It also suggests Tam was a young man when he made this trial flight. If so, and my findings are found to be correct, it would mean this whole story most probably took place in the 1870's, rather than 1860s. i.e. the recollection of the smith is wrong by 10 years. This is quite probable considering it was Mr Templeton's son telling the story, and I think he got the tale wrong by around 10 years. He would have needed somebody slight, perhaps younger to assist with the overall weight of the aircraft. By 1881, Thomas was married to Ellen Taylor and they were living at Govan with a growing, large family. There are no other Thomas Taylors in any census for Blantyre between 1841 and 1881, so I think this was the man! I would love for this to be proven, perhaps by a Taylor family member, if only to stop an incorrect date from perpetuating further.

DESIGNING THE COTTAGE HOSPITAL

Loved researching this and never seen it written about before. During the first decade of the 1900's the growing frequency of mining accidents and requirement for medial care promoted the need for a local Cottage Hospital in Blantyre. In February 1906, a public meeting was held in Blantyre to elect a committee and to discuss raising funds to create a new Cottage Hospital for the town. Mr. Andrew Miller Bannatyne of Milheugh was elected as chairperson and Mr. George Campbell, manager of the Clydesdale Bank was appointed honorary secretary and treasurer of the new group. It was agreed a fund should be set up, added with fundraising whatever means possible.

By 1908, with land secured at Bardykes, architects were then invited to produce a design with quotations on costings. It was decided by the committee to hold a competition for the design and it is known to have attracted 2 entries.

Architects David Bateman Hutton and Thomas Lumsden Taylor of "Architectural Practice Hutton and Taylor" (formed in Glasgow 1906) put their names forward in 1908.

The competitors for the design were William Forrest Salmon, his business partner John Gaff Gillespie and William's son James Salmon, all of the architectural firm, "Salmon, Son & Gillespie". Salmon's Practice called themselves "Phagocyte" and under that name submitted their design under that alias. (Phagocytes are associated with white blood cells and perhaps they hoped that the medical board would see their extra effort!)

Figure 49 Can you imagine this design being built on Bardykes Road in 1908?

The design Salmon's team came up with is as shown. Almost fairy-tale like, this hospital design was proposed for Bardykes. It is little wonder Salmons design had this almost Bavarian romantic design, for the architects had travelled extensively a couple of years before through Romania, Hungary, and Switzerland. They proposed Staff should live in a tower at one end, and the hospital connected by a veranda. The design had a pitched roof, with red tiles and a mixture exposed stonework and roughcast.

With the architects permitted to have all of 1908 to submit and cost their designs, plans were handed into the committee at the start of March 1909. At the same meeting of the committee, W B Dow was appointed Quantity Surveyor/ measurer. The committee took just that one meeting to decide upon the winner.

However, Salmon's design proved too expensive to implement and "Hutton and Taylors" more practical, yet equally unique and beautiful design was chosen, that is the design we see today. The chosen hospital was of a 'solid pavilion type' with male and female wards, an operating theatre and administrative accommodation.

Figure 50 Bardykes Cottage Hospital winning design

After £4,162 was collected, the hospital was built at Bardykes Road, overlooking the Calder Braes. Construction started on 6th March 1909. Initial budgets of £3,000 rose during the build and ended up close to £4,000. The Blantyre Cottage Hospital officially opened on 25th June 1910. It was the first local Cottage hospital to be constructed in Lanarkshire.

(Side note: On the back of their success Hutton and Taylor achieved success designing several Glasgow Schools and churches. The disappointment for Salmon's practice would have been apparent for it was the third in as many years of unsuccessful competition designs. They had earlier been runner up for the Mitchell Library, Rutherglen Town Hall, Hamilton Academy and Hamilton Municipal Library. However, in the month following the hospital award, Salmons practice was engaged successfully to design Stirling's Municipal Buildings.)

In October 1922, such was the demand for Maternity space in the Hospital in Bellshill that the sick children there were moved all over to Blantyre, to the cottage hospital on Bardykes Road. It is noted in local news reports, this filled the hospital in Blantyre to capacity, but eased the Bellshill situation hugely.

On Saturday 5th February 1927, a case of blood transfusion was reported from the Cottage Hospital Blantyre. Attempting blood transfusions was still quite a risky and dangerous thing to do. The patient was a young man of thirty years of age, and the doctor decided this course in the hope of saving his life. Volunteers were called for locally, and seven men presented themselves to assist. Three of them emerged successfully from the blood test. They then tossed a coin for the honour in performing the transfusion. The blood transfusion took place, and the patient improved slightly, but sadly died at the hospital two days later. The Hospital closed in the late 1930's and it is now a private home.

Alison Glen told me on social media, *"Being an architect, I love that we live in this great piece of Blantyre history and that it's been in my husband's family since the 1940s!"*

HOSPITAL THEFTS

Jean Helen Taylor McNaught would certainly have remembered 1932 as being a bad year. The probationary Glasgow Nurse was living and working in Blantyre at the Cottage Hospital on Bardykes Road. At the end of March 1932, she appeared in court where she pled guilty to stealing 3 shillings from a boy patient's wallet and also to the theft of the matron's pocket watch.

The case continued for a week, for the Fiscal could not understand how a woman could steal from a young boy and wished that the nurse were medically examined, presumably for any sort of mental illness. The nine-year-old boy was a patient in the Blantyre hospital and had gathered up 3 shillings in small pennies from his various visitors. With so many friends bringing him small change, he eventually had enough that his father decided to buy him a purse/wallet to keep them in, which was held in his bedside locker.

On the pretence she was going into the locker for a library book, the accused nurse deliberately took the wallet with the intention of keeping the contents for herself. Suspicion fell upon her, as she had been the only person witnessed going into the locker. The hullaballoo passed over, but surfaced again a month later when the matron noticed her pocket watch was missing. The day after, the accused nurse failed to turn up to work, which was unusual and the police were called.

Police officers went to Glasgow and turned up at the door of the accused nurse who appeared to be in fine health. She told the officers she had quit, but under pressure from questions, eventually admitted she had pawned the watch that morning. When the officers inspected her house, they found the boy's wallet.

The Fiscal concluded, *"This woman is a menace to the community as she is 'tarry-fingered.' It is not the first time she has been before a court. She has abused the chances given to her. Her father is a very respectable man and this is the cross he has to bear."* The medical examiner concluded there was nothing wrong with the girl, either physically or in state of mind and with a prison sentence imposed of one month and termination of her employment, the young nurse, left the dock in tears.

CHRISTMAS RAID

Sentence of 30 days imprisonment was imposed on William Sommerville Ritchie, a young unemployed farm servant, who appeared in custody before Sheriff Brown Hamilton Sheriff Court on Boxing Day 1933. He had pleaded guilty to 2 charges of breaking into a shed situated in Barnhill Nursery on Hunthill Road, on December 25th and opening two lockfast desks and attempting to steal there from; and stealing six stones of potatoes from the Barn situated in the nursery. William admitted three previous convictions for theft. The Fiscal explained that the accused was 24 years of age and an unemployed farm servant. He broke into the shed using the true key, which was hanging on a nail. He entered the shed with a pair of pliers or some other equipment and forced open the desks. The accused then stole a bag of potatoes weighing about 6 stones, which he hid in a wood. The police then kept watch on the wood and apprehended the thief when he came back for them. When charged, William said he would do the same again until he got Parish relief for himself and his wife.

On December 1st, just 3 weeks earlier, he had got married and had been living with his wife's family but over the last few days they had been living in a dug out on the banks of the River Calder. Mr David Baird, court writer, said Ritchie had been working as a farm servant until five weeks ago, when he became unemployed. Accused made application to the Public Assistance Department for outdoor relief. He was offered accommodation in the poorhouse, which he refused to accept. William Ritchie wanted money. He had no income whatever, and his wife had only 6 shillings per week by way of National Health Insurance. Accused's motive for committing the crime, while a foolish one, had been to bring his claim for relief more forcibly to the notice of the Public Assistance authorities.

Stopping for a second, it must have been a dire situation to be living in a little shack on the edge of the river Calder, as a direct result of being made unemployed 5 weeks earlier. Even worse, to know that it was Christmas day, and the situation called for breaking into empty premises to steal potatoes. I hope William's life story ended better.

Barnhill Nursery is now a modern home sitting on the corner of Broompark Road and Hunthill Road.

STOLE COAL FROM BING

On 26th August 1955, Patrick Docherty, a labourer of Hut 6, New Dechmont Camp (Whins Camp) and a 13-year old boy pleaded guilty to stealing coal with two other people unknown, from the refuse bing at Bardykes Colliery on 2nd August.

Docherty was 21 years old. During a patrol, 2 police offers saw 3 men and 1 boy on the Bing that afternoon, each carrying a small sack, and returning it to a hidden cart in the bushes.

When Docherty and the boy reached the bottom of the Bing, the police apprehended them, but the other 2 men ran off, their identities hidden by Docherty. The police took possession of 7 bags of coal amounting to 4.5cwts.

Figure 51 Former Bardykes Colliery in 1940

Docherty and the 13-year old boy were each fined 20 shillings, with the alternative imprisonment of 10 days.

The situation appears more desperate as August that year was particularly warm and pleasant, with good temperatures, even in the evenings. It is assumed the coal was needed to heat water at the camp or was being sold off to others.

JOHN BROWNLIE BAIN

Figure 52 John Brownlie Bain in 1933 at cottage door

During 1933, Mr John Brownlie Bain, stood at the door of a cottage once in the ownership of his family in Barnhill to mark an approaching important occasion. The cottage had been there allegedly nearly 400 years, the date on the lintel painted on as "1536". Brownlie Cottage sits across from the then Barnhill Tavern, at Barnhill. The Brownlie family had owned the cottage for much of this time.

John was the older brother of Aggie Bain, whom in 1933, lived at this cottage. Aggie was brought up by her aunt Marion Brownlie, who passed the cottage to Aggie, following her death in 1919.

Brownlie cottage, or Aggie Bain's Cottage incredibly is well on its way to becoming 500 years old and should it still be standing, will be an incredible half a millennium old in 2036.

The cottage for many years was presumed to be the oldest inhabited property in Blantyre, although has recently relinquished that title to the renovated Crossbasket Tower in 2015. The beautiful cottage is still there today and is now officially called Bardykes Cottage, and was put on the market for sale in October 2018.

The nearby Barnhill Tavern, now the Hoolets Public House, opposite the cottage is thought to be the oldest Public House in Blantyre dating to around 1701 (previously thought to be 1745), although it may be in name only, as it should be noted, it was almost entirely rebuilt at the start of the early 20th Century.

I've included this high-resolution image of John seen in good detail here for the first time.

WILKIE'S PALOMINO STALLION

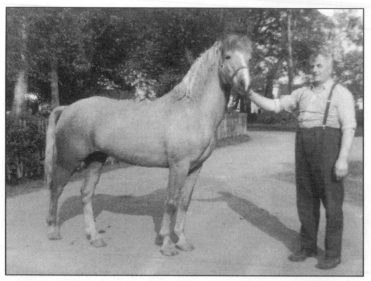

Figure 53 Peter Wilkie (1960s) with Palomino Stallion

This photo is from the mid 1960's and pictured is Peter Wilkie at Bardykes. He's standing beside beautiful Golden Monarch, a Palomino Stallion put out to stud at Bardykes. The photo is kindly shared here by Sandy Wilkie.

Gordon Cook, local historian told me, *"This reminds me of the night he brought, what might have been this horse, up to a field at Priestfield Street in High Blantyre. It was kicking and jumping and he had frightful time getting it out because the horse had already spied the mare in the field. This would have been around 1966/67"*

WEST END BAR

It's a fond farewell in summer 2018 to Maura, Steven and Michael, owners of the West End Bar, as the pub is sold on. With the sale of the West End Bar now concluded, new owners Harry Hood's 'LISINI Pub Co' can look forward to ushering in a new, exciting era for the old public house, which sits at the corner of Glasgow Road and Bardykes Road. The pub went through a brief transition period with customers informed.

Maura, Steven and Michael issued a statement on 2nd July 2018 stating, *"Would just like to say a big thank you to all our customers as we say our final goodbye to The West End Bar. Some great memories from the past 10 years with loads of laughter, endless debating at the big table, great functions, live acts and many friendships made. Sadly we also saw the departure of some great characters and the arrival of new ones. We would like to wish the new owners, LISINI pub Co all the very best in their new venture."*

LISINI also own the Parkville further along Glasgow Road. It's understood that the sale of the West End Bar attracted interest from several bidders. As with all new business ventures, we would like to wish Harry and his staff all the very best for this new endeavour.

CHAPTER 5
STONEFIELD

Stonefield is a fairly large area of Blantyre and a former hamlet certainly known for its retail and industry, as well as public buildings. A population centre going beyond the well-known spine road connecting High and Low Blantyre and actually spread over much of Glasgow Road and surrounding areas too. The identity of this hamlet is now somewhat lost, mixed and merged with mid parts of the town including Low Blantyre. Stonefield looks to date from the early 1800's, the name coming from the farm, which would become Hastie's. Pictured during 1915 is the bottom of Stonefield Road, a scene now hugely different with all the buildings at the back and right now gone.

ATTACK AT BINNINGS CHANGING HOUSE

In my 'Glasgow Road South' book, I exclusively explored the older history of the Stonefield Tavern, before it became a pub in the 1880's. It was formerly a changing house, a place to change over the horses and have a rest, right across the road was Blantyre Toll, at the corner of what would become Station Road.

I was excited to uncover the forgotten name of the changing house in the 1820's, forming another piece of the puzzle that is the Stonefield Tavern (Teddies). So here is a great story from 1824, nearly 200 years ago and around the time of the very birth of Stonefield itself.

On 6th December 1824, John McDonald a Blantyre cotton spinner ran amock in that rural area, which was surrounded at the time entirely by open fields. The former name of the Tavern was "Binning's Changing House" and on that day, a party of several young men and women were enjoying themselves inside the building. They were to be accompanied by a man named McKenzie who was walking with his sweetheart and approaching the changing house at Glasgow Road. However, they didn't get there. About 20 yards from the changing house, a group of Irishmen appeared, one of whom was John McDonald. On seeing McKenzie and his sweetheart, they hurled abuse and set about McKenzie, punching his face, as he fell to the ground. John McDonald, set about McKenzie with a stob, for no apparent reason, drawing blood, as the stricken man's girl shouted "murder" and for help.

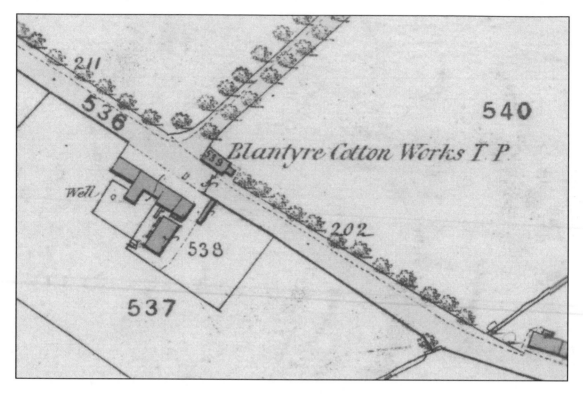

Figure 54 Binning's Changing House 1859 (where Glasgow Road met Station Rd)

Assisted Retreat

The whole party came out of Binning's Changing House and tried to help, but set about by the Irish Mob, they were forced back in again to retreat. The Irish party tried to follow inside, but the landlord had locked the door. A rammy ensued as the attackers demanded to be let in. When refused, they set about breaking the windows of the house, demolished the door and window shutters, causing considerable alarm to those inside.

It was later established that John McDonald has started the riot. McKenzie's head wounds were so severe, it was difficult to assess if he was to make it. A month in bed followed although he lived to tell the tale.

McDonald found himself in court in May 1825 where the judge took a firm stance, commenting, "You may have been connected with such affrays in the country of your birth, but it won't be tolerated in Scotland. Suitable punishment must follow that prevents you doing this again." John McDonald spent the next SEVEN years in jail on hard labour.

STONEFIELD BURN

When the 59 acres of land was up for sale in Stonefield in 1851, including the Stonefield farm steading (Hasties) and fields where the public park is today, its starting price of £2,000 ended up at £2,750 due to keen competition. The buyers were the Forrest family. They may not have realized the extent of some of the issues on the land however, for much of the fields which would later become the public park, would never be built upon, poorly drained and with a burn running right through the middle.

The burn rose far to the south off Stonefield Road, near where the Bowling club is today and ran north eastwards over fields, even determining where Dixon's Rows was to be built. It ran near Stonefield Farm and down to Glasgow Road, long before any tenements crossing, under the road at a low dip slightly west of where Annfield Terrace/Victoria Care Home would later be built. No building would ever be built on that small, low dip just before the Toll Brae rose, not even to this day. North of Glasgow Road, beyond where the park would be, the burn crossed the field, under the railway and to the River Clyde. It may have had the nickname, "Christie's Burn" after John Christie in the 1865 Valuation roll as nearby landowner and weaver's agent.

In November 1962, to relieve flooding at Stonefield Road, Glasgow Road and Stonefield Public Park, a large outfall sewer was completed crossing through Blantyre. The sewer was a dual pipeline and was of sufficient capacity to permit the capture of both sewage and stormwater from all the nearby housing estates at Stonefield Road and the surrounding district, ending up going through the Public Park and out towards the Clyde.

WESTNEUK CONCERT HALL

Perhaps one of Blantyre's least known and hardly explored buildings in Blantyre was the former 'Westneuk Concert Hall' on the south side of Glasgow Road. Incredibly this plot of land devoted to public entertainment would later become a house, then in future years once again serve the community for purposes of their enjoyment as a fondly remembered community centre.

The humble beginnings of this Victorian concert hall date back to the 1840's when Hugh McPherson, a merchant of Haughhead, Blantyreferme bought a long, rectangular plot of land on Glasgow Road, directly opposite some dense woodland. The plot was situated not far from the junction of what would become Stonefield Road and was near Clive Place and immediately to the west of Stonefield Cottage. It was on the western extremity of the hamlet of Stonefield, its western corner, and naming would have been easy with the word "Westneuk", quite literally meaning the 'western corner.'

Hugh McPherson was born in 1800 in Shotts and was in his 40's living in Blantyre with family by the time he constructed the concert hall. Built of stone, detached and 2 storey, it may have had intricate stonework features that set it aside from other buildings in Blantyre. At the rear, a small house was constructed separately to accommodate the hall manager or licensee.

Westneuk was initially built as a Public Entertainment Building, hosting plays, live music and recitals. It must have been a welcome retreat for the hard working people of Blantyre and somewhere to let off some steam! When Queen Victoria took to the throne, Scotland was undergoing a period of critical change. The industrial revolution led people to move from the country to the emerging villages and towns in search of work, resulting in the adaptation and rejection of rural traditions. Like the village pub, the urban public house became an important social space. By the mid nineteenth century, village life offered an increasingly wide range of leisure activities including sporting events, music and exhibition halls meant to cater for the tastes of the working and middle-classes who valued and were prepared to pay for their entertainment.

Figure 55 Early Concert House proved popular all over

The new audiences wanted music, dancing, spectacles and excitement, and many theatres such as Westneuk began to meet public demand offering alcohol on the premises. In the mid nineteenth century, such venues presented musical concerts, ballets, gothic dramas, melodramas and pantomimes. It would have been a noisy, rowdy place at times and not a place women would have frequented. The location was likely chosen carefully, at the corner of Blantyre, next to open fields with nothing westwards, at the time of its construction on Glasgow Road until you reached Blantyre's boundary at Priory Bridge.

Hugh McPherson's ownership of the concert hall was short lived. He died in the early 1850's and Westneuk would pass to ownership of his Trustees. Around 1855, the McPherson family let out the concert hall to incomer, Gavin Muirhead, who acquired a license to sell alcohol on the premises.

Born in Bothwell in 1815, Gavin Muirhead, a grocer came to Blantyre around 1855 and rented the house and garden behind the hall at Westneuk for £18 per year. There, he lived with his wife Sarah, some 16 years his junior and their young family. However, the important short, few years between 1855 and 1859 would seal the fate of Westneuk.

The End of Westneuk

It would appear Gavin Muirhead was simply 2 decades too early for his concert hall. In the 1850's, Blantyre's population was still relatively small and business was not good. Neighbours complained of the noise, the disorder of regulars and for unknown reason, whether through lack of custom, mismanagement, or excess, Westneuk was not the thriving place it was intended to be.

In March 1858, only 3 years after taking over the concert hall, Gavin Muirhead had other problems brewing in the form of mounting pressures and complaints from neighbours.

For example, Charles Ford renting next door at Stonefield Cottage had recently lost an infant child. Perhaps wanting peace, he was fed up of the entertainment public house next door and disorderly behaviour emanating from it at all hours. Charles involved others and it went to court.

The Edinburgh Evening Courant reported the case. MUIRHEAD V. FORD AND OTHERS states, *"The pursuer sells whisky and other liquors at Westneuk Blantyre; some of his neighbours petitioned to Justices that he might not get his license again, as he kept a disorderly house, Ford raises action against Muirhead."* On Thursday 11th March 1858, the Court held that there was no necessity for issue of 'veritas convicii' (an excuse) but that the truth of the complaint was in malice and want of probable cause. In other words, Muirhead got away with it, and Charles having to retract complaint.

This was no victory though. Neighbours ill feeling and falling or inadequate custom did not make a successful business.

By December 1858, only 3 years after coming to Blantyre, Gavin Muirhead was declared bankrupt, forcing a move out. He left Blantyre for good sometime shortly after 1861.

With the closure of Westneuk concert hall for good at the end of December 1858, so too, the name 'Westneuk' would permanently disappear.

Stonefield House

However, Westneuk's story does not end there. The building after all still existed in 1859. The name-book for the Parish that year describes the property as "a superior home formerly used as a public house of entertainment. The property of Mr. McPherson."

Westneuk was renamed in 1859 to 'Stonefield House' perhaps to compliment the adjacent 'Stonefield Cottage.' The building's hall would be renovated and split into functional homes, indeed enough for 2 spacious homes, 1 on the lower floor, 1 on the upper, accessed by stone steps at the back. A central path led from Glasgow Road up to the front doorway.

The houses continued in ownership by the McPherson family from 1859 let out to miners until they changed hands, bought over by Hamilton Brendon McDougall, of Hamilton Villa, Park Road, Kirn during the 1880's. This family would own Stonefield House for the rest of its years well into the 20th Century. Around the time they acquired the property, the opposing David Livingstone Memorial Church was being built on the north side of the road, directly across from the 2 houses, still with wide, open Wheatlandhead fields to the south and west.

It is known the Harvey family were renting in the 1880's, a daughter born to William Harvey on 9th February 1884 in one of the homes. The Harvey family shortly after moved eastwards to rent at Henderson's Buildings.

It is thought also that during the mid 1880's, William Small, the prominent Secretary of the Miners National Federation may have lived there a short time between censuses, before moving to Forrest Street. By 1895, James Powell a flesher and James Malone, a mining Contractor were renting from Hamilton Brendon McDougall for £16 and £14 per annum respectively.

At the turn of the 20th Century, as with many properties in Blantyre, the property was further sub-divided to maximize rental potential. The 2 homes became 4, with two on the lower floor and 2 on the upper. In 1905, one house was empty, two were occupied by miners William Stewart and Adam Yanker. The remaining house and stable to the rear was occupied by Thomas Reid, a fruit dealer. The stable would have been used to store his horse and cart for his deliveries. Thomas Reid was in the news a couple of years earlier.

In July 1903, Lord Kyllachy heard evidence in an action of divorce by Thomas Reid of Stonefield House against Mary Stirling or Reid, Lochore Bridge, Lochgelly, Fife. Thomas, the person who raised he action was a blind man. He said he had married on 14th April 1876, and there were three surviving children. He had been a miner, but in 1883 he had an accident, by which he lost his sight. Since then he had been hawking fruit and tea. Four years after the accident his wife deserted him, and he had learned that she had gone to stay with a miner named Phillips at Lochgelly. Other evidence was heard and the divorce decree was granted.

Figure 56 Our Line Diagram of Former Westneuk (Stonefield House) in a modern context

By 1915, the name Stonefield House was being used less and indeed does not appear in valuation rolls after that time, replaced simply by 291 and 293 Glasgow Road.

In the 1910's to 1930's, the 4 homes within Stonefield House were let out to miners and their families, all under the ownership of Hamilton Brandon McDougall, although by 1925 Nellie McDougall, a family member took ownership through inheritance. Rents in 1925 were £14 per annum. The stable was gone by that year too.

In 1935, all 4 houses lay derelict and empty, condemned by the council and were subsequently cleared as part of the slum clearance later that year. Stonefield House does not appear on the 1936 Blantyre map, a time when the County Council took ownership of that plot of land.

The ground lay empty for a few years, before being used again when a Public Entertainment building was built, in the form of a brand new, Council owned, Community Centre, itself now long since demolished.

Today, there's no trace of Westneuk, Stonefield House or the Community Centre. The site, today accommodates modern flats at Mayberry Grange, which were somewhat sympathetic in design by adopting a similar footprint, certainly at Glasgow Road as the old "Westneuk".

SWEENIE'S THE BUTCHERS

During the 1960's and 1970's Mr James (Jimmy) Sweenie had a butchers shop at 8 Stonefield Road not far from the bottom of Stonefield Road near the Old Original Bar. The Sweenie's appear to be incomers to Blantyre during WW2 years. It was adjacent to Gilbert the Bakers at that time.

It was not to be confused by the small sweet shop his wife ran on Broompark Road. The Sweenies lived at 53 Broompark Road. Their daughter Irene taught at Whitley's Business College in the 1960's. It is often said Jim Sweenie's shop had the most delicious sliced sausage in the town. Before Sweenie's Butcher shop, it was known as Arbuckles. Today, the shop is now Tan Unique.

Figure 57 Gilbert the Bakers & Sweenie's the Butchers

WALTER STEWART – MASTER OF BLANTYRE

Walter Stewart, the Master of Blantyre only son of Charles Stewart, 12th Lord Blantyre would have inherited the title on the death of his father. Unfortunately, he predeceased his father, dying on 15th March 1895 aged 44, and when his father died on 15th December 1900, the title of Lord Blantyre became extinct. Born on 17th July 1851, as a young man Walter went round the world, climbed the Rocky Mountains, met with a few adventures, had some narrow escapes and saw some of the finest scenery in America, New Zealand and many other countries.

The late Neil Gordon wrote the following article on Walter. "He returned to Scotland and settled near the north east coast, as tenant of a large sheep farm called Sciberscross in the Parish of Rogart, Sutherland, a few miles from Dunrobin Castle, where he remained for 12 years.

He took a great interest in all parochial matters and was warmly accepted into the community, being elected to the School Board and made captain of the Rogart volunteer company. After his acceptance of the captaincy the strength of the company advanced rapidly until it became numerically more than double what it previously was and by far the strongest company in the battalion. His kindness and unwearyingly helpfulness to the poor, and his frequent assistance to others in need of aid, secured for him the warm regard and sincere respect of all sections of the community.

In the winter and spring of 1879-1880, phenomenal snowstorms raged throughout the Highlands and were considered the worst weather in living memory. Many in Rogart, as in other localities, experienced great difficulty in producing fodder for their cattle and even if it had been available, did not have the means to pay for it. Many families found themselves on the verge of starvation and Walter was their means of survival

Figure 58 Master of Blantyre, 1880

as he battled throughout the winter to provide people with the essentials to see them through their suffering.

Later, at a public meeting in Rogart, he was presented with an illuminated address and a silver salver with suitable inscriptions as tokens of heartfelt gratitude and the deep regard felt towards him by all classes in the neighbourhood. Walter then purchased Eilanreach farm in the village of Balmacara on the north shore of Lochalsh, directly opposite the Isle of Skye. He resided there for 10 years until his death at Balmacara House. He served the community as a member of the Glenelg Parochial School Board, as a County Councillor and a Justice of the Peace.

After his death many ordinary people came forward with recollections of his kindness towards less fortunate townsfolk. Fishermen spoke of the many times he had taken their small boats in tow behind his, the Eilanreach, as they struggled to return to Glenelg with their catch. When his shepherd, Ewen Cameron, lost his wife, the Master sailed his yacht to Loch Hourn and brought back the funeral party, with the mourning husband and his children, and showed the kindest sympathy towards poor Ewen afterwards, even during his long last illness. The pursuer of a steamer related the following story regarding the kindness of the Master of Blantyre. "On a cold winters day, a number of years ago, as the ferryboat of Glenelg was waiting to take passengers ashore, a gentleman followed by his highland servant came along. As he was stepping into the boat, he saw a poor woman and her child crouched and shivering upon the deck. He at once took off his plaid and threw it over them, going ashore himself with only a light coat as protection. On making enquiries afterwards as to whom the gentleman was, I learned that it was the Master of Blantyre".

Crofters also talked of his kindness and the consideration given to them in times of need. Two Glenelg shepherds remembered the time when the Master, sailing home down Loch Alsh, observed them and their dogs trudging along with tired feet many miles from Balmacara. He sent a boat to bring them on board the Eilanreach, and save them the toilsome walk over the mountains to their homes. The Master of Blantyre was a very religious man and was missed not only at Glenelg, but throughout the Highlands, Inverness and elsewhere.

He did much to improve Glenelg in the 10 years he lived there. He made a post-path from Ardintoul, kept it in repair and also got a daily post provided. He secured a telegraph wire by giving a large guarantee to the company. He built good houses for his shepherds and kept 3 pairs of horses that he did not require for himself, but used to plough the crofters' lands for them. He also grew potatoes, oats and turnips to give people employment; even though it would have been cheaper had he bought them. Notice that the Master's funeral would leave Eilanreach at 6 o'clock on the Monday evening was given in all different churches in the district and a large gathering assembled, notwithstanding a continuous downpour throughout the day. Tea was prepared for all, it having been the Master's express wish, "*Now mind, no whisky*".

At the appointed hour, the coffin was brought out and set down on the grass in front of Balmacara House amongst the people. Rev Wilson, minister of Kintail offered a prayer in Gaelic and after readings from the scriptures by other ministers, the coffin covered in the green plaid was carried by 24 men, in sets of eight, and followed by his household and friends, to the Eileanreach, which was berthed at Quarry.

Three ministers led the funeral, which was followed by schoolchildren from the Master's School and over 200 people from the surrounding districts. There would have been many more mourners in attendance but for the terrible weather conditions, which prevented those from around Lochalsh getting over the water. Many tears were shed as the white boat sailed into the darkness on her way to Glasgow, from where the coffin was conveyed to the burial place of the family at Bolton, near Haddington. The Master of Blantyre was buried in the sarcophagus that stands in the Kirkyard of Bolton Church, close to the Blantyre's family home of Lennoxlove House."

DONATIONS FOR NEW CHURCH

From the Glasgow Herald, Friday March 1st 1878, page 9, there's a letter telling of the need for people to donate subscriptions towards the cost of the Stonefield Parish Church Construction on Glasgow Road, at the corner of Church Street.

"NEW CHURCH AT STONEFIELD, BLANTYRE - Manse of Blantyre, 28th February, 1878. Sir - Will you kindly insert in your journal the enclosed circular, which I recently issued, and in which I plead for subscriptions to defray the expenses of a new church that is now in course of erection in my parish. The population has so vastly increased that there is urgent need for this new church. The mass of the people is poor, being miners and their families, who consequently cannot afford to give much. The people of Scotland have nobly responded to the appeal, which I issued in behalf of the many families who were rendered destitute by the recent terrible colliery explosion. I feel assured that I shall not now plead in vain for sympathy and help to meet the spiritual wants of those who are still with us. I am, STEWART WRIGHT, Minister of Blantyre."

GASWORKS ROW

Gasworks Row was a former block of 6 little single storey houses, situated adjacent to the north of the yard gates of the Blantyre Gas Works on the mid eastern side of Stonefield Road. Built around 1880, they were partially demolished during the Second World War, leaving just 3 existing for some years post WW2. During the early 20th Century, to their north was Dixon's Rows, to their south, the Gas works, which would later become Letham's Garage.

DIXON'S ROWS

Dixon's Rows or Dixons's Raws were former single storey, small miner's houses consisting of 8 streets totalling 340 houses, of which 306 were lived in, the others being used as stores and a hall. They formed a large concentration of homes, packed into a small area near the northeastern end of Stonefield Road.

Figure 59 Park Street, Dixon's Rows 1920's as restored by A Rochead

Construction started in early summer 1872. All the homes, including a public hall at Stonefield Road were owned by Mr. John Mann Thompson (b1836 – d1899) John was an iron-master, a wealthy prominent man who forged his business on the back of the Dixon family and was a cousin of the Dixon family. William Dixon at this time was William Dixon the third. During 1872, John found himself the Chairman of the newly formed Dixon's Collieries in Blantyre, and was essentially "their big chief". It should be noted that John personally owned the rows. William Dixon & Co did not own them at that time, as you may have read elsewhere.

The small homes, essentially originally hovels were built to provide the housing requirements for employees of Dixon's collieries, initially at Priestfield at High Blantyre. Considered adequate at the time for single miners, they were far from being ok for families.

Figure 60 Miller Street , Dixons Rows 1912

In an area, which today is Calder Street, Stonefield Road, Camelon Crescent and Boswell Drive, 4 of these 8 old streets ran in a northwest to southeast direction (Park Street, Hall Street, Dixon Street and Calder Street), the other four ran in a northeast to southwest direction, criss crossing the others (Burnside Street, Miller Street, Govan Street and Carfin Street.)

The houses were basic. Built of brick, with slate pitched roofs, the single storey houses were terraced consisting of blocks of 4 houses, each with 2 rooms. On the front of each house were a door and one window, with 2 windows at the rear. The windows had wooden shutters to close over at night. It is rumoured that in the original days these houses had earthen floors, but it is more likely that they had some sort of flagstones down and it was subsequently reported that the floors were of timber by 1910, an effort to combat dampness. Of the 2 rooms, the main living room was known as "the kitchen" and the bedroom was simply known as "the room." Both rooms contained two "set in beds" into recesses in the wall, also known as "hole in the wall beds". These arrangements would quite often not be adequate for the large mining families who would end up living there over several generations. The kitchen had facilities for cooking over a fire. Originally there was no sink or plumbing of any kind within the houses. Some of the homes had only one room.

Dixon's Rows did not get off to a good start. Although construction started in 1872, by springtime 1874, only 160 houses had been erected from the 340 quotas. At the same time, 139 miners occupied about 110 of the houses, Of course with them were their families, averaging on 6 people per house. Water was non-existent unless you went to a mudhole nearby into which, the common sewer also ran into. This had been reported to the Sanitary Inspector who did nothing and it took until September 1884 for a proper supply of clean water was obtained for the rows, albeit still outside.

In April and May 1874, miners went on strike and William Dixons decided to act swiftly and decisively, using the legal right to evict not just the miners, but all their families too. Some of the men had been on strike for over 7 weeks. A standoff commenced, with officers serving warrant papers amidst wild scenes. Ultimately, the miners had to leave and so did their families, around 500 people homeless. By the end of May, the newly built Dixons Rows, again lay empty and derelict, with

500 people taking to the streets of Blantyre looking for a shelter. Salvation for the evicted miners and families came from a source nearby, and the miners, in defiance of Dixon's ended up moving to a temporary camp set up in a field near the Anderson Church. The field was called Pilot Acre and the encampment was set up on the front half acre opening out on to Stonefield Road (the other half acre was the Bowling Club, who had recently moved to that location from nearby Barnhill) However, it is known many families did not want to live in one open-plan large wooden temporary building 105 foot in size, along with so many other families, and so some of them moved away from Blantyre.

Dixon's Hall was located on the eastern side of Stonefield Road at the end of Hall Street. Its length ran alongside Hall Street and was long and narrow. It later had official address 43 Stonefield Road. For some considerable time prior to the opening of the St Joseph's chapel-school in 1878, Mass was celebrated and Sunday School conducted in a block of houses in Dixon's Rows, the inner walls or partitions having been removed. Such accommodation, however, proved wholly inadequate to meet the wants of the Catholic population of the district, so negotiations commenced for the purchase of a site at Glasgow Road more suitable. St Joseph's was formed as a mission in Blantyre in 1877. To the south west of the rows were the Gas works further up Stonefield Road. To the north east a colliery owned, L shaped shop at the corner of Stonefield Road and Calder Street known as Jackson Place.

It would be amiss, whilst discussing Dixons Rows, not to mention the terrible Blantyre Mining Disaster at Dixon's Colliery in October 1877. There was hardly a home untouched by grief at Dixon's Rows, the community effectively wiped out by the deaths of over 200 men and boys that fateful day, in what remains as Scotland's worst mining disaster. The heartache must have been unbearable and as the cottages were all tied to the deceased employees, the colliery owners later infamously ejected their widows and families, although a fund was set up beforehand to alleviate their plight.

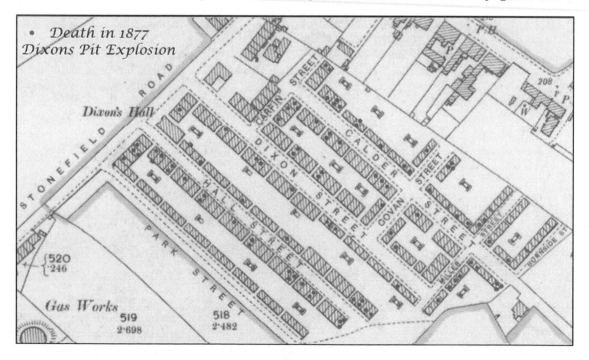

Figure 61 A circle marks every life lost from Dixon's Rows on 22nd October 1877

Another disaster happened on 2nd July 1879, not 2 years later where the lives of 28 miners were lost at Dixon's Pit number 1. Many of the fatalities were again from Dixon's Rows, further devastating a community, already in grief.

John Mann Thomson, the owner of the rows died on 12th March 1899, aged 63. He had been quite the shrewd businessman. Upon his death in 1899, the William Dixon Ltd board may have bought the rows from his estate, or inherited them at his will, but in any case by 1900, William Dixon & Co owned all the rows and continued to lease them all out separately to their own employees.

It was a condition in the tenancy of these tied miners' homes that the Father or the eldest son must have been employed in Dixon's collieries. A poem by Joe Corrie, describes this well, *"So, ah'll follow the gaffer wherever he goes, I'll say aye tae his ayes, an naw tae his naws. For ah'll lose ma job an house in the raws, should I faw oot wi the gaffer."*

In an extract from *"The Housing Condition of Miners"* Report by the Medical Officer of Health, Dr John T. Wilson, in 1910 noted that Dixons Rows had 420 employees living there. It was not unusual for a whole family of up to 10 people to be living in those cramped conditions with facilities outside. The reports mentions, "The mine-owners' houses are known as Dixon's Rows and are situated at Stonefield. They consist of: 149 Two-apartment houses Rental £5 17s. to £6 10s and 157 One-apartment houses Rental £3 18s to £4 11s. Erected about 33 years ago – One storey, brick – no damp-proof course – Walls not strapped and lathed, plastered on brick – A few wood floors, unventilated; majority brick floors – Some walls slightly damp – Internal surface of walls and ceilings good – No overcrowding – apartments large – No garden ground available, wash houses with water, no coal cellars – Water closets recently introduced, in the proportion of one closet to every 4 tenants – No sinks – drainage by open channels – Water supply from stand pipes in street, the well being at a distance varying from about 12 feet to 200 feet from the houses. – Scavenged at owners' expense, but houses are now included in Blantyre Special Scavenging District." The report suggests the houses were built in 1877, but this is incorrect, and I'll correct it by stating that 1872 is the correct date. Some evidence for this date correction is that the Glasgow Herald on 16th October 1872, published an article about the death of Thomas Docherty, residing at Dixon's Rows, Blantyre who was killed in a mining accident at nearby Greenfield. I take delight in being able to correct inaccuracies of dates wherever I see them!

On 25th March 1914, Evidence presented to Royal Commission, commented, "These rows cover a very extensive area, and are situated in the centre of the Blantyre district. They were erected some forty years ago, and are owned by William Dixon, Limited. They consist of 157 single- and 149 double-apartment houses. The rent per week, including rates, is 1s. 11d. for single-apartment, and 3s. 2d. for two-apartment houses. They are a most miserable type of house, thrown together with bricks in the cheapest possible fashion, with floors consisting largely of flags laid down on the earth. They are in a district well supplied with water, but are only served by means of standpipes at long intervals along the row."

The report continued, "They have recently been included in a special scavenging district, which has greatly improved the sanitation of the place. There are no sculleries or sinks; consequently all the dirty water has to be emptied into an open gutter that runs along the front of each row. There is a washhouse for every 4 and 8 double- and single-apartment tenants respectively. There is a water closet outside for every 3 and 5 double- and single-apartment houses respectively. Dustbins are in vogue, with a daily collection of refuse. There are no coal-cellars. There is a man employed locally for cleaning up the place." Relying on the previous report for dates, the mistake of 1877 being the construction date of the homes is carried over into this report.

At the field behind Dixon's Rows, the employees of Dixon's Collieries held an annual sports day in the field between Victoria Street and Boswell Drive, which would later become the playing fields of Blantyre High School.

Around 1930, a sink was provided in the main living rooms of each home but incredibly there was still no water supply. Water for cooking and washing had to be drawn from a communal well located in the street. The 4 families of each block shared an external toilet and a large washhouse, which was located at the rear of the rows. Gaslights were later installed and situated near the fireplaces.

Around this same time in the mid 1930's, the clearance of Dixon's Rows had commenced. Govan Street and Miller Street were the first streets to be demolished as part of the slum clearances, cleared to make way for the new houses at Priory Street and a revamped Calder Street, the houses you see today. At the time of the new homes being constructed in 1936, many of the remaining Dixon's Rows homes had been condemned and also in the early part of that year, the County Council took over the ground from William Dixon & Co.

Throughout the 1940's the abandonment and demolition of Dixon's Rows progressed. The last block of houses to be demolished was the former block of 4 homes, which had been used as a hall adjacent to Stonefield Road, in 1958.

REFUSE DESTRUCTOR

A Refuse Destructor was located at the very end of John Street, over the railway in vacant land surrounded by fields, to the north of the railway line.

It was opened in November 1910 built by Messrs Hughes & Stirling of London for the purpose of getting rid of Blantyre's rubbish. This new technology cost £3,500 and was situated away from people on the Braes overlooking the Clyde not far from Blantyre Railway Station.

It was accessed via John Street and was capable of destroying 45 tonnes of refuse per day shovelled into the furnaces as collected by dustmen and bin collections known as 'scavenging.'

Inside the building was an engine and dynamo room where electricity for lighting was produced, as a by-product of the burning operation. By the 1920's electricity for lighting was supplied to the Parish of Blantyre by the Clyde Valley Electrical Power Company, centralised and produced away from this facility. The destructor was disused by 1930. Another functioning destructor was located that year at Auchinraith, owned by the County Council of Lanark. To this day, tips are still located at Auchinraith beyond Blantyre Industrial Estate with refuse managed from a Council office to the side of the estate.

These days with re-cycling so prevailing, the tip is subdivided into many different access points for wood, metal, garden waste, clothing and the like. In these days of infrequent fortnightly bin uplifts, the tip is always busy with a constant stream of cars and vehicles throughout the whole day. Sadly, it is widely believed excessive charging for commercial waste in recent years, as much as £140/load has given a sharp rise to "fly tipping" in our scenic surrounding areas like the Calder.

SINGLE BOOT WAS HER REMINDER

Figure 62 The Boot was kept in a drawer

Many people reading this will now be aware of the fateful disaster on 22nd October 1877 where 216 men and boys lost their lives at Dixons Pits 2 and 3, High Blantyre. This sad tale remembers the grief one of the mothers endured.

Mr & Mrs George McLachlan lived at No 1 Jackson Place, Dixon's Rows. Sadly on that day, they lost THREE of their sons in that disaster, something I can't imagine how they ever recovered from. The youngest boy, William, was only 13 years old and was a pony driver in No2 pit. His young body was so badly burned that the only means of identifying the boy was by one of his socks and a boot.

His mother took the boot home, cleaned and polished it, then wrapped it in brown paper and kept it in a drawer of her sideboard, forever treating it with great care. Time and time again she would take the boot out, clean it and return it to its hallowed place. Some 30 years later (around 1917), the woman was dying and said to her daughter, *"William's boot means so much to me, bury it with me, when the time comes".* Her daughter did as she was told. Mrs McLachlan is buried in High Blantyre Cemetery and beside her in the coffin, is the boot her young son wore that terrible day.

BLANTYRE POLICE CENSUS

In 1924, the police completed their annual census of Blantyre Parish, and they were indebted to Sergeant George Logie for the following particulars. The population was returned at 18,703, a record peak for Blantyre of which there are 9,592 males and 9,111 females.

Aliens (immigrants) number 495 and consist of:

Russians. 404
Italians. 68
Germans. 18
French. 1
Austrians. 4

"The houses occupied number 3,483; 26 are returned empty and they are in the course of erecting 51 making a total in all of 3,560." In the parish there are:

26 Public Houses, 11 Licensed Grocers. Number of dogs 633.

Only in Blantyre could there be over twice as many pubs as grocery shops!

CHILDREN AT BENHAM'S WINDOW

I love this photo. Some Blantyre children in 1921 peer in the window of William Francis Benham's Shop at 11 Stonefield Road. This was near the bottom junction not far from Valerio's Cafe de Royal. The date and location are confirmed accurate.

Figure 63 Children on Stonefield Road peer in Benham's Window 1921

The window is a good source of finding out what Benham's sold. The tobacconist, hardware, confectionary wholesale and fruiterer was well known in Blantyre but Frank would only live another 4 years after this photo was take, the business passing to his daughters. During recent research, I found that Frank was the owner of the opposing Old Original Bar for a short time, following the death of publican Robert Craig. Frank lived in Glasgow Road and was well known in Blantyre.

Contrary to popular thought, nearby Valerios did not have monopoly on selling cigarettes and cigars in Blantyre, with Benhams, almost next door competing with them on that front.

Zooming in, under jars of sweets on the top shelf, we see window displays of fruit. Grapes and Watermelons were a surprise to see, but more commonly apples in the window, not so much. Tins of tomatoes are on the front shelf but with so much perishable produce, this is likely a window display that would need to be changed often.

CHILD'S THIRD CONVICTION

Figure 64 Birch Rod could often draw blood!

A **remarkable case** of juvenile precocity was heard in the Hamilton J.P. Court on Saturday 24th January 1925. Not yet nine years of age, a boy from Burnbank admitted the theft of tin of butterscotch from a confectioner's shop at Glasgow Road in Low Blantyre.

The wee eight-year-old boy incredibly had 2 previous convictions fro theft. Once in 1923 then another in 1924. The judge stated, "There must be some sort of punishment to make him realise the error of his ways, even his exceptional age." Sentence of six stripes of the birch rod was passed.

On hearing the sentence, the little fellow went into a fit of weeping. Reactions on social media to this story were not surprising:

Henry Hambley said, *"No evidence that corporal punishment did any good. We need to love and cherish children and all will be good though I admit there will be some problems along the way."* William Watson completely agreed.

Elizabeth Weaver added, *"I agree with Henry too – it's disgusting that children were abused like that and of course corporal punishment was used daily in schools until the 70s. I often wonder how anyone could claim that it worked! If that was the case, why was it the same poor kids who were belted day after day at my school (Auchinraith)?"*

BOYS NARROW ESCAPE

John Boyd was a miner who lived at 177 Glasgow Road in the early part of last Century. On On Saturday 23rd October 1926, his 6-year-old son had a narrow escape from death.

The boy had been to a baker's shop, and in crossing to his home just opposite he allowed a bus to pass by him, but upon stepping out into Glasgow Road afterwards, he failed to observe that another was coming close behind. The bus travelling at speed caught the child in front, knocking him down flat on the road. However, his life was saved by the prompt action of the driver, who suddenly swerved into a side street and halted. The boy had been knocked down to the ground, clipped by the front of the bus, but, fortunately, he had been between the wheels and had stayed down whether intentionally or not as the pass passed clean over him. His injuries consisted of a deep cut on the head. As frightened onlookers ran to the scene, they were most "relieved" to see injuries rather than a lifeless body in the road. They attended to him immediately by calling for medical help.

ANDREW LITTLE'S BAKERS

Pictured exclusively here in the 1930's is the shop front of Andrew Little's the well-known former bakers who were situated on the north side of Glasgow Road for 51 years.

Figure 65 Isabella Little (b1903) stands at her shop doorway 1930s

Andrew Little's shop opened in 1928 and was located at 200 Glasgow Road. (Opposite the bottom of Victoria Street close to the old entrance to the park.) In the photo is Isabella Little who was born in 1903. Brothers James, William and Andrew Little later ran the business working at the bake house at the rear of the property, and also the shop facing out on to Glasgow Road.

Many people in Blantyre fondly remember little's Bakery, and especially the delicious rolls. The shop unfortunately became a casualty of the Glasgow Road redevelopment and opened for its last day on 17th February 1979, when the till rang for the last time with the sale of a wedding cake for William's daughter. James, William and Andrew were present and worked on that sorrowful day.

Gordon Cook told me, *"I used to call in every morning at the bake house round the back of Little's shop to pick up freshly baked rolls after coming off the nightshift. They were still hot when I got home and the butter just melted right into them, delicious. Inside the bakery, there were usually three men working, all mature gents, and then there was the cat. This cat had the run of the place and was more often than not padding along the counter leaving footprints in the flour."*

BULLOCKS IN THE BAKERS

Great excitement prevailed in Blantyre on Tuesday 8th March 1932, when three bullocks which were being driven along Glasgow Road got out of hand and ran wild for a time, ending up in baker's shop. This was at a time just after trams on a newly renovated road.

Figure 66 Bullocks ran right though the shop

The animals were being driven to the county abattoir in Forrest Street when a passing motorcar apparently frightened them. They ran along the street and pedestrians scattered in all directions.

In their wild stampede the animals ran through closes and into various backyards and gardens causing alarm. They eventually found their way into a tearoom and baker's shop owned by Mr A. Benham, at 146 Glasgow Road much to the complete surprise of his customers and staff. The back door of the shop was open and two of the excited animals dashed through, finding their way behind the counter of the front shop.

Mrs Benham was serving a customer in the tearoom at the time, and she made her escape by leaping over the counter. The drovers were quickly on the scene and, by skilful handling, got the animals out of the shop, and they were driven off.

Former address, 146 Glasgow Road was on the north side of the road not far from where the sports centre is now.

LETHAM'S GARAGE

The Garage was located on the site of the former Gas Works on the Eastern side of Stonefield Road, about halfway down the street. Today, the ground lays vacant with a few home, which after a lengthy delay of many years as of November 2018, are finally being completed.

Figure 67 Letham's Garage on Stonefield Road pictured during 1950's

On social media, people clearly remembered Lethams' commenting:

Paul McDermott *"I used to get chased out of there by a huge German Shepard as a kid!!! "*

Sheona Thomson Brennan *"I remember one summer one of the buses was set on fire...Stonefield Road was filled with thick black smoke, cant remember what age I was maybe 9 or 10, as I lived right across from it. That damn dog barked 24 hours a day!"*

Thomas Barrett agreed, *"That garage could tell a lot of stories."*

Wilma McNulty added, *"My aunt Helen Gallagher cleaned them when I was a wee lassie. I loved to go in and help her ha ha xx"*

Linda Torlay Wood commented, *"My husband worked there for about 12 or 13 years."*

Andrew Baillie said, *"I recall one or two of the buses going up in smoke around 1985/1986!"*

Alan Lappin told me, *"I'm sure Letham's closed in the early 90's. Our family's home looks on to it from Kinnoull Place, can remember them being there, and also remember seeing their buses being in use and seeing them in Blackpool frequently around that time."*

COMMUNITY CENTRE CHILDREN

This picture is from 1978 and these are just some of the many Blantyre kids who enjoyed a summer of fun at the former Blantyre Community Centre at Glasgow Road.

Figure 68 Blantyre Community Centre on Glasgow Road 1978

It marked the start of 4 weeks of summer school holiday fun, which got off to a great start, despite earlier fears that the events may not go ahead due to lack of supervision. The Elizabeth Scott Centre and the Glasgow Road Community Centre dually ran the Play scheme events and they attracted youngsters in their droves! The idea was to stop children being bored in summer, but still give them something interesting to do in the company of many friends.

On a separate note, over 60 young children who attended Blantyre Community Centre Playgroup were confined to their homes in mid March 1979 after being all hit by a virus.

Doctors confirmed at least 2 of them had dysentery and were at a loss as to what was causing it. Centre staff took the outbreak seriously, asking parents to keep their children at home. All the play equipment including many toys were destroyed and professional cleaners hired to bleach the entire place.

Dysentery is a contagious disease and needs isolation. Dr David Colville at Blantyre Health Centre told staff that Dysentery was a much more serious disease than the usual tummy bugs encountered in day to day children's playgroups. It is very easily spread by hands and mouths.

Thankfully the crisis calmed down with children returning almost 2 weeks later.

THEY FLOCKED TO ST JOSEPHS

Here's a slightly more modern story for you. This photo dates between 1998 and 2000 and

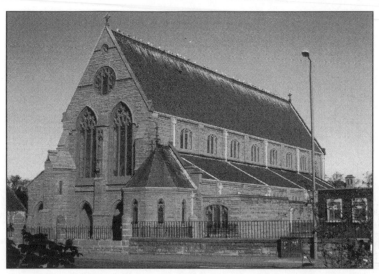

features St Joseph's church, Glasgow Road, Blantyre. Photographed and shared by Robert Stewart, if you look closely you'll see an unwelcome flock of seagulls on the roof. Perhaps attracted by the heat from the ridge that winter, the birds chose St Josephs to rest. Robert noted that nearby David Livingstone Memorial Church had no birds on it, which was peculiar.

You can see the mess that's being created on the St Josephs roof from their stay. Robert told me, *"I bet the local priest wasn't too chuffed with his new flock."*

Figure 69 St Joseph's Church, Glasgow Rd, 1998 by RDS

SUMMER IN THE PARK

I may go on a little about how beautiful the Public Park used to be at Stonefield in previous

decades. Sometimes however, it's good to take a step back and note at certain times, the park still IS very beautiful. It may not have all the trellises and rose gardens of the 1950's and 60's, but it does have some nice semi mature trees, which can be especially beautiful in full bloom, like this photo in summer.

A reminder, Blantyre does have some attractive green, park spaces within our town and its not all doom and gloom. The council general do well with upkeep of our green

Figure 70 The Park does look green and nice. Summer 2015

spaces. In Autumn 2018, with the demolition of the eastern side of Clydeview Shopping Centre, there are now views down to this park, from ASDA carpark and even Craig Street. Glasgow Road is once again in 2018 going through large, sweeping changes that will last generations.

DEMOLITION ST JOSEPH'S PRIMARY SCHOOL

I record here the date, 7th January 2016, a sad day for many Blantyre residents. The day the old St Joseph's Primary School in Glasgow Road got bulldozed to the ground. The popular school was well known and attended by many people living in Blantyre ad beyond and I'm sure will have a lot of fond (and perhaps not so fond) memories for many. It took contractors until 29th January, to finish the demolition.

Figure 71 Demolition of the old St Joseph's Primary School. Photo by Jim Donnelly

With the new modern school already built behind it, the scar that this site left in Blantyre now is truly massive and as of November 2018 is still vacant. Despite being enough for a whole new housing estate, a brand new state of the art care facility is confirmed by planners, with the expected closure of Kirkton Care in High Blantyre in the near future.

COLLISION WITH NEWSAGENTS

At 2.15pm on Sunday 22nd January 2017, a silver Astra vehicle crashed through the plate glass window of the Newsagents (Mauchline's) Shop on Glasgow Road, near the top of Station Road.

Thankfully, the young man driving the car was uninjured and had recently passed his test. The shop staff were also uninjured but the incident was alarming as 2 fire brigades, 2 ambulance and 2 police cars arrived on the scene, closing the full Glasgow Road off, giving rise to considerable alarm amongst Blantyre residents before the outcome and nature of the accident was announced.

LEANING POSTBOX OF BLANTYRE

John Ward Duffy shared this photo of the postbox at the bottom of Stonefield. I'm told it is an Edward VII box. If we can look beyond the rather 'saucy' photo in the window of Tan Unique, you'll notice of course that the pillar box has a remarkable lean, something that has been there since at least the 1970's. Even by Royal Mail standards, that's a long time in nearly half a century in not fixing it!

This post box located near the former Benham's shop and now beside Valerio Court was once outside Blantyre's main post office in the early 20th Century.

I turned to social media for answers:

Jo Kelly said, *"I honestly thought it leant like that from being tapped by buses turning the corner!"*

John Cornfield added, *"Not a mark on it the foundation must have moved."*

Bruce Baldwin commented, *"It was like that when I was postie the best box story was the box Stolen from Glasgow Road at Springwell."*

Davy Thomson suggested, *"It's been caused by people in Craig's Pub staggering oot and bumping into it over the years, true story!!!"*

Margaret Liddle rounded off with *"Probably the 263 bus coming round the corner off Glasgow Road had something to do with it."*

Figure 72 Stonefield's leaning Postbox

CHAPTER 6
AUCHINRAITH & PRIESTFIELD

Auchinraith and Priestfield are two separate but relatively close areas of Blantyre not far from each other. Auchinraith spans from Causeystanes in High Blantyre at Cemetery Road eastwards to the timber houses. It also covers a large area northwards, encompassing the housing estates around Auchinraith Road and into Springwells. Several prominent roads like Victoria Street, Craig Street, parts of Main Street, Auchinraith Road make up this area, once a hamlet in its own right.

Priestfield is another old area of High Blantyre, to the south of Main Street stretching from as far as High Blantyre Cross at Kirkton along a route towards Hillhouse in Hamilton. Dominated in the past by two Farms, (Priestfield and Back Priestfield) the fields eventually gave over to mining operations by Coalmasters Dixons. Today, Priestfield in name is remembered by the hall and early 1980's Cemetery of the same name. The colliery buildings and their tied rows are long gone.

Photographed above on 20th April 2015 in our cover photo is the relatively new restaurant and pub, "Redburn Farm Inn". Construction commenced in Summer 2014 and the popular eatery is now well frequented. The pub is sited on the exact spot of the Blantyre Mining Disaster of 1877. Indeed, the old Dixons 3 pit itself had to be capped before construction could commence. It is hoped that management will take heed of the wishes of the people of Blantyre and treat this important site with utmost respect. Surprisingly, there was little objection to the restaurant being built there, perhaps due to the land being vacant for decades and the fact that Blantyre already has two different memorials to the terrible disaster that happened deep below the ground on that spot.

The addition of Priestfield as a separate section into this particular book is a first for this series, created at the request of residents in High Blantyre for further representation of the area they live in. We note that Priestfield "on paper" now falls outwith Blantyre ward 15, classed as Hamilton as of 2018, and whilst that may be for electoral reasons only, we consider it very much to still be part of Blantyre as a whole.

DIXON'S VENT PIPE

Figure 73 Vent Pipe in 2015

Betty McLean in Canada asks, *"I remember someone saying that there's a pipe in the ground where the miners were brought up after the 1877 explosion and it's near the current roundabout at Priestfield. Just wondering if this could be found and perhaps a memorial plaque placed at the spot as something of historical interest."*

There is indeed a pipe in the ground and it's my understanding it's used to vent the ongoing gasses, that still exist at those depths. The pipe is relatively modern and sits a few metres off the footpath on Hillhouse Road, on the Hamilton Technology Park side. It is located on the bend, before Priestfield Cemetery in amongst the bushes and trees. In October 2015, during a historical walking tour, Alex Rochead took this photo. It may not be the exact location that the men and boys were brought up from below, but the spot is definitely poignant and worthy of some kind of future marker or memorial.

JERUSALEM HOUSES

Thanks to Stephen McGuigan for sharing this photo, which was taken in the early 1980s, from High Blantyre's Forres Street, looking over northwards towards Main Street, High Blantyre.

The photo demonstrates exactly why this housing estate, built in 1970, had a local nickname of being *"The Jerusalem Houses"*, a term some people still use today despite the modern pitched roofs added later.

Alan Dorricott said on social media, " I remember the roofs leaking every winter! I will say though that the neighbours were fantastic and there were many parties had out the front during summer weekends. The flats had really big rooms and blow heating, a big change from the coal fire we had in Springwell."

One winter, some of the flat roofs blew off in strong winds and there's even an urban myth that somebody was sunbathing on the rooftop in summer.

Figure 74 The Jerusalem Houses, 1980

HOISTING THE FLAG

Figures 75 - 79 Raising the Flag at High Blantyre, Nationalising the Mines, 1947

These wonderful photos were taken on the 6th January 1947 as the NCB flag gets hoisted above Dixons Pit 1, High Blantyre on the day the mine was nationalised. It attracted a large crowd of spectators from all over, including the families of the miners themselves. As well as Andra McAnulty attending, Councillor Jimmy Beecroft and other officials from the colliery watched on as the miners who had long waited this day, got the chance to hoist the NCB flag, high above the offices. The large crowd assembled on land, which is now Priestfield Cemetery watching the flag being hoisted up over the colliery offices and for many people this signified the future.

The photos are permitted stills from an old coal mining film reel. Dixon's Collieries had been in this area since the early 1870's and formed a huge part of mining life in Blantyre. They employed many thousands of people during their existence and of course brought immigrants and others looking for work, many of whom settled here permanently.

Crowds coming to Priestfield that day in 1947 packed into the area. To the left are the offices and Priestfield Terrace. In the background in High Blantyre Parish Church steeple and the horizon is actually High Blantyre Main Street.

Figure 80 Crowds flocked to usher in the new mining era in 1947. Pictured Dixons 1

The delight on everybody's faces indicates what a popular event and achievement this was. Not even a couple of years after WW2, this signified new employment opportunities, new conditions for workers, welfare and hopes for the future. However, their hopes were not to be realised. Little did anybody know that the mines throughout High Blantyre would be closed, exhausted of most of their resources in as little as a decade later.

Andra McAnulty, the noteworthy campaigner for miner's rights who assisted raising the flag that day was described nicely by the now defunct Blantyre Gazette.

As he unfurled the National Coal Board flag at Dixon's Colliery in High Blantyre, the paper said "*This old war horse still going strong.*" At the time Andra was 86 years old. In his address to the large crowd pictured, he told them he had been in the mining industry since he was 10 years old. He went on to say how he had been associated with the pitmen's champions like Keir Hardie, Bob Smillie and William Small. He went on to say how proud he was to be president of the union from 1920 -1924 and how proud he was to have lived long enough to see the aim of these men, the nationalisation of the mines, realised.

Figure 81 Andra McAnulty in 1947 at Blantyre

Andra had been particularly elated when he found out the coal mines were to be nationalised. It was an ambition of his for 70 years beforehand to see that day and it is said by his family that on the day the flag was unfurled in Blantyre, they were fearful he was so excited he would have a heart attack. An enormous crowd turned up at High Blantyre Dixon's collieries to see the event. The standing ovation given to Andra by what seemed to be the whole population of Blantyre, appeared to go on for an eternity. The feeling of euphoria almost caused a disaster. As Andra was being assisted from the temporary platform that had been erected for this occasion, so many people wanted to either pat him on the back or shake his hand that he was in great danger of being knocked over. Only the intervention of several burly miners prevented this calamity, as they quickly formed a protective cordon around his slight figure.

Andra died on 12th November 1949 at the home of a married daughter Mrs George Patterson, at 105 Parkville Drive, Springwells, Blantyre. Thank you to the book "A Blast from the Past" for these snippets. In our photo, Andra's left hand is resting on James Kellachan's shoulder. On the far right of the picture, with the cigarette is Councillor Jimmy Beecroft.

ROMAN FIND AT PRIESTFIELD

Next, a newspaper article from nearly 250 years ago! From the Middlesex Journal London, May 17th – 19th 1770.

"A few days ago, while some labourers were employed in sinking a well at Blantyre in Scotland, they dug up a couple of copper vessels full of antique Roman silver coins, struck in the reign of Augustus."

Figure 82 Roman Coins similar to those found in Blantyre

The old Roman coins were found by labourers sinking a well at Priestfield in High Blantyre. We know Romans occupied the area, evidence of which can be found just a mile or two away at the ruins of the Roman Bathhouse at Strathclyde Park. The coins found may have been similar to those found. Question is, do more treasures exist buried in the fields in and around Blantyre?

JAMES ALEXANDER

James Alexander was a late 19th Century shoemaker in High Blantyre, according to Naismith's Directory of 1879.

Born in 1826 in Blantyre at Auchinraith to David and Margaret, James was a middle child from a cotton worker family. During the 1850's, he left Blantyre whilst in his late 20's and was absent during the 1861 and 1871 Blantyre census. However, he returned to his hometown to the Hunthill area of Blantyre sometime between 1875 and 1879 when he was in his late 40's or early 50's. Perhaps attracted back by the growing population, business opportunity or simply having married to Annie Greenshileds in 1875, he initially rented a house named "Adams Cottage" from Mrs Betsy Weir, who owned Braehead, the large house next to the Calder.

In 1881 James was 55 years old and was living at Hunthill with his wife Annie, aged 49. In 1885, he paid £3 and 10 shillings rent per annum. In the 1891 census James was 65 years old and still working, self-employed, but not with any employees. James and Annie (b Ayrshire) did not have any children. By 1895 James had retired and moved home to the top of Broompark Road, renting a house from Arthur Blakely. The address suggests he lived across the road from the public house in the former tenements at the junction of Main Street. Mr Blakely had built the pub and the tenements around the same time in 1894. James Alexander, bootmaker died in 1897, aged 71.

MARY NICOL NEILL ARMOUR – BLANTYRE ARTIST

Mary Steele was born in Blantyre on 27th March 1902. She lived with her parents at their home near Victoria Street and when just 12 years old, she won a scholarship to attend Hamilton Academy. Leaving behind Auchinraith Primary School, she attended the Academy between the years of 1914 and 1920. She was a gifted pupil, immersing herself especially in art, drawing and colour (perhaps on reflection to escape the grey, dirty world Blantyre was back in those coal mining era days). Her talent caught the eye of her art teacher, who had a word with her parents and persuaded them to let Mary attend Glasgow School of Art (GSA). Mary Steele studied at the GSA from 1920 until 1925, when after a post-diploma year and teacher training; Mary Steel became an art teacher.

Figure 83 Mary Armour during 1970's

In 1927 she married the landscape and figure painter William Armour (1903–1979), settling in Milngavie on the outskirts of Glasgow city.

By then Mary Armour was an accomplished artist, painting still life, landscapes and portraits in oils and watercolour. Mary Armour was to exhibit regularly at the Royal Academy; the Royal Scottish Academy (winning the Guthrie Prize in 1937); the Royal Society of Painters in Watercolour, the Scottish Society of Artists and the Royal Glasgow Institute of the Fine Arts. In 1941 she was elected an associate of the Royal Scottish Watercolour Society, becoming a full member in 1956, and became a Royal Scottish Academician in 1958. Armour taught still life painting at Glasgow School of Art from 1951 to 1962 when she retired from teaching and returned to painting full-time.

In 1972 she was awarded the Cargill Prize at the RGIFA (Royal Glasgow Institute of the Fine Arts) becoming a full member of the RGIFA in 1977. In 1982 she was awarded an honorary LLD from the University of Glasgow. Armour was also elected Honorary President of the Glasgow School of Art and of the RGIFA, which awards the annual 'Armour Award' for a work of distinction by a young artist. Mary Nicol Neill Armour died on 5 July 2000, aged 98.

Her paintings sell for many thousands of pounds and since her death; her stock has been rising in value. Her work is displayed at many Scottish museums, including City of Edinburgh Collection, Aberdeen Art Gallery and of course nearer her hometown, at David Livingstone Centre too. A Mary Armour early painting is displayed in the Centre, which was gifted there to commemorate the opening of the centre in 1929.

Figure 84 Armour Painting

THEFT OF OATS

On Friday 19th December 1862, a week before Christmas, police constable Andrew Cooper was going about his rounds on Burnbank Road when he saw three well-known characters of the same family.

John Cook (the father), Sarah Cook (the wife) and also Sarah Cook (daughter) were in the dark street carrying something bulky, struggling with its weight. He immediately pounced upon the trio demanding to know what was in the sack. When it was opened, he saw large quantities of corn,

beans and oats. After a little resistance, he apprehended all three of them taking them to the lock up.

On the following morning, whilst they were still locked up, police enquired at several Blantyre farmhouses where it was found that the barn at Auchinraith (Burnbrae Farm) had been entered into by force.

Crops matching those stolen were found inside, the farmer and police concluding they had been taken from that very barn without permission. Mr James Scott, the farmer concluded also that a theft had taken place.

Figure 85 Oats stolen from the barn

The trio of family thieves were examined before the Sheriff that same day and sent to prison for 1 week, spanning the Festive holiday.

AUCHINRAITH NURSERIES

Pictured here in an aerial photo from 1955, are the greenhouses and gardens of Auchinraith Nurseries. Located on Main Street, at its junction with Auchinraith Road, the nursery served Blantyre well and was run in the early to mid part of the 20th Century by the Pattie family. Frank Pattie in the 1950's supplied floral tributes for all occasions, the nurseries specialising in growing flowers of all types. Prior to this, Matthew Campbell ran the nursery for many years.

Figure 86 Auchinraith Nurseries in 1955 corner of Auchinraith Road & Main St

Matthew was born in 1839. He is not noted as being in Blantyre until the 1881 census, suggesting he was an incomer. In 1881 Matthew was living at Nursery Cottage, Main Street, High Blantyre with his wife and children, good confirmation that the nurseries existed then.

In 1891, Matthew aged 55 was still living at Nursery Cottage with his wife Catherine and their 6 children. Joseph McNich, an elementary teacher was boarding with them. 22-year-old James Gilchrist a practitioner lived with them, as did 15-year-old Peter Gilchrist, an accounts clerk. 36-year-old Minnie Anderson and her 5 children lived with them too. Mr Anderson was apparently a cigar merchant. The large amount of people suggests Nursery Cottage or cottages were fairly large offering accommodation for all these people.

However, it was all change in 1901, at the age of 62 Matthew was living at Nursery Cottage only with his daughter Jeannie, aged 19. His son's Matthew Jnr and John were to continue the family businesses at expanded locations working from 'Milton Burnbank View'. Matthew Snr died at the nursery aged 76, on 20th August 1915 during WW1. He was buried on Tuesday 24th August 1915.

In February 1915, 6 months before Matthew died, an advert ran in the newspaper for "M Campbell & Son, Nurseries, High Blantyre", stating they sold ornamental trees and shurbs, privit hedges, roses, wallflowers, primroses, with flower and vegetable seeds available from a catalog.

We can trace the start of the nurseries back to the 1881 census, suggesting they may have been there even in the 1870's. They are certainly there on the 1898 map, with greenhouses and gardens laid out on extensive fields. Access was from Main Street itself, entering a courtyard area, with a large house belonging to the owner. In 1898, at least 8 large greenhouses existed alongside numerous smaller ones. A pump in the back garden provided water. By 1910, the business had expanded hugely with over 16 large greenhouses, of an impressive size.

By the 1930's the same number of greenhouses existed, but the open fields surround the business, now gave way to modern homes at Muir Street and the aptly named Nursery Place. Some of these properties and gardens looked directly into the nursery itself. The nursery still owned a large piece of land, including vacant ground at the corner of Auchinraith Road.

In the 1970's following the demolition of the greenhouses, when the sheltered houses were built on the land, a new road called Braehead was created, leading in off Nursery Place. Braehead is easily missed and leads to a dead end and sits on the exact land where many of the greenhouses were once located. In mid 2018, the modern Kirkton Care Home, which is located on the very same spot as the gardens, was threatened with imminent closure, once again meaning this site looks destined for another use in future.

ALLANGOWAN MANSE

Allangowan was the name of a former house at 9 Auchinraith Road, which appears to have been constructed between 1897 and 1905. By 1905 the detached house was owned by Peter MacIntosh, then following his death between 1915 and 1920, passed to owner and occupier, Margaret MacIntosh.

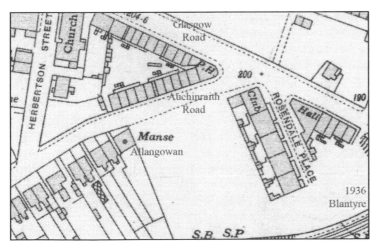

Figure 87 Allangowan (Manse) shown on 1936 Map

It sat on the south side of Auchinraith Road at the end of a row of semi-detached homes. It was initially beside a track that led over the nearby railway to the south. In those early years, there was a neighbouring blacksmith, not far from tenements named Rosendale. Between 1920 and 1925, the building was sold on.

In 1925, Rev. D.W. Thomson occupied it. By 1930, according to the Valuation Roll, Allangowan belonged to the managers of the Blantyre Evangelical Union, part of the Congregational Church. That same year Rev. Thomas Shanks lived there, indicating it was likely the church manse. The house was still there in the mid 1930's, but is now demolished. It sat on land, which is now the monoblocked car park on the right hand side of the entrance to Gavin Watson Printers.(former JR Reids)

ORIGINS OF VICTORIA STREET

Unlike the other streets leading south branching off Glasgow Road, Auchinraith Road and Victoria Street joined Low to High Blantyre, cutting right through Blantyre and has many homes and public buildings. Let's look at Victoria Street.

During the 19th Century until the mid 1870's, small track led up a slight gradient from the Glasgow to Hamilton Road, up towards the Stonefield Farm (Hastie's) ending at that property. The farm was elevated overlooking fields at that time and the small, expanding village hamlet of Stonefield, itself then only a few homes and shops. This track was extended during the 1870's and 1880's leading up to what is now the crossroads at Calder Street, providing easier access to Netherfield Place and Dixon's Rows. The track was known as "*the Clay Road*", a good indication that it likely did not have a good surface.

During the late 1890's, Blantyre was still going though rapid population growth due to the expanding coalfields. At this time, upgrading the narrow paths and thoroughfares was an important reinforcing of infrastructure. The Clay Road was then further extended during the 1880's and 1890's from the crossroads right up to Main Street on High Blantyre to the South. The track generally inclined upwards the further south you travelled as it does today and was narrow, muddy and frequently used by miners as short cuts.

The track had previously simply been a field boundary for Stonefield Farm. It was essentially a route over fields, with no buildings at any side. Indeed this track was so roughly constructed; it simply had the topsoil and turf taken off. In the first decade of the 1900's, the Clay road was widened and constructed over with a more permanent surface forming what is now Victoria Street. A section of the original Clay Road still exists today at the very top of Victoria Street at the junction of High Blantyre Main Street. The road at that point significantly narrows back to the size it was then, which was not much larger than the width of a horse and cart. It's for that reason cars cannot exit off Victoria Street directly on to Main Street today.

Victoria Street was named so, following the death of the Monarch Queen Victoria in 1901, coinciding with a new century and the 'Clay Road' name abandoned, it had been given the name "Victoria Street" by 1910.

Buildings on Victoria Street

During the late 19th and 20th Centuries, some very prominent and public buildings were constructed on Victoria Street, some still existing! On the eastern side behind the school was the Schoolmaster's house and the Police Station near the impressive Calder Street Junior Secondary School. Today, ASDA warehouses occupy this space. On the eastern opposing side there were shops, the Health Institute as well as, further to the north, a Hospital for Infectious Diseases.

Across from the Health Centre for many decades of the 20th Century a fine park for children had been laid out. Now going into Winter 2018, a newly constructed housing estate is about to open.

Alongside the schoolmaster's house and Victoria Place (tenement houses for miners nicknamed 'the Honeymoon' behind Stonefield Parish School), there were privately built stone homes and huge expansive council estates built in the mid 1920's. It is perhaps the quality homes and number of families that lived in Victoria Street that defined it as a popular residential place. Centrally located, the street was and still is close to many public amenities.

JIMMY DUDDY

Mr James Duddy was born in 1871 in Mountpleasant, Church Hill, Donegal, Ireland, a son for Michael Duddy and Mary McCay. He moved to Scotland seeking employment and became a miner in Hamilton, where he met and married a local girl Mary Jane Wallace (b1872) on Hogmanay 1890. Children soon followed. Sadly, their daughter Susanna, aged 2 and a half died on 12th June 1898, prompting a fresh start and a move away from memories and heartache.

They all moved to Blantyre in 1898 deciding to settle down at 73 Merry's Rows (near current Elm Street). James, more commonly known as Jimmy was employed as a "shanker" at the Auchinraith Colliery, owned by Merry and Cunningham. By 1901, 30-year-old Jimmy had a growing family. Little Maggie, John, Mary and Lizzie all aged between 1 and 9 years old lived at the little cramped house together with their mum and dad. I say cramped, for amongst them was a lot of workshop equipment, for Jimmy had quite the flair for invention and fixing things. Around this time, motorcycles were a new invention and to those lucky enough to own one, when it broke down, they would bring it to Jimmy to fix. This skill for fixing all things mechanical, led him to have a part time job carrying out repairs on the projector at Blantyre Electric cinema on Glasgow Road, the town's very first silent cinema.

However, there is another story for which Jimmy is best known. A fanciful story, but delightful nonetheless. It is said the Wright Brothers first flight in 1903 sparked Jimmy's interest in taking to the air. Sometime between 1903 and 1913 he had installed a lathe and machinery in the back part of his miner's row home where he took to inventing, constructing parts from scratch. It is alleged that Jimmy constructed a small machine, labelling it a "manned aircraft" and constructed from his own manufactured components. Stories of Jimmy flying over the rooftops at Stonefield were told, but having no means to land safely, the aircraft always crashed and each time had to be brought back and reassembled. Its thought he made contact with the Patents office, but not known if anything was ever registered.

Figure 88 Jimmy's Children & Partners in 1940s

At the time of the 1911 census was taken, he was visiting his mother Mary back in Ireland, whom by that time was 75, although this is known to have just been a holiday. He was soon back to Blantyre.

Sadly, Jimmy didn't live a long life and indeed didn't see the First World War. On 19th July 1913, aged 42, he died in a pit accident at Auchinraith. He had been summoned to Auchinraith to take off broken plates on pump rods, near the top of the shaft. He stood to the side on to a scaffold board, which gave way underneath him, causing him to trip and fall to his death down a frightful 113 fathoms. (203 metres!) One cannot imagine if he was alive for the duration of his fall! The racking that kept the scaffold in place, had for some unknown reason come off. At the time of his death, he left behind a wife and 9 children. Pictured are Jimmy's daughters and their husbands in the 1940's. Jimmy Duddy was clearly a man with a flair for invention and will be remembered here as such.

RIVER RESCUE

A dramatic river rescue took place on Sunday 20th May 1923. The Auchinraith Silver Band, Blantyre had set off from Calder Street and had the luxury of travelling to Airdrie by motorbus that day. As they left Blantyre, heading down the Whistleberry Road towards Bothwell Bridge, the passengers heard screams coming from the nearby River Clyde.

The bus halted at the edge of the road to investigate and James Barrie, a bandsman from Blantyre jumped from the vehicle when heard screams in the river, this time more loudly. A small lad was being carried out to midstream near Bothwell Bridge.

James at once jumped into the river with no thought for his own safety, and succeeded in bringing the lad to safety, amidst the applause of his fellow bandsmen standing on the verge and a growing large number of spectators. James Barrie was a hero that day, his story remembered here.

WHISKY AFTER HOURS

At the Hamilton J.P. Court, on Monday 28th January 1929, a charge was made against Hugh McKenna, a publican residing at Uddingston for having sold excisable liquor after 9 p.m. from his public bar in High Blantyre.

Hugh was the landlord and owner of the Auchinraith Vaults on Main Street, which in more modern times we may know better as Matt's Bar. On the 1929 night in question, around 9.18pm, McKenna's younger brother had been preparing to close the premises when he was disturbed by a woman knocking at the side door. She stated that she wanted some whisky for her neighbour who was seriously ill. Now, with the pubs closing at 9pm in Blantyre that decade and alcohol not permitted to be sold after that time, passing the woman whiskey would be an illegal act.

After some deliberation McKenna gave the woman her whisky. However, their actions were not being ignored. When she went outside two policemen accosted her. Quickly on being approached, the woman stumbled towards an open doorway and threw the bottle of whisky inside. The constables, however, observed this action and regained the full bottle as evidence. The law places the breach on the publican, not the person buying it.

Hugh McKenna did not attend the court, but instead sent along an agent on his behalf. The agent had been instructed to plead guilty, McKenna obviously accepting in advance that he was going to have to pay some sort of fine. A fine was indeed imposed of 20s with an option of spending 10 days in prison instead. McKenna's agent chose to pay the fine. Nobody knows what happened to the bottle of whisky, and I wonder if it was "*kept in the police station*" as confiscated evidence! Thank you to Scott Allison for sharing this photo of his precious bottle of whisky. Dating from 1970, the bottle is unopened, a gift from former Hastie's Farm.

Figure 89 Hastie's Whisky

THE GLAD EYES GANG

The "Glad Eyes Gang" were a gang of young men in Low Blantyre during the mid 1920's.

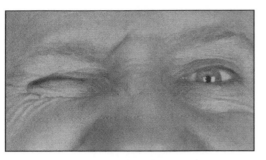

Their rather strange name came from their self-belief of being able to attract a lady or two. (The meaning of 'Glad eyes' being the glance given to young women indicating an advance of a romantic nature!). Their most common meeting place was at the many Blantyre dances each weekend and they did NOT take kindly to Hamilton or Burnbank men coming into Blantyre each weekend, on their patch, and dancing with Blantyre's beautiful women!

Figure 90 The Glad Eyes Gang

One story goes; on the evening of Saturday 9th January 1926 a dance at the Co-operative Hall near Rosendale was taking place. Hamilton man Neil McLaughlin decided to attend the dance and found himself in a pickle when asking a Blantyre woman out, whom four members of the *"Glad Eye Gang"*, each had their interest in.

However, Neil was a miner from Wylie Street, Hamilton. A well-built man of such build that gave any onlooker the impression he could protect himself. He was not afraid of 4 smaller built gang members.

It was alleged that when the dance finished, some of the Hamilton men, including Neil got to know that the *"Glad Eyes"* were waiting for them outside in Glasgow Road. Neil McLaughlin lifted a bottle in his hand and made a blow at a Glad Eye member, Hutchison, but the bottle missed him and struck another gang member Richard Waters in the left eye and cheek. M.cLaughlin then shouted *'Come on then, Glad Eyes! Boys...let's get mucked into them!"*

A crowd of Blantyre Glad Eye gang members then rushed into the midst of the attack and some of them received a general mauling before managing to get out the fight. Police were called and Neil McLaughlin was arrested, along with 4 of the Glad Eye members.

Fiscal Hiddleston had that remarkable story to tell at Hamilton J.P. Court on Monday 11th January 1926 when Neil McLaughlin described members of the gang known as *"The Glad Eyes."* but to no avail. Neil being the one brandishing the broken bottle, had to plead guilty to the charge of assault and breach of the peace.

The court, annoyed at the growing fighting of Hamilton and Blantyre men stated that that when any of the members of these type of gangs were fined anything at Court, there was a simple collection made amongst friends, and the fine is paid over quickly and without any real detriment or punishment. He said, *"I think any monetary fine is not punishment at all."*

The Chairman. Mr Dunn. J.P of Bothwell characterised the offence very serious. McLaughlin had been previously convicted of assault, the Court considered that a heavy penalty must be imposed and so he decided to make it one of £5 (about £300 today), with the alternative or thirty days imprisonment. Time to pay the fine was refused.

GIFTING THE WELFARE PLAYPARK

Considerable discussion took place on Wednesday 24th October 1936, at the Fifth Lanark District Council (Blantyre and East Kilbride), whether or not the council should take over the children's playground with its amusements, offered by the Blantyre Miners' Welfare Committee (at the ground in Victoria Street, opposite the medical centre).

It was proposed the play park should be conveyed to the council as a gift, including the cost of transference fees. County Councillor Edward Daly, who presided, asked the council to consider the gift as one of utility and pleasure to large number of children. On a vote, three voted for acceptance and three for rejection. Mr Daly gave his casting vote in favour of acceptance and the Miner's Welfare graciously handed over the Play Park and land to the council for permanent safe keeping and maintenance. Three members did not vote.

Figure 91 Victoria Street in 1928, Quiet yet recognisable

The land in question is shown to the left of this photograph, taken a few years earlier than the Welfare's decision. The play park was maintained for several decades but as we're sure many Blantyre people will know, it's now closed, the playthings removed. The land was suitable for development for many years and it took until 2017 for Lovell Homes to build a brand new housing estate there, which is still being finalised in November 2018. It makes us feel quite sad that the Miners Welfare voluntary gave up their land which was supposed to be for Blantyre's children and that the price of progress has ultimately meant children are not benefiting anymore. This area may very well have nice new homes on it now, but it is sadly another example of the removal of a much-loved Blantyre Play park. We can't help but feel the three councillors who voted 'no' wishing to let the Welfare continue to maintain the land all those decades ago, were probably right in doing so.

Lynn MacFarlane said, *"Great memories of park in Victoria Street especially the Punch & Judy show that came every year in the early 70s and me running up to my grans at 72 Victoria Street because I was terrified of the puppets."*

END OF AUCHINRAITH PRIMARY SCHOOL

Pictured, in this previously unseen photo is a photograph taken by a very distant relative of mine David Ritchie, of Auchinraith School in the 1910's, the school, clearly in its prime.

Figure 92 Former Auchinraith School pictured in 1910's by David Ritchie

Jump forward in time. Blantyre organisations were shocked in the first week of November 1979, to learn that the derelict building formerly the Auchinraith Primary School at the corner of Craig Street and Auchinraith Road would NOT be turned into a renovated community centre.

Springwells Tenants Association and the Boys Brigade had been especially interested in using the school, so it was a blow to learn that the Government had turned down an appeal for cash and decided there was no future for the building. Despite some sentiment, which still exists even today for the old building, it was the right decision in this instance. Many years of neglect had committed the building into a state beyond dereliction, vandalised beyond all description. However, it was the independent survey of the fabric of the building itself that ultimately sealed its fate.

The report in November 1979, recommended that the Auchinraith School was beyond saving and recommended it should be demolished. Severe subsidence caused by the immediate proximity to the former Auchinraith Colliery had put almost the stonework of the windows and doors out of alignment, with severe cracks to the walls. The report went on to say there was a strong possibility of the roof collapsing, the complete lack of wiring and plumbing, no heating and dangerous lead pipework throughout the building.

Local Councillor Malcolm Waugh wasn't surprised having made all the points before. He had been instrumental in getting the building closed as a school in the first place due to its dangerous condition. It was not fit for purpose and could never have been saved. One of the groups hit hardest was the *"Blantyre We Care Group"* consisting of mothers of handicapped children who had been hoping to move there and had hoped renovation would allow it to be used as a creche. The fate of Auchinraith School had been sealed by December 1979 and was subsequently demolished in 1980.

Henry Hambley said, *"Happy memories of Auchinraith P School which I attended from 1954 until 1961. Mr Dunlop was the headmaster. Other teacher included Miss Grieve, Mr Burt, Miss Blair, Miss McGreavie, Miss Francis, Miss Allen, Miss Hamilton, Miss Forest and Mrs McMinn."*

Davy Thomson added, *"the subsidence was pretty bad, at one of the kerbed entrances you couldn't see the end of the kerb it was sunken so much."*

Elizabeth Weaver remembers, *"Outside toilets with no roofs! Not to mention non-flushing toilets, and no doors on cubicles, so you had to get a pal to stand in front of you if you wanted privacy. And the stink!"*

ZEIGFIELDS

Nightclub owner James Mortimer bought the Hastie's Farm development at 16 Victoria Street in 1985 as part of his Lanarkshire Holdings. He altered the rear Hastie's Restaurant into Zeigfields Nightclub and the front, formerly Bananas Disco, into 'Barnums'.

Figure 93 Zeigfields Advert

Friday, Saturday and Sunday nights were Disco nights initially in 1986 from 10am until 2am. Admission was £2.50 on a Friday, £3 on a Saturday and £1 on a Sunday. Zeigfields 50/50 Thursday night was also incredibly popular. On Thursdays, it was 50p to get in, and then 50p for a drink. People may remember buying a pint of diesel (snakebite and blackcurrent) or Pink Panthers. Amongst the workers was Gus Sillars. The phone number was 826060. On Wednesday 5th February 1986, a local talent competition took place with the winner receiving £1,000. Tuesday 25th February 1986 was Ladies only night with a male stripper on show, including a basket meal for the £4 ticket price. The venue was also host to many birthday and private functions, but will forever be remembered for people in their teens, 20's and into their 30's that enjoyed the weekend discos. Zeigfields closed in late 1989, a casualty of dropping trade from nearby competitors like Caspers and the growing popularity of clubs in Hamilton. The building lay derelict for almost a year when on Hogmanay 1990, the roof caught fire and the building was subsequently condemned, scheduled for demolition a few years later. Zeigfields, (or Ziggy's as it was nicknamed locally) remains a popular memory for many people whom, for their entertainment would often jump between Casper's Nightclub across Victoria Street and Ziggys, sometimes even on the same night!

CALDER STREET SANDSTONE

I was invited in November 2015, to take a photo at Auchinraith Primary School, something interesting from days gone by, now in the playground. Two of the four original sandstone blocks, once saying "Blantyre Parish School Board" on the front of the former school, were salvaged in 2010 and are now used as a benches for the children of the new contemporary, modern school.

Figure 94 Blocks from the former school now form modern benches

They look in good condition, the Blantyre block being in prominent position across from the Police Station, the other block behind this and nearby. Like saving the old bell, it's good to see at least a nod was given to the location of the previous school, which was attended by so many people over the years, since opening in 1912. Calder Street School was demolished in Summer 2010, with the new school (Auchinraith Primary) constructed later that year and into the next.

P.s Over a hundred years ago, Andra McAnulty had put forward a proposal to use concrete blocks or the like to build the school, to save money, but was outvoted. Like Blantyre Cottage Hospital, the design of Calder Street School was the product of an Architects competition in 1909. Eight architects were asked to design to a budget of £10,000 (an impressive £1million in today's money). The winner was announced on Christmas Eve 1909. Construction started in 1910 using red sandstone obtained from Corncockle Quarry in Dumfriesshire. The old school was completed and opened in 1912.

CALDERSIDE MEDICAL PRACTICE

Calderside Medical Practice is a contemporary health practice at Blantyre Health Centre in Victoria Street. It's situated on the left as you go through the main door. Open from 8am until 6pm, it has postcode G72 0BS and is currently occupied by Doctors Mary-Jo Sommerville, Dr Graeme Bingham, Dr. Mobeen Ashraf and Dr. Kieran Dinwoodie.

Mrs. Fiona Rowe is the practice manager and has overall responsibility for the running of the Practice. She looks after staff and patients as well as overseeing all services. Sister Hogg and Sister Keegan are the Practice Nurses. They are both specialist nurse practitioners involved in chronic disease management and health promotion.

The office manager is Anne Clark, the secretary is Elaine Murdoch, the Data Administrator is Pauline Cunningham and IT administrator is Sandra Kilby. A number of receptionists work in the practice including Anne Callaghan, Anne Brennan, Jackie Beale, Jackie Nisbet, Eleanor Smith, Karin Williamson, Frances McCulloch and Mandy Allan. The District nursing team offer a full range of domiciliary nursing services and there are health visitors, who have special training in health education particularly with regard to paediatric assessment and development.

The practice has a couple of treatment rooms as well as each doctor's room and is well maintained, clean and tidy. Home visits are possible by booking in advance. All medical practices are contracted to provide essential services, primarily the basic treatment of ill people. Calderside Medical Practie hold a contract with NHS Lanarkshire Headquarters in Bothwell.

The practice is also actively involved in teaching medical and nursing students from Glasgow University, Caledonian University and the College in Hamilton. Patients are welcome from Blantyre and Drumsagard catchment areas and are treated with respect and privacy with 24-hour medical advice available.

CHAPTER 7
THE VILLAGE & LOW BLANTYRE

With Blantyre very much a town, the term "Village" relates to a certain well-known part of Blantyre, that is the northern area, a legacy of Blantyre Works Village. Residents of Blantyre know 'The Village' as a busy area, predominantly branching off Station Road and incorporating several large housing estates, the David Livingstone Memorial centre and Blantyre's railway station. Pictured above near the River Boundary of the village area is the Blantyre Weir, shown in this photo exclusively seen for the first time in this book. The photo dates from the 1890's.

This chapter also explores "Low Blantyre", perhaps once one of the most populated areas. The term Low Blantyre dates from the late 19th Century, appearing firmly on maps and giving an area of Blantyre its own identity with focus around Glasgow Road and the streets leading off it. One theory as to why a distinction was made between Low and High Blantyre was the construction of High Blantyre Station in the 1860's, causing a need to separate the names of each station in Blantyre at that time. Newspaper articles refer to 'Low Blantyre' from around that time, although the term is not widely used on postal addresses and in the opinion of the writer, may actually be in decline.

BLANTYRE WEIR

Monks in Paisley were granted various extensive charters to net and to construct traps (yairs) in the year 1452AD for catching salmon in Loch Lomond, Rivers Leven, River Clyde and the Gare Loch. During the early 1700's, long before the construction of Dales Mills, a dam had been built on the River Clyde at Blantyre. The area was then known as Millhaugh (the land of the Mill) and the dam most likely assisted that early industry. It is known a mill existed at this location on the Blantyre side of the river before Dales 1785 mill, for baptism records of folk who worked there, exist for the mid 1700's. Lord Blantyre was the constructor of the little dam which was known then as "the Small waulk" of "Fulling Mill", for the thickening of the "Hodden Grey" of the Lairds of Blantyre, which was preceded by the "Little Cotton Mill" first built, and that through the "Triffing Dam Dyke" then existing, plenty of water flowed for salmon to pass freely up the river. The 1747 map shows this little Blantyre Mill directly across from Bothwell Mill.

Figure 95 Blantyre Weir in the 1930's, the old bridge visible in the background

In 1771, dredging of the River Clyde for navigation and easier upstream access commenced. An escalation in the rate of industrialisation, including construction of a number of weirs hindered the passage of adult salmon, notably including Blantyre Weir on the River Clyde (1785) and Partick Weir on the River Kelvin.

Blantyre Weir was built in 1790 during a 7-year construction period when Dale and Monteith were building their nearby mill works at Blantyre. The original 1790 weir was 16.5m wide to allow the works to get started, then extended in 1796 to 63m to serve the growing expansion of the mills.

By 1798, it was noted many sewers discharged directly into the River Clyde and this started to affect the freshwater fish, salmon included. According to FRS Freshwater Laboratory, by 1808, there was a noticeable decline in Salmon in the River Clyde, the fish seriously impeded by the man made obstacles, with pinchpoints like Bothwell Bridge, upstream of the obstacles abundant with plentiful fishing. In 1814, the Blantyre weir was widened again to 109m to service the new Turkey Red Dye Mill and lade and finally in 1836 expanded again eastwards fully to 127.5m. That expansion saw not only the weir dam span the entire river, but actually repaired a large part of it which had broken away in a flood during the spring of 1834. The sluices were on the west side, the small salmon ladder on the east, on the opposite side from where it is today. The salmon ladder was built into an eastern sluice, which was accessed by a small footbridge from the Bothwell side.

Robert Wallace of Kelty, MP for Greenock, raised an action in the Sheriffs Small Debt court at Glasgow in December 1838 against Henry Monteith, the proprietor of the Blantyre Mills for violating his rights as a proprietor of "salmon fishings" further downstream. Wallace claimed compensation amounting to £8 8s. 6d for loss and damage to his fishing at Weems (Wemyss) Bay, four miles distant from Blantyre Dam by illegal obstructions to the course of the salmon up the River Clyde caused by the collection of water to supply Monteith's cotton works at Blantyre. (It is worth mentioning that Wallace may have misled the court in stating his fishing right at Wemyss Bay were only 4 miles down the river in an effort to suggest he had rights to that part of the river!)

Mr Wallace, who brought the action not only on his own behalf, but also as a representative of other proprietors, one of whom was the Duke of Hamilton, stated that the salmon fishing at Weems was out in the sea and that any fishermen on the coast could, in theory come forward with a similar claim. He also maintained that unlike other proprietors, such as the Duke, he did not want the removal of the dam, as he knew the value of waterpower to the country, and only requested that the fish should have access to their natural habitat. While the Blantyre Company took enough water to keep their works going, they should leave the comparative driblet, which would allow the fish to pass up and down the river. He claimed that the present sluices (1838) and Salmon "chace" were unsuitable and that poachers from near and far were "cleeking the fish" as they lay dead or dying below the Blantyre dam. Some poachers who stayed all day at the dam had their meals brought to them by their families!

After hearing all arguments for and against the dam, the Sheriff of Lanarkshire declared that he found that salmon got past the dam easily during rains and floods. On 5 or 6 runs a year, salmon could not get past the dam, and so the dam, as it stood, was an illegal erection. The Blantyre Company had unquestionable right to use the dam for the purpose of their machinery, and therefore he could not have it stopped or find a way to preserve the breeding of salmon in the river by the upper and lower heritors. The Sheriff awarded compensation to Mr. Wallace but found that for 80 to 100 days a year, the fish got over the Blantyre dam easily. He noted that the company would make alterations at their own expense to secure the passage for fish to the upper reaches of the river. In the end the case resolved nothing, because the dam was modified and raised to its present height shortly after, which restricted the salmon even more and one can't help but wonder at how irate Monteith must have been at these salmon who caused him so many financial problems.

Around 1850, shortly before the construction of Monteith's Suspension bridge, the height of Blantyre Weir was increased, to the sizeable height and barrier we see today.

By 1900, occasional salmon were still being sighted at Blantyre weir. Throughout the 20th Century, water purity improved hugely with legislation to prevent dumping waste and effluent into the Clyde. With it saw a gradual return of Salmon to the river and the building of a new, modern Salmon ladder next to the Hydro building. We're pleased to say, Salmon are often seen leaping the ladder, much to the high expectations of waiting heron often poised beside the top. Blantyre Weir was and remains a fairly dangerous place and stories of casualties and even fatalities at that area are commonplace throughout its existence to date.

Graeme Walker added, *"There were significant repairs undertaken and that the weir was raised slightly when the mill was converted to hydro power in the 1940's. The fish pass was actually an integral part of the new hydro proposal."*

JOURNAL OBSERVATIONS

Mary Berry was an English Aristocrat born in 1763 and died in 1852, who wrote about her well-travelled life for over 70 years.

During Miss Mary Berry's residence in 1805 with her friends at Bothwell she took the opportunity of visiting the Blantyre cotton-mill established in the neighbourhood. The following detailed account has been provided to Blantyre Project from Mr Jack Daniels, and shows the regulations and arrangements in force around Blantyre Works in 1805.

If this account by Mary is to be believed as factual, what follows is a real, exclusive revelation that Blantyre Works mills initially was a huge operation involving child labour on a scale never previously written or published about!

Figure 96 Mary Berry 1805

Mary wrote in her journals;

"Tuesday 8th November, 1805 —Walked to the cotton mill upon the Clyde, just above the grounds of Bothwell, on the opposite side of the river. Nine hundred persons employed about it, of which about 100 are artificers of various sorts, smiths, carpenters, etc., etc., to keep the buildings and machinery in repair. The remaining 800 are all employed in the various operations of making the cotton ready for the weaver from the rough state in which it comes home in bales. Of these 800, nearly 500 are children from six to twelve or fourteen years old, and of the remaining 300 there are many more women than men.

The children are for the most part apprentices, bound to the manufacturer for six or seven years according to their age, for their food and clothing. After this time is out, they either continue on to receive wages or go to some other business. I am sorry I did not ask what proportion of them continue on at a business of which they must have had such a melancholy experience, for all these children, as well as all their fellow labourers, are employed fourteen hours a day, from six o'clock in the morning to eight at night, of which time they are allowed an hour for breakfast, from nine till ten, and an hour for dinner, from two till three; after which, they continue uninterruptedly at work till eight at night.

I need not commemorate their in general forlorn and squalid looks; they are, God knows, painfully enough impressed on my mind. What a beginning, gracious heaven! For the dawn of human animal life and human intellect! A number of these children are sent from the parishes in London. They have just now have thirty-six or forty from the parish of 'St. Martin's in the Fields'. God help them, poor souls! Never to be blessed with the fond endearment of any creature caring for anything but their mere existence and their labour, and condemned to pass the playful years of childhood in a wearisome sameness of employment, to which childhood is so particularly averse. This subject has been so often enlarged upon, I did not mean to have allowed my pen a line upon it; but it is impossible to have had it brought immediately under one's eyes this very day, and not express one's feelings somehow."

This incredible journal entry, was not put into a published book, but was simply recorded in one lady's diary of the time. I see no reason for her to embellish her observations, but to state that over 60% of the millworkers were children is fascinating and truly horrifying too. Did the mills engage in child labour so abundantly and did something happen to change that? Little has been written about the early period of the mills, and perhaps children *were* exploited to this extent.

Figure 97 Former Blantyre Cotton Mill on the Clyde, pictured around 1903

Pictured just over a hundred years AFTER Miss Berry's visit, is a brand new photo, (previously unpublished) of Blantyre Powerloom Factory at the derelict Blantyre Mills in 1903, showing where all those little children and adults alike, worked in those long hours and in those terrible conditions described. Condemned, the building was demolished shortly after.

DYE WORKS BURN DOWN

On Saturday 28th April 1821, in one of the very first documented articles about fires in Blantyre, the former extensive dye works at Blantyre Works, near the River Clyde, burned down. The loss was total, despite desperate attempts to save it and from keeping it from spreading. The dye works, situated on the bend of the river, was however renovated and rebuilt, ensuring this time it was kept separate from the adjacent cotton mill. It burned down several times that Century!

MURDER BY COBBLESTONE

Figure 98 Picked up a Rock

On Friday 26th August 1836, two males who were employed at Blantyre to cart some stones and rubbish ended up in a quarrel. The row was over some trifling matter relating to the performance of the work, which resulted in one of them, named Cameron picking up a heavy stone and with it, struck the other a severe blow behind the ear to the head.

The man fell down to the ground, dead instantly. Scared off, the assailant was later apprehended and taken to Hamilton jail. The name of the dead man was David Hamilton, said to be a quiet, industrious man.

BLANTYRE WORKS PARTRIDGE NEST

Some excitement occurred at Blantyre Works Village when a Partridge nest was spotted in a field near the River Clyde on 20th February 1846.

The field belonged to Messrs Henry Monteith & Co and the discovery of 11 eggs in the nest at that date, knowing it would take 20 days or so to lay 10 or 11 eggs, meant that the nest must have been ready at the end of January. Something ornithologists at the time found this quite hard to believe. Birds were nesting so early still in winter. The story appeared in the papers deliberately in March to allow time for the eggs to hatch first, showing even then, our Victorian Ancestors had some compassion for this beautiful bird.

VILLAGE PRANK GOES WRONG

Figure 99 John lost his sight in one eye

An eventful event occurred at Blantyre Works on Friday 29th August 1851. John Alexander, aged 10 and his friend, another boy were playing with a makeshift bow and arrow in the village. 'Spicing' up their game a little, they bound a nail to the end tip of their wooden arrow and continued with their summer boyish game.

The alarm was then called when one of the boys proved to be too good a shot! An accident had happened, where the nail on the fired arrow went cleanly through John's eyeball rendering his sight. Indeed, the nail went in to the back of the eyeball, something that must have been extremely painful and John permanently lost his sight, the story making newspapers far and wide.

LIVINGSTONE'S HOMECOMING

Figure 100 Dr David Livingstone

On Wednesday evening, Hogmanay 31st December 1856, the Blantyre Works Literary and Scientific Institute entertained and welcomed Dr David Livingstone, the distinguished Explorer, back to Blantyre his birthplace, for the first time in 16 years! A grand soiree was arranged at the Blantyre Works School for the popular visitor, something, which attracted a crowd.

Description of the Soiree

Precisely at 6pm, the Doctor accompanied by Mrs Livingstone, daughter of the distinguished missionary Mr Moffat, were led on the platform with their 3 children, a girl and 2 boys aged eleven, eight and five, the eldest girl bearing a strong resemblance to her grandfather Mr Moffat.

Dr Livingstone in his appearance that day was a tall, thin, wiry man described as having something of a 'Yankee' look about him, perhaps a reference to fashion. When he began to speak, it was at once apparent that he was not accustomed to speaking in public, stumbling from word to word, although his energy, willpower and intellect soon got him underway. As he warms on each subject, the audience intent on listening with interest, soon forget that their speaker has not spoken at length in his native dialect for nearly 20 years! David added a touch of humour to his speech, the audience warming to him quickly and finding the whole thing fascinating.

The crowd in the room was varied. From true merchant princes, wealthy businessmen to the lowly weaver or piecer who worked in the mills, just as David once did. All walks of life were crammed into the Blantyre Works School Room, side by side, gleefully showing their admiration for the Blantyre boy who had succeeded so brilliantly in the large, open world. The Blantyre Works School room once was where the turning point is on modern day Fagan Court. i.e. this soiree took place where this tarmac is now.

Detailed Description

The evening had started with prayers and when Dr Livingstone was called initially to that platform, he was received with enthusiastic applause, the whole audience standing with prolonged cheering and applause. When the applause subsided, David began by apologising for his inability to speak due to having a cold. He was back in Blantyre and announced that his cold was the first he had in 16 years! He continued, *"I hope it will be another 16 years before I catch another!"* [Loud laughter from the audience].

The Lion Attack

The Doctor then gave an interesting account of some of his adventures. He stated he had received "a shake" from a lion. The tribe with whom he had been living were greatly annoyed by lions that came down the mountain in great numbers seeking their cattle. His advice to them, was confront the lions and kill one and the others would surely take a hint and leave. The tribe went out a few times, coming back empty handed believing now they were cursed. David decided to go with them the next time.

Figure 101 Livingstone Statue in Centre Grounds

The plan was to encircle one of the lions and then gradually make the circle smaller until a lion could be speared at close range. The party went out and soon found a lion sitting on a rock at elevation. One of the party threw a spear but missed, hitting the rock. David had a gun and took the opportunity to fire upon the line, firing off 2 bullets. The tribe called out that the lion had been shot, but whilst David was engaged in reloading his gun, the injured and irate lion seized David by the shoulder, shaking him like a terrier would do to a rat, and broke his arm! As another man ran to assist, the lion turned his attention of him instead, leaving him also with injuries.

The statue in David Livingstone Centre grounds today depicts this story very well. The statue once had a bronze gun, but vandals kept coming back making progress in chiselling it out. The centre staff thankfully noticed the damage and decided to remove it themselves for safe keeping, as it was bronze and before it went missing!

Further Adventures!

Figure 102 David in Africa

David had other dangerous adventures, sometimes clashing with other men. Seven times his life was in danger from tribal chiefs. People though generally in Africa treated David's expedition very well, giving them food, good hospitality and even apologising for what little they had. However, one tribe near a Portuguese settlement was another story!

They gave them nothing to eat and despite the freedom within Africa to move place to place, wanted payment to pass. Livingstone had no money on the expedition. Not one farthing and no payment could be made. He had 27 men on this expedition with him and when the Portuguese said they wanted "one black man" from the expedition as payment, Livingstone replied it was never going to happen and they may as well take him instead. They were immediately surrounded and threatened with guns and spears and eventually had to make their way off in a different direction.

Another tribe approached them from behind in a dense forest. The trees were high and thick with only a small, narrow winding path leading through it. Ambushed, some of his men were knocked to the ground. Being head of the party, Livingstone found himself suddenly face to face with the chief of his attackers. Livingstone found no alternative than to draw his gun and point it at the chief, who responded quickly that he wanted peace, despite some injuries to Livingstone's expedition. The revolver was definitely the pacifier! Livingstone also told him, he was a man of peace and asked the chief to leave them alone. The chief was willing to do so, but feared being shot by Livingstone in the back, if he turned his back, and so on that day, the tribe retreated, walking backwards, whilst all the time facing the barrel of Livingstone's gun!

The soiree ended with Mr Andrew Bannatyne of Milheugh House moving a vote of thanks to Livingstone and hoping that the town could present him with some sort of token of their gratitude in the near future. A few days later Livingstone received the key to the Burgh of Hamilton.

WOODBURN FIRES

On 2nd September 2016, Woodburn House, a beautiful family home on Woodburn Avenue, Low Blantyre burned down, leaving owners, the Scott family who had lived there for 55 years, devastated. This nice family had been plagued by youth disorder for some time around their home and the issue had at one point been escalated to the council and local politicians. Pictured is the fire brigade in the aftermath of having put out the flames. You may be surprised to know however; it's not the first time Woodburn has been totally gutted by fire!

Figure 103 Woodburn House Fire during 2016

James Spreull was living at Woodburn in 1859 when he attended the inaugural meeting of the Rifle Volunteers and when the Name Book was written up, he had a firm of Writers in Hope Street, Glasgow, and like many business men of his day, having a house at the station like that meant he could commute quite comfortably. The house had eight rooms, a kitchen, washhouse, and it had gas from the mills piped in as well as water. It was a desirable, comfortable place to live. It was located on an acre of ground which, in those early days was well stocked with fruit trees and up to 300 hundred black-current bushes. Described in 1859 as, *"A superior house on the south side, & near the Railway. Occupied by J. Sproul Esquire, Proprietor"*. The house was listed for sale in 1862 and then again in 1869. Enter Mr William Stiell, a retired Glasgow leather merchant.

The 1873 Woodburn Fire

Mr William Stiell or Steel was quite hard of hearing. On the night of Tuesday 22nd July 1873, a thunderstorm began. The thunderstorm was particularly severe and would claim many lives across Scotland that night.

There are a couple of versions of this story. One goes that Mrs Stiell was quite frightened, so much so she felt something bad was going to befall them, so she woke up the servant girl, then they woke up her son, and these three were making their way to the upstairs. Mr Steill was sleeping in one of the attic rooms oblivious to the great crashes of thunder and bright flashes of forked lightning.

Just as Mrs Stiell opened the room door, a bolt of lightning shot down the chimney across the floor of the room and out of an open window, the metal grate had been blown out of the fireplace and also the lightning had left a trail of fire in its wake. The furniture also caught fire. The flames began to spread rapidly, and the four occupants hurriedly made their escape in their nightclothes. The men had left their pocket watches under their pillows, in fact all the family valuables, jewellery, and money were left in the rush to get out of the house. Some of the less expensive furniture was able to be reached.

According to reports in the Edinburgh Evening News, the family were hardly out the house before it was all ablaze. The neighbours rallied round but the fire had taken too good a hold on the property for them to do anything. The house was burned to a stone shell, just the bare stone walls, totally gutted.

The Stiells were taken in by Mr Pettigrew who lived just the other side of the railway. The house was partially insured and was rebuilt with additions. In another version of the story, it was Mr William Stiell (the son) who had the premonition of danger after being awakened by a fearful crash of thunder.

Sadly the house was completely demolished in September 2017. The land around Woodburn went on fire again in late Summer 2018, perhaps set by vandals. We have to say, it would not surprise us in the slightest if this quality, prime piece of land gets sold off to developers for flats, a crying shame given the name, "Woodburn" has been so well known in Blantyre for such a long time. Whatever happens next at least there's Woodburn Avenue adjacent to ensure the name is remembered and continues.

MC'CORMICK SCANDAL

Pouring over Blantyre census information these last few years, I've started to get an eye for patterns. Perhaps a trend here or there, familiar names and bookmarking interesting information to look at? One such thing has turned out to be quite the scandal, which is explored here.

James McCormick or McCormack was born in Ireland in 1861. In 1884, at the age of 23 years old, he scandalously got 13 year old Jane, (a girl from his village) pregnant. This must have been fearfully hidden away and Jane's family would likely have gone to great lengths to make sure neighbours didn't know!

In 1889, when James was 28, Jane was by then 18 years old and of age to leave home. So together they both left Ireland taking their 5 year old daughter little Annie Eliza McCormick with them. It's noted they had married around this time. The family found themselves in Blantyre at Shuttle Row, at the home of James's brother William McCormick. Both James and William were employed as Pit Labourers. That same year in 1889, Jane was pregnant again, and at the age of 18 gave birth to her second child, young William James McCormick.

The 1891 census shows the family as James McCormick 30, Jane McCormick 20, Annie Eliza McCormick their daughter aged 7, son William J McCormick aged 2, and also William McCormick (James's brother) aged 22. The family next show up in 1895 Valuation roll, still at Shuttle Row with James paying £2 a year rent and William his brother paying £3, 10 shillings, indicating he was likely living in slightly larger or better premises.

Unfortunately then the trail runs cold. There's no mention of the family in Blantyre after 1895/1896. They are not in any future Scottish census and we can only presume they returned back home to Ireland or emigrated. What happened? Did the scandal catch up on them in Blantyre and drive them away again? Did they simply miss family and need to return home to Ireland? Did their own families forgive and forget a generation later and accept them openly? This was an uncomfortable story for me to look at, but interesting nonetheless. Such a tale would certainly be a crime punishable by jail these days. Was it so back then in Ireland? So many unanswered questions and perhaps somebody out there is able to tell us, just what happened next?

LIVINGSTONE CENTENERY

Celebrations marking a hundred years since the birth of explorer, David Livingstone took place in 1913. These were undertaken nationally and locally throughout that year – the Rt Hon.Earl Curzon of Kedleston, as Chairman of the Geographical Society said at a meeting at Burlington House, London – "As a missionary, Livingstone was the sincere and zealous servant of God". Locally, in Blantyre a statue of David Livingstone made of bronze by Mr. A.Kellock Brown, Glasgow was placed in the niche reserved for it in the tower of Livingstone Memorial Church on Glasgow Road. The statue fully six feet high and showing Dr. Livingstone with a Bible in his left hand and his right hand extended in preaching attitude, was unveiled by his daughter, Mrs. A.M Livingstone Wilson. The inscription reads- *"This statue erected by public subscription to the memory of David Livingstone born 19th March 1813, at Blantyre, died 4th May 1873 at Chitambo, Illala, Africa. Unveiled by his daughter Mrs Livingstone Wilson 15th March 1913."*

ILLGEAL STILL AT STATION ROAD

Next is a story about making booze illegally on Station Road. From 1924 newspaper, *"Sheriff Shennan, at Hamilton yesterday, imposed a fine of £75 on Alexander Dunbar Nicholson, who admitted having had an illicit still in his premises at 30 Station Road, Blantyre. The accused's house was raided at midnight by the police, and the Fiscal stated that with the apparatus which was found the Revenue could have been defrauded of several thousands of pounds a year. Mr Nicholson declared he had been the tool of others, who had induced him to let them put their stuff in his cellar, and then threatened to report him to the police when he asked for the payment he had been promised."* Picture is not of Blantyre and used just to illustrate a 1920s still.

Figure 104 Illegal Booze Making

POISON IN THE SUGAR

A unanimous verdict of " Not proven ' was returned in Glasgow's High Court jury on Thursday 8th July 1926 in the case of James Boyle, a Blantyre man charged with attempted murder by poisoning. Boyle was accordingly discharged.

Figure 105 Poison in the Sugarbowl

It was alleged that in his house at 100 Station Road, Blantyre, he put poison, a substance containing phosphorus, into a bowl of sugar, which Joseph McDermott kept for his consumption, hoping that McDermott would ingest the substance.

A further allegation was that James had previously had ill will against McDermott by threatening him. An alternative charge against Boyle was that he administered poison with intent to do McDermott grievous bodily harm.

Sugar with a Smell

The young miner, Joseph McDermott, was married and he had rented a kitchen in the house at 100 Station Road, his landlord being James Boyle, the accused, who also happened to be his uncle.

On 31st January 1926, Joseph's wife went to hospital. In the evening her sister made Joseph some tea, and put sugar from a bag into the sugar bowl, which was empty. The bowl usually stood on the kitchen table. Next morning, when he returned from his work (he was on the nightshift), he detected a peculiar smell coming from the bowl when be was making tea for himself. He examined the sugar bag, but there was no smell from it. However, the smell was coming from the bowl and there was darkness in the sugar in the bowl, as if something had been poured in.

Joseph went to bed, and when he wakened later in the day he took the sugar basin to his mother's house, suspicious of it. Next night he went to the house of Nicholas O'Brien, his father-in-law where he mentioned the incident about the sugar. He then brought the bowl out. Mr O'Brien tasted a little of the sugar in the bowl. He immediately turned red in the face and looked as if he was choking. He was also immediately very sick.

Told the Police

That night Joseph McDermott accused his Uncle James Boyle of interfering with his sugar. Boyle called him *"a liar,"* and struck him. There was a fight.

Joseph afterwards took the sugar to the police and said that a month before this Boyle had abused him and his wife. Joseph had retaliated and struck his Uncle at that time and Boyle declared, *"I'll get my own back."* Joseph told police that he and his wife were at breakfast a few weeks ago when they detected a curious smell coming from the sugar. He thought nothing of the matter then, and suggested mice had been the bowl but neither of them had taken any of the sugar.

Before this incident Joseph and Boyle had quarrelled in what was clearly an argumentative household. Mary McDermott (19), the sister of Joseph, corroborated him regard to the filling up of the empty sugar bowl. She said that when her brother brought the bowl to their mother's house she detected a smell from it.

Sick for a Week.

It was explained Nicholas O'Brien (47) miner, that when he tasted and tested the sugar from the bowl he was sick for a week afterwards, and he had a pain at his head for three weeks. Cross-examined, he admitted that although he was sick he could still take beer.

Describing an analysis, which he had made of the sugar in the bowl, Mr Walter Brown, County chemist, Lanarkshire, said he got 42 grains of brownish pasty substance in the bowl. Grains of sugar adhered to the substance. He examined the substance and got the presence of one-third of a grain of phosphorus.

Professor Glaister stated that from information he had received, he considered symptoms shown by O'Brien were characteristic of the effects of an irritant poison. He held that a third of a grain of phosphorus might cause death in an adult and certainly would in an infant.

Charge Denied.

In court, James Boyle, whilst in the witness box gave a denial that he had put anything into the sugar bowl. Speaking of the night when McDermott accused him of interfering with the sugar, Boyle asserted that when he opened the door McDermott said—" *It is you I am waiting for. Take off your jacket. I'll give you it for trying to poison me."* McDermott struck him and caught him the throat. He declared he had not threatened McDermott at any time. Boyle had trouble with his Nephew about the payment of rent after the incident, and had not spoken to him since by the time of the trial. Cross-examined, he denied ever buying rat poison. A verdict of not proven was returned, James Boyle let off.

AFRICAN HUT

Pictured here in the 1930's are visitors to the former replica African Hut, reconstructed in the grounds of David Livingstone Centre. The hut was a reconstruction of the place where David Livingstone died, whilst in Africa in 1873. This was part of the original tourist attractions when the centre opened on 5th October 1929 and was located where the current Africa gardens are.

Figure 106 Replica African Hut in Livingstone Grounds 1930's

Blantyre's climate had a lot to do with it being demolished, and there are no photos or mention of it after the mid 1930's. It does, even then look quite fragile. A week after the museum opened in October 1929, the Arbroath Herald wrote an interesting article that mentioned this little hut.

"Away at the farthest corner of the ground that has been bought along with the house to make a playing field for the children, there stands a tiny little straw house, and it was this that drew the attention of the young people.

It was a small place, just about half the size ordinary room, with a tiny door at one side, but how the children clustered round it. So much so that kindly old gentleman standing by took a hand in arranging things. "Get into line," he said "and pass round it. Now just a peep inside today, for there are others." And queue they did. Walking to the door they peered in, and what a fine thing it was to watch these young faces as they did so."

There was nothing inside but few sticks laid for a fire, but to the children there was all the excitement and the thrill of adventure as they pictured the great explorer on his adventurous last journey through Africa. You all remember how David Livingstone died, how his servant found the noble man on his knees beside his bed, worn out with pain and suffering for the sake of Africa. The little hut, that has been built close to the Scottish river Clyde in the village that was David Livingstone's birthplace, is an exact copy of that one in far-away Africa where the last scene in the great explorer's life took place, and these children looked into the little dark house they could see in imagination something of the story that great Scotsman's work in that unexplored country in the great continent of Africa.

The Thrill Exploring.

Of course every boy loves exploring. Every man has been like that ever since there were boys, and there are no stories that thrill the boy like those that tell about going away into unknown places where no man has ever been before. And so because David Livingstone was an explorer and spent his life going where white man had never been, boys, and girls too, find his life story a real thriller. But it is not only the excitement and the wonder discovering new places that makes the explorer set out on a long dangerous journey into unknown parts. He has something else in his mind. It may be to discover a way for a railway, or to find if there are gold mines or anything else that will bring wealth to people if it bought and sold in the markets of the world. Or it may just to add to the knowledge of the world.

When David Livingstone left his one-roomed home in a high tenement house in Blantyre to go away to the undiscovered parts of Africa he did not go to have good sport shooting lions and tigers, nor did he to discover gold and diamonds and ivory to make him rich—though there are all these things in Africa. It was as a doctor and a Christian missionary as well as an explorer that he went. And it was the people of heathen Africa he lived to help. We in Scotland are proud of David Livingstone, and we shall grow more and more proud of him, I think, when we see how people from all over the world will visit this memorial to him. From it we can learn all about his life from a boy to the time he died in his little straw hut.

We see the little one-roomed home in which he was born, with everything just it would look when his parents and brother and sisters lived in it. Then we see a big spinning jenny," the same as worked at as a boy making his first shilling to help the home, and learned his Latin from a book propped on the machine.

We see in picture many things that happened when he became an explorer and a missionary, and we learn that to the boy of grit and perseverance and purpose all the world is open to him. David Livingstone had above all a great purpose, and the other things helped him to carry' it out. I hope that all of you will some day see the David Livingstone Memorial. It will interest you to know that a big tablet on the wall tells us that it was largely through the efforts of Sunday School children of Scotland that the Memorial was bought and set apart for all time in honour of a great and noble son of Scotland. No wonder the children who could be there at the opening on Saturday felt proud and happy!"

SALMON IN THE CLYDE

Gerry Chambers sent in this cracking photo adding, *"Hi, the Clyde at the David Livingstone Footbridge was teeming with running salmon, like this jumper, yesterday afternoon, 25th October 2015. They were trying to negotiate the weir in their efforts to get upstream. How awesome nature is on our doorstep!"*

Figure 107 Salmon in the Clyde photographed by Gerry Chambers in 2015

DAVID LIVINGSTONE CENTRE REFURB

July 2017 saw an astonishing, huge announcement for Blantyre with the release of the exciting news that the David Livingstone Centre had at last secured many millions of pounds of funding to renovate the centre and grounds. The project to renovate the local museum dedicated to Scots explorer David Livingstone was awarded more than £6 million in funding, aiming to turn the centre into a top tourist destination.

I was thrilled to be invited amongst 50 distinguished guests on 3rd July 2017 for the official public announcement, which had been a closely guarded secret for some time and one, which should put Blantyre firmly back on the map. Following coffee and introductions, staff, volunteers, funders and Blantyre Community Committee were there for the historic moment and all met in the lower floor in the Livingstone Shrine room to hear the announcement.

It was confirmed the Scottish Government will invest £1.375 million with £4.1 million coming from the National Lottery and £575,000 from Historic Environment Scotland. The £6m will completely transform the centre, cafe, shop and grounds. The interpretation of around 3,000 internationally significant artefacts will be modernised and visitor facilities such as the café and shop upgraded.

Born in 1813 in Blantyre, David Livingstone spent 30 years exploring southern, central, and eastern Africa, often in places where no European had previously ventured. International Development Minister Alasdair Allan said that day:

"David Livingstone remains to this day a deeply inspirational and iconic figure to many people here in Scotland, in Africa and across the world. Principles of global humanitarianism and solidarity lay behind much of his work. The reinvigoration of these historic buildings and surrounding grounds, aided by the Scottish Government's £1.375 million funding, will create new spaces and opportunities for people to learn about the important legacy of one of Scotland's national heroes. It is appropriate that the project gets underway during this, our Year of History, Heritage and Archaeology. The other partners, the Heritage Lottery Fund, Historic Environment Scotland, the Scotland Malawi Partnership and South Lanarkshire Council are to be congratulated for working with the David Livingstone Trust to support this exciting project."

Various speakers commented on the funding, heritage and what this means for Blantyre and surrounding communities. Speeches were heard from Tom McCallum (Provost), Dr Isabel Bruce the Chairperson of David Livingstone Trust, Neil Wilson the great grandson of David Livingstone himself, Rev Murdo C Macdonald the new David Livingstone Church minister, Lucy Gannon of Historic Environment Scotland and Dr Alistair Allan, Scottish Minister.

Figure 108 Livingstone Minister Murdo MacDonald with Hazel (left) and Arlene of Blantyre Community Committee, invitees to the official Livingstone Trust announcement in 2017

Volunteers and Hazel's Butterfly Bakery served refreshments up in the cafe afterwards as all warmly received the welcome news. As I left, a meeting was taking place with Architects, the centre staff keen on progressing the plans immediately. Speeches recorded that historic day are available online on Youtube. As of Summer 2018, the centre is closed for a year whilst work is underway.

CURE OF 3 YEAR COUGH

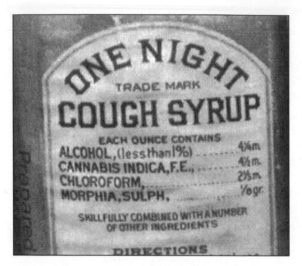

Figure 109 Cough Miracle Cure

These days, we take medicine for granted when it comes to curing simple ailments like a cold or a cough. But, in the 19th Century when remedies weren't so readily available, finding the right medicine and cure could sometimes take a while or prove difficult, which often led to ailments becoming worse through time. Sometimes the ingredients themselves could make things worse unknowingly, like this advert showing chloroform in the recipe!

So, you can almost hear the delight when this Blantyre man wrote to a doctor in Glasgow in 1858, thanking him for the remedy. Writing into the Paisley and Renfrewshire Advertiser George Irvine was an early resident of Low Blantyre, an emerging district in our town, then still a village. He wrote:

"To Mr Henderson, Medical Botanist, 60 Commerce Street, Tradeston, Glasgow, – Dear Sir, I have much pleasure to inform you that you have succeeded in effectually curing me of Cough, accompanied with a Spitting of blood, Shortness of Breath, and Palpitation of the Heart, of which I was afflicted for upwards of Three Years, during which time I was under the treatment of several medical gentlemen, without having any desired effect, and they all latterly gave me as being in Consumption. I have quick pleasure to inform you, or any person you may refer to me, that from the time I commenced taking your medicine, I gradually got better, and in the course of nine or ten weeks I was as well as ever I was in my life, and would be happy to give any information to any other person similarly afflicted I was.— I am. Dear Sir, yours, GEORGE IRVINE."

NEARLY CAUSED A RAIL CRASH

On 30th December 1862, a pointsman was arrested whilst drunk at work in Low Blantyre and nearly caused a huge rail accident!

That Tuesday night, the county police apprehended a pointsman on the Hamilton and Glasgow Railway, named Archibald Kennedy, residing at Blantyre. They accused him of culpable and reckless neglect of duty. It appears that on the evening of Saturday 27th December 1862, a passenger train left Hamilton station at about a quarter past six o'clock heading for Glasgow. Upon the train reaching the junction of the Hamilton and Strathaven Railway, near Greenfield Farm (Betram Street Burnbank), at which Kennedy was pointsman, the pointsman (who was worse of liquor) set the points there for the Strathaven line running through Springwell, instead of allowing the train to proceed along the main line towards Glasgow.

He thus caused the train to run off the main line to a distance of about 400 yards, along the Strathaven Railway through Springwell. Fortunately no accident occurred, and the train, being backed up again on to the main line, proceeded, without any long delay. The prisoner (who wore on his breast a war-medal in court, was above forty years of age) and was examined before the Sheriff was eventually committed to prison.

BROOMKNOWE COTTAGE

There's a little one storey, detached cottage, which still exists to this day at 259 Glasgow Road. Sometime between 1876 and 1880, the Gray family who had already built their neighbouring tenement, constructed a small cottage, as home for their son, grocer John Gray. His first child was due in 1878 and the cottage may have been built in time to coincide with that life event.

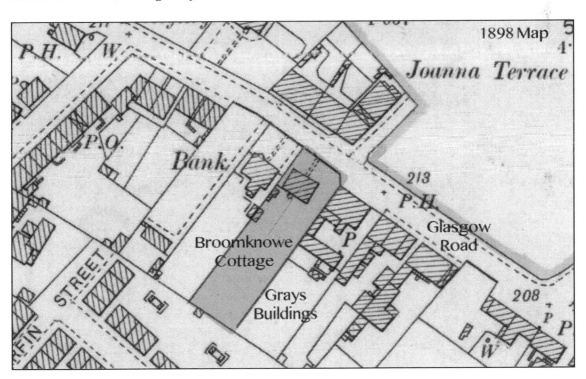

Figure 110 Broomknowe Cottage highlighted by us on the Blantyre 1898 Map

Original ownership and the likely constructor was Mr. Robert Gray, the father of John, who initially called it *"Milne Cottage"*. The name would change in that first decade to become "Broomknowe Cottage", a name that is still even today the official name of the building.

The cottage was set back slightly from Glasgow Road, but still opened out on to it. Situated on a long, rectangular plot, it had a path leading from the road up to the doorway, with plenty room at the back gardens. Being a family of grocers, this land would have been put to good use and it is telling that during their occupancy, the back gardens were never built upon. They would have provided an ideal place to securely grow vegetables for sale in their shop at nearby Gray's Buildings.

In 1881, the occupants were John Gray (36), wife Agnes (35), son Robert (3), daughter Agnes (2) and domestic servant Jane Hamilton (18). John is noted in that census as being a grocer employing 1 man and 1 boy. Following the death of Robert Gray in 1879, the cottage passed to his widow, Mary Gray who continued to rent it out to her son John right up until her own death in 1901. In 1895, the rent was £18 per annum. In 1901, John Gray, who had been living and renting this cottage for over 20 years, inherited it. He was still living there in 1905, but before WW1, as he became older, (perhaps to retire) he moved next door to the upper flat at Grays Buildings. His son Robert junior then rented Broomknowe Cottage. By 1915, Robert Gray (37) was an electrical engineer, considered in age to be 'too old' for the wartime initial draft and so in those rough years, he continued to rent the cottage for the modest rate of £18 per annum and conducted his grocer business, established by his grandfather 2 generations earlier. Robert continued to live at Broomknowe Cottage before moving away.

Figure 111 Broomknowe Cottage on Glasgow Road (South) during 1979

During World War Two and immediately after, the Aitkenhead family lived in the cottage, occupying it solely as a house. In the 1950's and 1960's, Mr. Felix McLaughlin, a car hirer conducted his business from the building, which had now become a business for the first time. Felix would go on later to establish a funeral parlour and had telephone number Blantyre 373.

The little garden once at the front was landscaped over with hard standing to accommodate parked vehicles for the business. Metal railings were erected in the 1970's to fence off the street and pedestrians. In later years it continued as a Funeral Parlour, taken over by Joseph Potts and has had that use for many years now at time of writing in November 2018. Premises at the back have been, in post Millennium years occupied by Kennedy Travel, then from 2015, Kennedy Coachworks.

ELECTRIC TELEGRAPH

The electric telegraph was a system that permitted communication via electrical signals. The first commercial systems using Morse code but later were able to transmit words. It meant quick transmittal back and forth of news as it happened, without having to wait for messengers to convey it by foot or vehicle.

In 1859, the telegraph in this region was described as "A line of railway between Glasgow and Carlisle. The "Clydesdale Junction" applies to that part of it between Glasgow and Motherwell. The Electric Telegraph is on the south side of the line. There are no Stations not in their Parish. It passes out of the Parish by a Viaduct over the Clyde." This comment conflicts with maps of 1859, which mark the electric telegraph to the north side of the line. It would appear the telegraph relied on proximity to the railway, perhaps making use of its land and equipment.

Use of the telegraph was particularly expensive, perhaps to validate the use of full time operators at each base. In 1872, it was 1 shilling for the first 20 words and 3 pence for each additional 5 words. Telegrams were therefore kept short and sweet.

There was no ability to telegraph out or into Blantyre in the 1850's and 1860's. This was to change in 1878, when the electric telegraph was branched off, into Blantyre, connecting the Post Office at High Blantyre to the National Telegraph system. The High Blantyre Post Office was located on that part of Main Street, which would later become the Masonic Hall. Mrs Grizel Penman was the postmistress. The post office later moved by 1898 across the road to a point what would later become the entrance to Kirkton Park. Then, finally in the 20th Century, it moved again to a tenement that stood on the corner of Main Street and Cemetery Road.

One of the first news items to be relayed out of the town was an accident in 1878, which happened at Dixon's Pit, killing 6 men. In 1880, a train crash was "at once telegraphed" to the authorities at Hamilton.

The ability to communicate quickly must have been a wonder, not just for reporters and business people, but also for local families who wished to communicate something immediately. Telegrams were here to stay for many decades and were still being used far into the 20th Century.

ORIGINS OF CHURCH STREET

Like all the southern side streets leading off Glasgow Road, Church Street had its humble beginnings as a field boundary between two fields, in particular at this location, on the former farm of Stonefield. The boundary became a track in the 19th Century and the track would towards the turn of the 20th Century, be renamed Church Street, after the Stonefield Parish Church built in the early 1880's. Like Jackson Street further to the east, Church Street was to be a dead-end street, a cul-de-sac if you like, just as it is today. During the 19th Century the street ran only the length of the church. However, by 1910, decent quality stone homes, mostly semidetached had been built on either side of the street, most of which still exist today.

ANDREW GILMOURS

Andrew Gilmours on Glasgow Road, is pictured here in this photo taken around 1904. Glasgow Road trams were up and running a year earlier. Andrew Gilmours wasn't just the clothing shop at the end, the signage also suggesting it was the whole building (Gilmour's Buildings) with another grocery shop to the left of the canopy. The postcard is confusingly titled "Main Street" but is of course "Glasgow Road", then considered the Main Street of Blantyre.

Figure 112 Gilmours Buildings on north side of Glasgow Road, around 1904

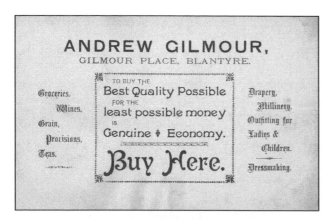

Figure 113 Andrew Gilmour Advert

Here's an interesting local advert associated with this shop. Gilmour's Buildings were officially known as *"Gilmour's Place"*, even although the frontage was on to Glasgow Road. Naming buildings after the constructor or owners was quite common practice in days prior to the 1920's and numbered postal addresses appearing along busy streets.

Andrew Gilmour also had premises at High Blantyre Main Street near the junction with Cemetery Road in a similar era.

CHURCH STREET INSCRIPTION

Michael Barrett shared this photo adding, *"There's an inscription in my workshop at 19 Church Street that says 'WA 1912', within the concrete. (The workshop is behind a bungalow built in the 50's by a footballer....Hibs I think). Do you know anything about what it could mean?"*

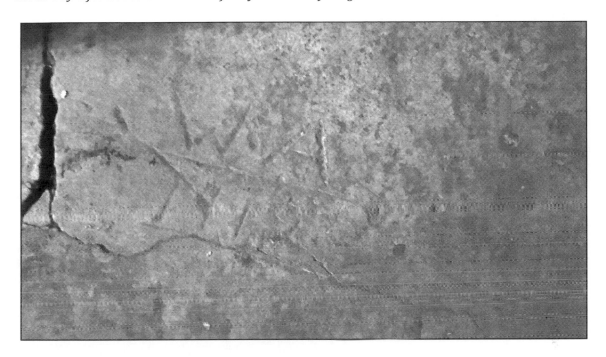

Figure 114 The '1912' Inscription on the garage wall at Church Street

Upon seeing this, I believe it to be the construction date of the building and perhaps the initials of the builder. Initially I thought William Aitkenhead Builders, but by 1912, William Aitkenhead had passed away and his business had become Robert Aitkenhead Builders. The small garage workshop wasn't on the 1910 map of Blantyre, so this being the constructors dating evidence seems likely.

Another suggestion is William Adam, the son of the well-known William Adam (Snr), the High Blantyre builder and joiner of that era. By 1891, the entire family including young William had moved to Shott House, High Blantyre. After William Adam (Snr) died at 174 Main Street on 27th August 1919, aged 78; the business was still named William Adam & Son.

Young William Adam was working for them at that time and it is him, who I think inscribed the date into the concrete, some 104 years ago. After William Adam (Snr) died his will was read at Hamilton on 14th April 1920 and he left an estate of £4,503. (About £230,000 today's money). His will was made on Christmas Eve 1909 and in it, his possessions were left to his eldest son, John Adam, whom by then was living at Archer's Croft in High Blantyre.

In this instance and unusually for me to entertain assumption, this is just a theory, so if anything to the contrary is known, please let me know!

MRS MEIGHAN'S RAMMY

Figure 115 A Blantyre Square go!

On 20th August 1922, residents of a particular Blantyre house had their grief interrupted when a neighbour barged into their house.

The family had lost one of their own that week and in fact the corpse still lay in the house awaiting the funeral. On the day in question, Mrs Meighan, a Blantyre woman and their neighbour, in an inebriated state came barging into the house creating a breach of the peace.

Mrs Meighan took one look at the family and piped up, *"Whit the hell are ye greetin' fur? She's got tae dee some time."* As you may imagine, this question was not well received and the family in their time of sadness was having none of it. Challenges were made to fight between the womensfolk and Mrs Meighan before police eventually called for.

Of course, Mrs. Meighan ended up in court. Mr Robert Weir, Fiscal, during the trial in Hamilton J.P. Court that October said, *"she had been married tor twenty-six years, and she had never been Court before. She challenged the inmates out to fight, and behaved in remarkable way whilst under the influence."* A fine of £1, with the alternative of going to prison for ten days, was imposed.

FITS AT CHURCH STREET

In Hamilton J.P. Court on Monday 2nd October 1922, Thomas Houston, a labourer of no fixed residence, pleaded guilty to being found in a state of intoxication and unable to take care of himself at the junction of Glasgow Road and Church Street.

Thomas was found actually on Glasgow Road after 10p.m on the previous day. Police were called when pedestrians saw Thomas appeared to be taking fits on the road. Police arrived quickly and removed him to the safety of Church Street where they noticed the man was having medical issued, apparently going from one fit to another.

They sent for doctor and the inspector of the poor. After they had examined Thomas Houston the doctor said he was suffering from drink and that this may have brought on the fits. Houston was fined 10s, or 5 days imprisonment although it is not known which he received.

Reading back on this, I can't help but feel Mr Houston would have received no help afterwards. I can only imagine his situation exactly the same upon leaving prison, with nowhere to stay and what money he had being spent on alcohol. I do hope he managed to get some help.

DAVID LAMOND COAL CONTRACTORS

This 1923 photo shows Blantyre's former business, 'David Lamond Coal Contractors' and has been kindly sent in by Australian man, John Maguire.

Figure 116 David Lamond Coal Contractors in Blantyre, 1923

John writes, *"This picture shows the coal lorry of David Lamond, contractor, Craig Street, Blantyre. It is typical of the coal lorries that used to deliver coal to the houses of Blantyre. A hard job. The young chap at the left is my uncle Joe Boyle, aged 19 in this photograph, which dates it at 1923. Your page keeps turning up beauties that keep Blantyre alive in many minds as well as my own."*

Digging a little deeper, I found out the Lamonds had their own buildings at Springwells. The lorry is clearly marked Craig Street, although I didn't recognise the buildings in the background as being Craig Street. Margaret McCrory emailed me recently saying, *"About the photo sent by my brother John Maguire, I think the photo of the coal lorry was taken at Hawthorne Place which was off Aucunraith Road near Elm Street"*. The Lamonds lived at 33 Craig Street during the 1920's and 30's (about halfway down Craig Street opposite the Miners Welfare). I don't have much information on the business, but I did find a traffic penalty imposed on David Lamond, and thankfully to save my embarrassment here, not against Joe Boyle! In the Dundee Courier on Wednesday 2nd October 1935, an article appeared, *"Penalties of 20s were imposed upon David Lamond contractor, 33 Craig Street, Blantyre, and Edward Kelly, motor driver, Auchinraith Road, Blantyre. Lamond admitted that, on 20th July 1935, at The Porte, Burntisland., he failed to comply with the conditions of his B " license by allowing twelve passengers on the back of the lorry. Kelly admitted that on that occasion he drove the motor lorry without a third party insurance policy in relation to himself."*

SWORN ENEMIES

In 1925, Hamilton Justices had to step in to attempt to restore peace between TWO Blantyre families. It was something that seems to have caused the Chairman a bit of a headache. The McGuigans and the Farrel families of Central Buildings, Glasgow Road had been at 'fisticuffs' for many years and finally in December that year, the law had to intervene.

Figure 117 Difficult time for the Judge

The families were sworn enemies and matters were taken to court in Hamilton when a female member of one of the families was put on a term of further probation covering six months for her 'behaviour' during a period of observation.

The Fiscal mentioned that at previous Court appearances, several relatives of the same family had been put on probation and observation, with the hope of restoring peace between the McGuigans and the Farrels. However, it was to no avail.

"This is an opportunity to cease this endless strife between the families," observed the Chairman. *"Should any of you come before the Court before the period probation has expired it will serious matter. It you carry there is no doubt that the Court will always win."*

There's no mention of what strife was caused to lead to the court appearances but certainly it appears to have been sustained for a long time, with each family thinking they were 'in the right' to reach court in the first place!

FLOODED OUT

In April 1925, Blantyre saw enormous flooding (as did much of Scotland). It caused SO many problems for businesses and individuals alike. In the area surrounding Blantyre, acres of fields were under water damaging new crops. On the tramway track, the flooding was most serious at Whistleberry Bridge near Springwell and at the other end of Blantyre at Spittal (Priory) Bridge, where the water was lying to a depth of three to four feet!

The early morning workmen's cars could not get through to Low Blantyre, and in consequence large numbers of workmen had to forego their day's work.

Westend Place, the large two-storey building at the corner of Bardykes Road was a building most affected by the flooding, completely surrounded by water. The sewers were unable to cope with the terrific rush of water, whilst at Auchinraith Bridge all traffic was suspended, four feet of water lying below the bridge. It took several weeks into May for the water to dissipate.

HORSES RESCUED

An alarming fire broke out on Saturday 26th February 1927 in buildings at Clark Street, Low Blantyre. The properties were owned and occupied by Patrick Murray, a coal merchant. Patrick was also a dealer in second hand furniture. When the fire brigade arrived, the buildings were well alight, but the firemen quickly got the flames extinguished. The roofs of the buildings were completely burned and the stock was greatly damaged by water. The fire was supposed to have originated in the hayloft above the stables. Two horses were rescued by the heroic efforts of five young men.

HORSES WILD DASH

There were several narrow escapes in Blantyre on the early morning of Saturday 22nd December 1928, when a horse attached to a milk float ran away from Thornhill Avenue near Glasgow Road, and continued its wild career for about a quarter of a mile, luckily clearing two buses on its way.

It charged right down Glasgow Road, with the abandoned milk float in tow, where it raced along the busy thoroughfare. At great personal risk, a local postman, Mr Andrew Moore, who was on delivery duties that day, rushed forward and hung on to the float. Clambering on board, he could not for a time catch the reins, but last managed to do so, and brought the horse to a standstill just as a crash with an oncoming passenger bus seemed imminent. Incredibly, interviewed later, the plucky postman commented, *"This is the third time I have done this in such incident!"*

AUDACIOUS PUB THEFT

Audacious Thieves carried out a double robbery in Blantyre on the same evening in January 1928. Blantyre police struggled in their searching for the person, or persons, responsible for one of the most daring burglaries ever recorded in the district, which took place at a public house, the Livingstonia Vaults, at the junction of Forrest Street and Glasgow Road. The public house at the time belonged to John Forbes.

The pub was locked up at 10pm as usual by the woman who was in charge. Shortly after midnight, the woman was informed by the police that one of the sidedoors of the pub was open. On her early hours arrival back at the shop, she made an examination of the stock, and found that nine five-gill bottles of whisky had been removed!

The premises were again made secure eventually at 3 o'clock in the morning and both police AND the woman left for their own homes.

Four hours later, as the morning shift arrived, it was found that the same premises had been broken into a SECOND time, on this occasion the break of a large window, four feet above the level of Forrest Street. The second haul made away with ten bottles of whisky and a large number of screw top beer. It is thought that, in the first instance, the burglar must have concealed himself on a ledge actually within the premises, locking himself in before it closed.

DOG'S LOYAL VIGIL

A tale of loyalty is next. To be more exact, the loyalty from a loved pet. Blantyre was astounded to learn of a night Vigil on the railway line. It was a night vigil of a different sort, which happened on Saturday 14th March 1931.

Figure 118 Dog's loyal Vigil

A retriever dog kept guard over the body of its master on the railway line at Blantyre from late that Saturday night until the discovery of a man's body on the Sunday morning. Mr William Miller, of Glasgow Road, found the body near a horse-loading station, while on his way to work on the Sunday morning.

The dead man was Mr. William Ross, aged forty, Deanbrae Street. Uddingston. Ross. An unmarried man he had been an unemployed sea cook. The railway line crosses a viaduct over the river Clyde at the Clyde Bridges between Blantyre and the Uddingston side of the river, north of Blantyreferme. It was believed that William Ross was making his way in that direction when he was struck on the head by something overhanging from a passing engine or carriage. He had a compound fracture of the skull, which would have knocked him out, perhaps even killed him on the spot. His retriever dog, ever faithful, sat on the railway bank, dodging further trains for the whole evening and throughout the night.

When Ross did not arrive home, his concerned relatives searched for him on the Sunday morning, and when they approached near the horse-loading station at the railway side, their attention was attracted by the known dog, which was immediately recognised, sitting by his beloved and deceased master. Certainly, this was a case of man's best friend.

RAILWAY GOODS SHED

Pictured on the next page in May 1963 is Low Blantyre Railway Station, photographed from Station Road, looking down on the Station. In the background are the houses at Rosebank Avenue. The old pedestrian bridge is roughly in the same position as where a pedestrian bridge is today. (The bridge was repaired during nightshifts in November 2018.) Station Road is just out the picture to the left. The white wooden fences, perhaps looking so good, as the Queen had visited Blantyre Station only a year before, part of a tour on the official opening of East Kilbride's new town celebrations.

In the background is the Goods shed. Between the shed and the railway lines, were further sidings, permitting the goods carriages to stack up, ready for loading and offloading. Out the picture to the right was a tall crane, opposite the modern day ticket office. The building appears to have been made of wood and corrugated tin, which may have later been replaced with asbestos.

This was actually the second goods shed at that location. Prior to 1910, a smaller shed existed immediately adjacent to the railway line, dating from the opening of the Station.

Figure 119 Blantyre Station in 1963 showing the Goods Shed

This building in the photo was constructed between 1090 and 1910 and was set further back from the railway and more away from nearby property Homeston, at Rosebank Avenue. It was built on part of an allotment site, although this small path at the side dates from WW2 years.

Figure 120 Goods Shed at Blantyre Station, 1963

On Sunday 18th July 1968, the goods shed at Blantyre Railway Station burned down. Two fire brigade units attended but the wooden structure was a raging inferno and left practically only the brick chimney standing. The devastation was so thorough that the structure had to be demolished entirely by British Rail the following Monday 19th July 1968. It was thought that children had set it deliberately alight.

Sandra Brightside said, *"I remember the goods shed well. The clanking of the carriages as they were shoved into the front door. What goodies lay inside? Was it more than just coal? We were always curious about the contents of the goods shed, but told by mother not to play near the railways."*

REID PRINTERS

Here's a great photo of the old JR Reid Printer's shop at 108 Glasgow Road, in the former Co building, pictured here in the 1970's. John Reid, who kindly shared this photo told me his windows were smashed out by vandals and rather than him incur the cost of replacing them, he simply boarded them over and painted them!

Figure 121 J.R Reid Printers former shop on Glasgow Road 1976

NAZARENE PROBLEMS

In spring 1979, the Nazarene Church (the first one) on Elm Street was constantly broken into and 2 organs were stolen. Right through that month, a systematic campaign of vandalism by youths saw the church decline rapidly. By the end of March 1979, an announcement was made that the Church was to be demolished. There were no windows left, all smashed out and the old building, boarded up. The wife of Pastor William Mackie commented, *"The vandals have almost demolished the place by themselves. They smashed the place up one particular night and must have had a van as organs were also taken away."* After the vandalism by March 1979, the Nazarene had given up on the premises and moved into the Stonefield Parish Hall on Stonefield Road. Blantyre didn't even have to wait for demolition contractors. Further vandalism created a fire later in 1979, causing the old Church to burn down completely, the 3rd church in Blantyre to do so in just 2 years. Another church on Elm Street was to be built but that took a few more years to come about.

<u>DEMOLITION OF POST OFFICE</u>

Makes many people feel sad. This is the demolition of the Blantyre Post Office on Glasgow Road, incredibly now 21 years ago! These sorts of pictures may not have been interesting at the time, but seeing them 2 decades later invokes feelings of nostalgia.

Figure 122 Demolition of Glasgow Road Post Office 1997

After the building was demolished, several Blantyre people were interested in acquiring the '1953' masonry date stone to protect and ensure it didn't get put in a skip. Amongst them was Blantyre man and historian, the late Jimmy Cornfield. Jimmy had struck a deal with the foreman of the wrecking crew, and when he returned with the cash he was told the deal was off, the worker saying his boss has told him it wasn't for sale and that someone else had taken it. The location of the stone is unknown, but perhaps another local person beat Jimmy to the 'prize'.

The Post Office then moved further along Clydeview Shopping Centre for a short time. Afterwards the post office relocated even further west along Glasgow Road to the rear of the Londis supermarket, on the same southern side of the road where it remains today. Difficult to park there, it feels perhaps a little inconvenient but remains an important, popular resource for the people of Blantyre.

This corner site at Logan Street was bought in 2017 by ASDA and incorporated into their development plans and as of November 2018, is currently being landscaped over behind the existing petrol station.

CLYDEVIEW SHOPPING CENTRE DEMOLITION

It was the end of an era in Blantyre on Thursday 19th July 2018, as contractors commenced the demolition of the eastern, redundant Clydeview Shopping Centre.

Figure 123 Demolition started in July 2018 of the Clydeview Shopping Centre

Glasgow Road and Low Blantyre is set to be transformed as the eastern side of the 38 year old shopping centre was pulled down to be replaced by modern units with new landscaped pedestrian spaces. Demolition of the old brick building started at the southeastern side near Logan Street around 9am that day. The following months saw completion of the demolition work and by October 2018, work had started to landscape over the scarred area of Blantyre, with ASDA postponing the building of new units, waiting renewed demand for them. The public didn't react well to this phased approach believing another part of Blantyre to have been lost, with no opportunities for small business to flourish. ASDA defended their position and although constructing a small kiosk for Timpson's key cutting to move to, many residents were not satisfied at the lack of action. A plus point though has been the new views from the car park down to Stonefield Park, a welcome sight.

As for building new units and shops? Let the clock start counting at November 2018 and we'll simply wait and see!

CHAPTER 8
PRIORY & CALDERGLEN

Blantyre Priory, the ruined 13th Century abbey is located to the north end of Blantyre on a steep cliff known as "Blantyre Craig" above the snaking River Clyde. The old ruins, the oldest building in Blantyre is in an ever-decaying state and stands looking towards the majesty of ruined Bothwell Castle on the opposite riverbank. The Priory playing fields are nearby and border Blantyreferme and the former area of Boatland. Nearby, to the south and west of Blantyreferme is Redlees Quarry and the former estate of Calderglen. Our cover photo above features the glasshouse in 1975, a decade or so before it was demolished.

Calderglen features for the first time in this series of books, a worthy addition given the amount of stories, information and photos recently acquired through inheritance that can now be published.

JANET ANDERSON, MILKMAID

Miss Janet Anderson died on Tuesday 27th May 1879. The dairymaid from Calderglen was killed under shocking circumstances on the railway near Blantyre. She had been at Hamilton and travelled by train to Low Blantyre Station, alighting there.

She decided then to take a short cut westwards along the line, which directly passed by Calderglen. She was walking between the rails of the upline and had her attention drawn by a mineral train on the downline, when a passenger train from Glasgow came up behind her at full speed. She was caught by the buffer of the engine and thrown 10 yards, dying instantaneously.

However, lessons were NOT learned at Calderglen, for only a few years later, the Calderglen owner's son, Pelham Cochrane died in similar circumstances.

BLANTYRE AMBULANCE

You may have seen this postcard, which features an Ambulance in Blantyre during World War One. Information published by others in a book is incorrect about this subject and the error is perpetuated online so I wanted to correct things here. (Let's get some things straight. It's *not* World War Two. This wagon is not pictured at Caldergrove Auxiliary Hospital, nor is it a Crossley 25/30 model which was never manufactured until 1919.)

Figure 124 Blantyre Ambulance in 1915 at Calderglen House

From October 1914, Blantyre residents were engaged in raising money to build and equip a motor ambulance waggon for the front. The intention was to gift the ambulance to the British Red Cross to help with the war effort, either at the front or at home.

The date is Saturday 1st May 1915 and this was the very day a brand new ambulance was presented to the Blantyre Branch of the British Red Cross. The wagon arrived in Blantyre that day and it proudly toured around various points in the Parish, including estates of Greenhall, Milheugh, Caldergrove and pictured above at Calderglen House.

It was big news too. At Commercial Place, just off Stonefield Road in the presence of about 2,000 people, a special dedication service was held, with all local ministers taking part. The Rev. Charles Turnbull, of the Parish Church, gave an interesting statement on how the money had been raised, and said that the idea of providing an ambulance waggon originated with Miss Bannatyne of Milheugh; Miss Cochrane of Calderglen; Miss Jackson of Bardykes; and Miss Mooreof Greenhall, and these ladies, with the assistance of a committee of other well-known ladies, had worked continually to make the scheme success.

In short, the Ambulance was the mastermind and effort of Blantyre's women.

The total money raised was £505 11s 4d and the cost of the waggon was £450. It was agreed that the other £50 or so should be given to name a bed in the Scottish Women's Hospital at Gorges, France. The order for the building of the car was given to the Red Cross Society. It was a Darracq model, which could accommodate patient's stretchers and eight people sitting, together with seat for an attendant. The car was to be under the control of the Red Cross Society and was kept in a garage in High Blantyre at Broompark.

As early as 5 days later, on the morning of Wednesday 5th May 1915 it was first called into service, assisting in the removal of wounded soldiers to Stobhill Hospital.

The women raised the funds from fetes and flag days. These collection days were popular throughout the town during WW1 years. For example a flag day later in Blantyre on 4th November 1916 raised over £34 in itself making a significant contribution for the Red Cross. A subsequent instruction from the War Office asked for raised funds to be used to buy ambulances throughout the UK. By the end of 1916, the National campaign had raised £70,000 promising a further 50 new ambulances.

CALDERGLEN TREE

At the entrance to the Calderglen Estate stands a large tree. It made me stop for a moment, when I saw the size of it. It surely must be as old as the house itself at a couple of hundred years. Its twisted trunk and lush leaves made it stand out from the others around it, which are far younger by comparison.

Figure 125 Large Tree at Calderglen pictured in 2014

This old tree stands proudly at the entrance to Calderglen House, at the far end of the long driveway in, just beyond Priory Bridge.

COCHRANE'S CHAPEL

Pelham Maitland Cochrane was the 21-year-old son of John Richard Cochrane who both lived with the rest of their family at the grand Calderglen Estate. During 1884, as their house was closer to Newton Station, than Low Blantyre, the family were in the bad habit of getting off at Newton and walking along the railway line (no paths) back to Calderglen. However, tragedy struck on Monday 14th July 1884 when army officer Pelham alighted at Newton as normal accompanied by friend, also an officer. Fifty metres from Newton Station as they walked back to Blantyre they observed a ballast train coming towards them from Blantyre. Pelham's friend stepped to the left of the line on to the verge, and Pelham stepped to the right, sadly on to the adjacent downline. With all eyes on the ballast train ahead, they both failed to see the rapidly approaching 'Hamilton Express' from behind which cut him to pieces.

His father J.R Cochrane, a merchant and tile manufacturer very quickly built a beautiful ornate chapel (near modern Jura Drive) in 1884. By all accounts in the weeks following the accident he diverted his employees to complete construction of the chapel. Pelham's body was interred near to the chapel and later, at least four other family members eventually ended up buried there too.

When the Cochrane family left Blantyre it seems likely the burials were exhumed and taken to Edinburgh, where the remaining family settled down for several generations. Calderglen was sold and the chapel fell into disrepair, vandalised and when the Priory Bridge housing estate was built immediately next to it, it quickly became an unsafe ruin, forcing the council to demolish it in 1990 (despite a controversy existing as it wasn't on their land). Today the site is woodland.

Rediscovering the Chapel

Figure 126 Chapel found!

In February 2016, on a particularly rainy weekend, in true 'Indiana Jones' explorer fashion, I set off with Gordon Cook and Alex Rochead to the location of the chapel, armed with a shovel, to see if we could find anything. The purpose primarily was to try to find the foundations, document the sizes of the chapel, and piece together how it was configured, which didn't appear to have been recorded before.

Our day at the bottom of Kirkwall Avenue, Priory Bridge proved very eventful, and knowing where the chapel was, we set about digging in the field to see what we could find ad were astonished to find not just the foundations, but also parts of the floor. We took great care to ensure nothing was disturbed and that everything, including dimensions and location was recorded. Nearby dog walkers and residents were curious and we did well not to be visited by the police after their alarm in seeing three men digging in the woods in the rain!

We were delighted to find parts of the chapel floor intact, and carefully removed the 100mm of topsoil to expose the tiles. The clay orange coloured tiles were about 80mm wide with 8 sides, infilled with darker smaller square tiles. Around the perimeter was a band of smaller, rectangular orange tiles and grey tiles. We found the chapel existed in an exact east-west direction, a Christian tradition, perhaps to let morning and evening light into the building. The grave markers, which were still there on the site were recorded as being placed between the 1930's and 1954, with the exception of the original marker stone for the chapel, dedicated in 1884. The gravestones were actually outside the chapel imprint, in what was a small memorial garden. Evidence of paths around this could still be seen, although the stones were toppled for safety by the council when the ruined chapel was demolished in 1990.

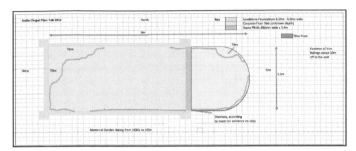

Figure 127 Recorded and put into Blantyre Library

At 9m wide x 3.5m wide the chapel was rectangular in shape, with a curved bow shape at the east end. I drew up a plan of our findings as seen here. Of course before we covered things up again, we took plenty of excellent photos. Little do dog walkers know that just 4 inches below the woodland surface, they're walking on this historic spot!

Figures 128 - 133 Uncovering the Chapel floor, temporary dig in 2016

Figures 134 - 140 Parts of the Chapel's Ornate Floor still exists just below the surface

Figures 141 -145 Further Photos of the Chapel Dig at Priory Bridge Housing Estate, 2016

This little known subject certainly sparked my renewed interest in Calderglen. Wishing to know a lot more about the Cochrane family, who lived such a privileged and extremely wealthy life, I decided to investigate more about these people who were a far cry, in the late 19th Century from the mass Blantyre population of traditional miners and their families. The 'holy grail' of Blantyre photos or illustrations was still missing too! *What did Cochrane's Chapel actually look like?* Then, just as the question had been asked, as if by magic and entirely coincidental, in February 2018, descendants of the Cochrane family now living in London contacted me. The family were emigrating and conducting a house clearance and seeing online my interest in Calderglen decided to kindly gift to me, some of the Cochrane family photograph albums from the 1870's onwards, including giving me…. the actual key to the Chapel!

Figure 146 Calderglen Collection

So it was in February 2018, two rather large parcels arrived from Alice Fookes in London. Her grandmother was Miss Kathleen Hickman whose mother was Louisa Cochrane, the daughter of JR Cochrane. Alice was attending to the house clearance and after things of sentiment and value were retained, she found she had SO many items relating to Calderglen and kindly selected some and posted them to me. For the small postage price, as you can see I obtained quite a haul! Needless to say, I was like a "*kid in a candy shop*".

Incredibly, amongst the photo albums was the elusive photo I've been looking for many years! A building previously unseen in any publication is now shown exclusively here. Here is a forgotten piece of Blantyre history, in pristine, perfect original condition photographed around the 1890's. My most treasured and wholly owned 'only known' photo of the former 'Cochrane's Chapel.'

Figure 147 Former Cochrane's Chapel at Calderglen, 1890's (from P Veverka Collection)

RETURN OF DEER

With recent housing estates being built at Newton Farm in 2018, roe deer have been getting ever increasingly braver and coming closer to Blantyre at Calderglen, Blantyreferme and the fields at Blantyre Priory. On some occasions they've even been seen within housing estates at Buller Crescent. Deer sightings may not be anything new, but the animals, so normally shy are certainly getting more curious and coming into urban areas, something This is likely caused by a reduction of their natural environment. Our northern green spaces are certainly reducing in recent years.

BOTHWELL CASTLE

Although Bothwell Castle is not in Blantyre Parish; we can't ignore the wonderful history that's sitting on our very boundaries. The history of the castle is briefly told here for all.

Bothwell Castle is one of Scotland's largest 13th Century castles. Its strategic location meant it became a key location during the Wars of Independence, being captured and recaptured many times in dramatic circumstances. The castle provides an excellent opportunity for investigation of the Wars of Independence and medieval castle life.

Figure 148 Bothwell Castle Ruins, above River Clyde pictured 2016

Historical background

Building of this mighty castle began with Walter of Moray after 1242 shortly after Blantyre Priory was built across the River Clyde. Repeated invasions and sieges meant the castle changed allegiances often and that the original design was never completed. What you see today is largely the work of the Earls of Douglas from and following the year 1400. The present castle is roughly rectangular. At one end is the massive donjon with an adjoining prison tower, which was the original part of the castle. The other end of the castle comprises the Great Hall, and the remains of two towers.

The castle played a key role during the Wars of Independence when it changed hands several times. In 1296, the English King Edward I invaded Scotland and captured Bothwell Castle. By this time only the donjon and prison tower had been completed. The Scots then starved out the English garrison in a 14-month siege in 1298-9. One has to wonder what role the opposing Blantyre Priory played in all these battles. In 1301 Edward I returned with a huge army and a siege tower, specially constructed to access the top of the donjon. The siege lasted just three weeks before the English took the castle for the second time.

The English then surrendered the castle to the Scots, led by Edward Bruce, after the Battle of Bannockburn in 1314. It was recaptured during the second Wars of Independence in 1336, when it briefly became the headquarters of King Edward III. In March 1337 a Scots army, under Sir Andrew Murray of Bothwell, took the castle once again. Though this was Murray's ancestral home, he ensured much of the mighty donjon was destroyed for fear it might fall into enemy hands once again, leaving it much ruined as you see it today.

By the late 1300's the castle (ruined) had passed to the Earls of Douglas. They repaired and extended Bothwell Castle. By 1424 they had constructed the two residential towers and a range between them, which included the Great Hall. They connected the rest of the castle with curtain walls. Bothwell Castle was the property of the Crown through much of the 1500's, and in 1669 it passed to the Earls of Forfar. In the late 1600's they abandoned the castle in favour of Bothwell House, a large mansion built nearby. Ironically the castle has outlasted this house, which had to be demolished in 1926.

In 1935 Bothwell Castle was placed in the care of the State, and today it is cared for by Historic Scotland, a popular tourist and wedding destination, perfect for romantic photo backdrops.

WILLIAM WALLACE MYTH

Figure 149 Wallace leaps from Blantyre Priory

A reference to the popular Scottish hero of the early 1300's being in Blantyre is made in a Victorian account. I have illustrated this article with a photoshopped picture, depicting how I think the scene may have looked. The tale, (which is very much an unproven myth) is described as follows:

"Tradition says that a vaulted passage under the Clyde formerly existed between the Priory and the Castle of Bothwell; and Miss Jane Porter, in the Scottish Chiefs, has taken advantage of this alleged subaqueous way to heighten the dramatic effect of her story, the scene of which—as most novel readers are doubtless aware—is partly laid here. On our first visit to the Priory—a goodly number of years since—our guide, a school-boy from the adjacent village, told us that according to a winter evening tale current in the neighbourhood, the popular hero, Wallace, in a season of difficulty once found shelter from his foes among the cowled inmates of this establishment.

By some means or other the usurping Southrons learning where their terrible opponent was concealed, a large party of them at the dead hour of night determined to secure him and earn the handsome reward offered for his apprehension. To effect this they surrounded the building, with the exception of that portion overhanging the precipice, which from its altitude they considered perfectly secure. While they were thundering at the portal, however, and demanding the surrender of the Knight of Ellerslie, that doughty chief, nothing daunted, flipped out by one of the windows, leaped at once over the rock, and fording the Clyde, made his escape undiscovered.

As a convincing proof of the truthfulness of the legend, we were then taken to see an indentation in the solid rock below, which bore some resemblance to a gigantic footmark, and which we were seriously informed had been caused by the foot of Wallace on that eventful evening. A fine spring issues from the ground at this spot, the waters of which flow into the sacred footprint; and we need hardly say that it was with a deep feeling of reverence for "Scotia's ill-requited chief" that, on the occasion alluded to, we knelt down and took a hearty draught from the alleged pedal mark.

Our faith, we are sorry to say, is not now quite so strong. On our present visit we scarcely discern the resemblance to a footprint which was formerly so obvious; and although we dip our beard in the gratefully cold and crystalline water, the delicious awe which we experienced then comes not again over our spirit."

<u>PRIORY RAVINE CARVING</u>

Let's return to extracts from the journal of English born, Miss Mary Berry, a well-travelled writer who lived from 1763 to 1852. For nearly 70 years of her life she visited many foreign places, writing daily about her experiences. She often visited Bothwell to see her friend and fellow writer, Joanna Baillie and on several occasions wrote about Blantyre. Her descriptive accounts are very special indeed. Here's a nice little entry from 1808 taken from her journals whilst she visited Bothwell House. It describes coming across the River to Blantyre to visit the Priory. Mary wrote:

"Saturday 20th August 1808 – Walked on the other side of the water to my favourite ravine, just under the remains of Blantyre Priory; again admired in singular beauty and the grandeur of its parts, though the whole thing is only a narrow gully. The day and the spot were so delicious for loitering about, that I began cutting my name on the bark of a tree in the ravine, whilst the others sat by. The view of the Bothwell ruins from the Priory is beautiful."

Mary carved the word *"Berina"* into a large tree in the Priory Ravine. Berina is Mary's name in Arcadian (Greek). It is stated in later correspondence to a friend, she carved the name into one of the largest trees in the ravine, which I strongly suspect is one of the huge trees along that riverbank still there today.

If anybody visits the Priory Ravine, please feel free to look for "Berina" carving. I admit, as of 2018, I can't find it. It would surely be still visible, at eye or ground level. If the tree still exists it would need to be at least 3 or 4 hundred years old! Now there's a challenge if ever there was one!

FATAL FALL AT PRIORY BRIDGE

Figure 150 Fatal Fall on Priory Bridge, 1817

On Saturday 21st June 1817 an open air stagecoach travelling between Glasgow to Hamilton was involved in a fatal accident on top of the Priory Bridge at Blantyre. As the coach approached the bridge, an oncoming horse and cart startled the horses pulling the coach, and the passengers on top of the coach were alarmed as they were thrown from the side, as their coach toppled over. The coach didn't topple right over, but fell leaning on top of the high Priory Bridge parapet wall, with such a movement and jolt that several passengers fell from the coach to the bridge.

One passenger however, was not so lucky. A young man, named Bennie was thrown clear of the parapet right over the side of the Priory Bridge itself, and fell below in the River Calder. He was hurt so badly, he lived for only an hour afterwards. His body was so shockingly disfigured, for he had fallen a great distance from above on to rocks below. No other person was hurt, although there were several outside passengers on the coach. Mr. Bennie was a millwright who had been working at Camlachie and had been travelling to see his father in Blantyre, when the accident occurred.

Those who know Priory Bridge will realise just what a great height this bridge is. The attached picture is a mock up of the scene I've created using an actual sketch of the bridge from a similar time period and showing an 'added' coach and cart of the day, poised ready for the accident to happen.

LOANEND COTTAGES

Loanend likely takes it name from *"Laun's end"* or *"Land's End"*, which is reference to the land at the edge of Cambuslang Parish. Knowing the cottages were tied to nearby collieries, I was surprised to see Loanend on the 1859 map of Blantyre, at a time before coal in the area. However, upon closer inspection, it wasn't actually the cottages, but instead it was the ruins of Loanend Farm, located to the South East of Flemington, not too far from Dechmont.

Not much is known about the old farm, but the buildings were situated in a U shaped arrangement, made of stone and even by 1859, were being described as "old". A good description is given in 1859, as *"An old Farm building occupied by servants employed by the lessee of Flemington. The property of His Grace "The Duke of Hamilton."* In effect the old farm was being used as servant's quarters for the main house nearby at Flemington. (At the time Flemington Farm, House and offices existed, built on the site of a former and more ancient 18th Century village named *Flemington*). Loaned sat fairly isolated, with fields all around, the only signs of industry being the nearby Drumsagard Tile works located across the single track road, further eastwards towards

Malcolmwood. The 1859 map shows a well in the gardens of Loanend Farm, the whole location sitting slightly north westwards of the later cottages.

By 1898 Loanend Farm is shown on maps as "ruined", i.e. derelict, with exception of an L shaped part of the building to the southeast. By this time the Tile works had been exhausted and was no longer there. It is probable that just a few remaining servants of Flemington lived in the old farm ruin. However, things were about to dramatically change for this rural and peaceful area. In 1908, Archibald Russell Ltd sank a shaft on a nearby field at Loanend and discovered coal. Dechmont Pit no 3 was established not far from the farm ruins and a small railway siding was constructed to transport the coal from Dechmont no 3 into Dechmont No 1 and 2, located near Spittal.

In 1909, the colliery erected Loanend Cottages, being forced to build them under newly created Building Bye laws. The cottages were built on the roadside, between the old Loanend Farm ruin and the Dechmont No 3 pit (also known even then as 'Loanend Colliery'). The colliery by 1910 employed 320 people, 280 of whom were underground. 20 of the miners were housed in the Loanend Cottages, with the remainder in rented home in Blantyre and Cambuslang. Described in 1910, Loanend Cottages consisted of:

16 Two-apartment houses Rental £9 14s
3 Three-apartment houses Rental £14 5s
1 Four-apartment house Rental £19
Each house has a scullery – One storey, brick built – Damp-proof course – Walls strapped and lathed – Wood floors, ventilated – internal surface of walls and ceilings in good condition
No overcrowding – apartments large
Garden ground available – wash houses – coal cellars
WC within each house
Slop sinks, with gravitation water, within each house
Drainage treated in small private installation
Common ashpit at the extremity of site
Scavenged regularly at owners' expense

Indeed, those homes are described in a much more healthy and favourable fashion than other miners' homes of the time. The larger homes would have been the colliery managers.

The nearby colliery proved as dangerous as others, when only a couple of years after opening, fatalities occurred. The Scotsman reported on 21st April 1911, *"A fatal accident took place yesterday morning in Loanend Colliery, Cambuslang, the property of Messrs Archibald Russell & Co. (Limited) Accompanied by a number of workers, Mr Robert Edgar the under manager, was about to undertake the stemming back of a quantity of gas which had accumulated in the pit, when they were completely overcome, and had immediately to retreat in a more or less dazed condition. All succeeded in regaining a clear zone with difficulty except Edgar, who was unable to crawl out of the danger. The alarm was speedily spread, and repeated heroic efforts at rescue were made, but without avail, as the fire-damp was exceedingly dense and occupied a considerable space. Dr Hutchinson was lowered into the pit, and lent assistance to the workers who had been affected by the fumes. Mr Low, the manager, was among those who endeavoured to reach Mr Edgar, but he met with complete prostration, and his removal to the pithead, where he gradually recovered, was imperative. There others needed attention, but the arrival of Doctors Macpherson and Beveridge relieved the strain. The accident occurred about nine o'clock in the morning, but it was about one in the afternoon before a young Cambuslang miner, named Duncan Dunn, succeeded in reaching the place where Edgar was. Edgar was dead, and all attempts at resuscitation failed. Edgar who was 36 years of age, resided at Loanend Cottages, Flemington, Cambuslang and is survived by a widow and six children. The colliery was thrown idle for the day."*

There were heroes that day. On 22nd September 1911, The London Gazette reported, *"His Majesty the King has been graciously pleased to award the Edward Medal of the Second Class to Walter Cullen and Thomas Macfarlane, miners working at the Loanend Colliery, under the following circumstances:- On the 21st of April, 1911, Mr. Robert Edgar, the under manager of the Loanend Colliery, Cambuslang, went up a highly inclined road to tear down a screen so as to disperse an accumulation of firedamp, and was overcome suddenly by firedamp. Macfarlane at once went to his assistance, but was in turn overcome and rolled down the road. Cullen, who is 60 years of age, then made two attempts to rescue the under manager, and on both occasions was helped back by Macfarlane, who had recovered, though still suffering from the effects of fire-damp. The under manager's body was not recovered until three and a half hours afterwards."*

During WW1, a Private Taggart was killed in action, who had previously been a miner at Loanend colliery. In summer 1924 the colliery was subject to a series of strikes. The Bing was on the Malcolmwood side of the rows and a mineral railway ran across the fields and under the Glasgow Road at the Flemington Cottages. By 1936, the colliery was disused and this must have forced the residents there to leave. The nationalisation of the coal board in 1947 saw Loanend Cottages become the property of the NCB.

Figure 151 Loanend Cottages in the late 1970's looking to Malcomwood

William Miller who is president of the Cambuslang Rangers Club gave me written permission to illustrate this article with this wonderful photograph of his father walking outside Loanend Cottages in the late 1970's. William took the photo and told me he always liked to get people into his photographs.

Blantyre man **Alex Rochead,** having been brought up nearby, was able to help me with the next part of the story. He said, *"I remember Loanend Cottages before they were converted into the present houses. I think that around 1965 – 1968. Robb the farmer at Flemington bought the cottages from the coal board. He knocked out the centres to make byres and feeding areas for his cattle. He kept one building of two semi-detached houses and converted it into one house for a worker, George Mare and his family. This was at the Flemington side of the rows beside what I think was the Colliery manager's house. In my teens I was friendly with his son Billy Mare although I haven't seen him for years."* **Gordon Cook** told me he could recall a small swing park at the back of Loanend Cottages in the 1960's.

Margaret Smith Edmond added, *"I was born at 4 Loanend Cottages in 1950 as were my brothers. My eldest brother was born at No. 3 in 1936 where my grandparents lived – probably moved there before 1915. I lived there until 1968. I think I spoke to the lady who now lives at No. 4 a couple of years ago when we took some Canadian relatives there. We also knew the Mair family. I remember everyone who lived there and we knew Willie Miller Snr very well. I also remember the Collins family and the McCallums. The railway bridge was taken down in the late 1950's I believe. When I was very young we didn't have any street lighting or a tarmac road. I think one or two of the residents were instrumental in getting this done and they also got the swing park built."*

William Miller added, *"My father walked all a round Cambuslang, Dechmont and Blantyre during his life. At the time of the photo, the properties were used as cow sheds. If you look further ahead you will see where the railway crossed the road into the pit."*

It is evident that in the following decade the farmer at Flemington sold off the cottages separately to private owners, with the central dividing walls reinstated to create individual homes again.

Today, the cottages are beautifully kept and home to many families. Whilst a little out the way, the residents currently enjoy excellent views of the surrounding fields, with abundant wildlife and very little trace of any of the previous industrial work. In recent years a wind mast was approved and erected behind the cottages, with the intention for a large wind turbine being placed there in future. However, following fierce local protests and a successful campaign against such intrusion on this beautiful landscape, planning overruled the decision, preventing it from happening and forcing the owners of the mast to have to remove their redundant equipment at their cost. Just one resident at Loanend was in favour of the turbine being built.

Loanend is a very small, but tight knit community, often feeling part of both Blantyre and Halway/Cambuslang. It is still surrounded on all sides by open farm fields and woodland, attractive and green for most of the year. It remains a desirable place to live, peaceful and quiet, if not for one or two large vehicles blindly following their misguided sat-navs each day.

DROWNING AT HAUGHHEAD

About 5 o'clock on Monday 17th June 1861, a collier named William Bishop, aged 17 went into the River Clyde at the riverbank about 300 yards west of Haughhead Bridge and didn't come out alive!

He entered the river on the north side and swam towards the Blantyre side, but unfortunately about only 6 yards from the shore, sank. Getting into difficulties, he bobbed to the surface twice, but sank a third time. The spot where he drowned was only about 9 or 10 feet deep. There were several people on the embankment at the time and some more people actually bathing nearby. However, none of them made any attempt at rescue until they realised when the man finally sank, that he was in bother. William Bishop was not a good swimmer and exhausted, it is supposed fear came on him, preventing him from having any power to save himself.

Two boats later arrived on the scene with grappling hooks and after a search of around 3 hours, the body was found nearby. Superintendent D Dewar of the County Police arrived also and took statements.

ROYAL VISIT TO THE PRIORY

Well, here's a discovery that took me surprise and hope it does to you too! Did you know that Queen Victoria's son, Prince Alfred visited Blantyre in 1864?

Figure 152 Prince Alfred in 1864, aged 20

Prince Alfred, born in 1844, was the second son and 4th child to Queen Victoria and Prince Albert. When Alfred was only 18 years old in 1862, the King of Greece abdicated and proposed that young Alfred should be the new King of Greece. Queen Victoria forbade it, having her own intentions for Alfred in Europe. So, the young Prince joined the Navy and decided to travel.

A tour of his own country was first and at 20 years old on Saturday 2nd April 1864, Prince Alfred arrived by carriage at Hamilton Palace accompanied by Lord Belhaven and a Royal Escort. After seeing Chatelherault and the Cadzow Oaks, his carriage went to Bothwell Bridge, then on to Bothwell Castle. The men then took a boat across the Clyde and visited the ruins of Blantyre Priory! Perhaps the first ever Royal visit to Blantyre! Their sightseeing journey that day ended with them travelling to Wishaw House. Prince Alfred was well travelled, usually by ship taking in Hong Kong, Australia, India and Africa during his life. He passed away in 1900 from throat cancer.

Prince Alfred is photographed here aged 20; the same age he was when he visited Blantyre.

OPEN DECK CAURS

Even in the vilest weather passengers on buses can travel between Cambuslang and Blantyre in comparative comfort with little chance of catching pneumonia, but for passengers 100 years ago, it was a very different case, especially those travelling by Priory Bridge on tramcars. It was a miserable experience being on a busy tram 'caur' in winter. During mid day journeys, men would often give up the shelter of the lower deck, being courteous in taking the upper uncovered deck and being exposed to winter weather. However, for "*rush hour*" and miners it was a different case when there were no women on the caurs first thing in the morning. Getting to work at Gateside, Dechmont or Priory was a short trip for miners. Congregating at Cambuslang terminus at 6 o'clock in the morning, they did not form queues and the clamours sounds of a tram as it came clanking around the corner was the signal for them to advance en masse and take up position where they thought the caur would stop. When it halted, the miners would storm aboard. To gain a place in the inside saloon was the primary aim of this 'assault party'. The unlucky ones of course had to go upstairs and if it was raining or even snowing, the prospect of starting their shift in the mine with wet clothes was not particularly pleasant! (Especially before the arrival of drying rooms and warm pit baths!)

The seats on the upper deck were of hard wood, slatted, reversible and downright uncomfortable. A protective knee-high strip of sheet metal with a safety railing enclosed the sides, front and back of the deck. Midway along the passage separating the rows of seats was 'the trolley' which carried the overhead boom. The trolley was a constant source of imminent danger to any unwary passenger who may be tempted to leave his seat and stamp about the deck to keep warm or go into the aisle whilst the 'caur' was moving. Indeed, in wet weather it was practically impossible for passengers on the upper deck to avoid being drenched. The pits are closed now. The caurs are gone. Those who remember those "far from fond" commutes are also now gone, but the memory of those miserable journeys live on in these words.

THE STOLEN PURSE

Isabella Stillie or Weir, the middle-aged wife of a pensioner, residing at Hamilton Road, Cambuslang, was before the Hamilton J.P. Court in October 1925 charged with having in July stolen a purse containing 8s and co-operative checks from the house of Mrs Chambers at Main Street, High Blantyre. A plea of guilty was tendered, and the Fiscal explained that Mrs Chambers was in the living room of her house when she heard a noise in the kitchen. On going there she found Isabella, who asked to be directed to a Mrs Montgomery. A direction was given to someone corresponding to Mrs Montgomery, and Isabella Weir, who was noticed to be little the worse of drink, left. Mrs Chambers afterwards found that a purse had been stolen from the top of a dresser in that room. Neighbours in the district had complained that a woman answering to the accused's description had called and asked to be directed to a number of different people whose names locally were not known. It was only with great difficulty, explained the Fiscal, that Police in Cambuslang traced Isabella. She latterly confessed that she had thrown the "store checks" and the empty purse over the Priory Bridge at Blantyre. A lawyer representing Isabella later explained that she being the worse of drink had succumbed to temptation. A fine of with the option of ten days' imprisonment was imposed.

The whole episode made me wonder that if over nine decades later the remains of that little purse are possibly still lying in the river!

CALDERGROVE WW1

Pictured in World War One, around 1917 are the nurses and doctors of Caldergrove House, which at that time had become a temporary Auxiliary hospital on the outskirts of Blantyre.

Figure 153 Medical Staff at Caldergrove House during 1917

As well as a fantastic picture showing the uniforms of the time, it also shows just how well manned the small hospital was and indeed is also a great photo of the former 4-storey house too!

FIRE AT PRIORY COLLIERY

About five o'clock on Friday morning of 2nd October 1931, the lamp cabin at the Priory Colliery, Blantyre, belonging to William Baird & Co Ltd., was gutted by fire and the lampman, John Doran, who resided at 5 John Street, Blantyre, was removed to the Royal Infirmary, Glasgow, suffering from serious burning injuries. On inquiry at the colliery, a press representative was informed that, before being removed the infirmary, Doran said he had been unscrewing the bottom of lighted oil lamp, when it slipped from his hands and fell into tray of oil. Immediately flames burst out all over the cabin, and he was badly burned on the arms and body. There were over 700 lamps in the cabin, some of them being lit with oil, but the greater number of them are lit by electricity, and these were temporarily rendered useless. In consequence, the colliery was totally idle on that Friday.

TEENAGE TRAGEDY

Nan Lyndon, aged fifteen, who lived with her father, a widower, at St. James' Place, Auchinraith Road, Blantyre, was drowned in the River Clyde at Blantyre on the afternoon of Monday 22nd January 1934 and is remembered here. The newspaper reports of the time told *"The body of the girl lay wedged in between boulders in the centre of the river for two hours. Police assisted by volunteer helpers tried to reach the body only to swept back by the current."*

John Cross, a fisherman, finally succeeded in bringing it to the bank. John Lydon, the girl's father, to his horror and shock, identified the body. There was one eyewitness to the tragedy, Mr. J. Cowler, Uddingston. He had been crossing the River Clyde by the walkway at Craighead when he noticed the girl walking at the edge of the water. Her actions seemed to him rather peculiar. A few minutes later he saw her in the water. He ran down the riverbank in the hope of rescuing her, but by that time she had been carried out to the centre of the river, which was in full spate. There's a dangerous current under the viaduct.

It was unknown what events led up to and caused this young woman either to take her life, or if the river actually swept her away in an terrible accident that day. There are countless stories of drowning's around Blantyre on the River Clyde, a reminder again of how dangerous the under currents can be.

TRIPS TO CALDERPARK ZOO

The date is early 1972. In the pram, is none other than me as a baby. My father obviously trusted the monkeys at Calderpark Zoo to let them as close as this to his first-born! It was a sad day when the zoo closed all those years later but well overdue with the animals clearly being neglected with attitudes changing towards that particular space near Uddingston.

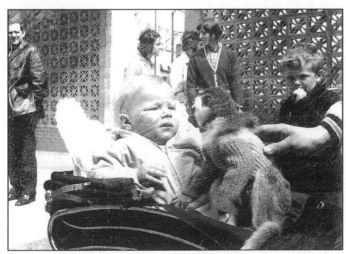

Figure 154 Baby Veverka at Calderpark Zoo, 1972

However, as a child, it was a great day out with many memories throughout childhood and so handy for Blantyre families to nip across the Blantyre Farm Road to such a popular tourist attraction.

The zoo was established by the Zoological Society of Glasgow and West of Scotland in 1947 and did pale by comparison to the mighty Edinburgh Zoo. Some of the animals always seemed constantly to be in danger of being moved elsewhere.

It closed in August 2003 after running up a debt of around £3.5m and failing to renew their zookeeper licence, having been unable to meet new standards on animal welfare.

18 HOLE GOLF COURSE

Redevelopment in Blantyre in 1979, did not just consider properties and shops. Recreation space was a major consideration too. Did you know plans and budget had been approved in September 1979 for a large 18-hole golf course for Blantyre on the site of the former Priory Bing?

The £1m set aside for Blantyre Golf Course was the subject however of much heated debate within Hamilton District Council. Much of the funding was coming from the Scottish Development Agency who were to prepare the former mining site, ready for the council to step in and lay a brand new 18 hole golf course, overlooking the woods, river and Bothwell Castle. It had been welcome news for many local people considering the site still contained remnants of the coal era and looked at eyesore.

The main Council objector was Conservative Councillor David Williamson stating that Blantyre

Figure 155 The Priory Fields Today

had been getting preferential treatment in recent council projects, at the expense of Hamilton trailing behind! A statement other councillors furiously disagreed with; given the lack of attention Blantyre had received throughout the 60's and 70's. Appalled, Councillor George McInally stood up for Blantyre and the golf plans asking Mr Williamson where he thought exactly Blantyre was *'romping ahead'*. Councillor Williamson replied that Blantyre was to receive a sports centre, which would be larger than any facility in Hamilton. Councillor McInally angrily replied that the sports centre hadn't even been approved yet with funding still in question. Discussion then turned to new community centres and care homes planned for Blantyre, which again Councillor McInally said put Hamilton at a disadvantage.

When Provost Charles Brownlie reminded Councillors that Hamilton alone had over 50% of the population of the district, it was clear he was siding with Councillor Williamson and opposed Blantyre receiving the new course. Unfortunately, with battle sides drawn, other more numerous Councillors in Hamilton expressed similar concerns, and ended with objection to the course at all. However, the District Council agreed in principle that the land should be bought for some sort of development, ideally recreation and the sale went ahead at a considerable cost of £36,000.

Blantyre did not get its course, but in Autumn 2018 Council discussion again turned to this land, which has been greenbelt with adjacent playing fields for some time. Recent proposals have asked that the land should now be classed as a Local Nature Reserve, a first for Blantyre, protecting it somewhat against future building and reserving it only for recreation and environment.

CHAPTER 9
CROSSBASKET & STONEYMEADOW

Although much of Crossbasket and Stoneymeadow actually fall into East Kilbride Parish, various postal addresses in this area say 'High Blantyre' and on the fringes to the west of the Blantyre, it's an area most well known and frequented lots by walkers. There is sufficient history and interest in the area for both Crossbasket and Stoneymeadow to be included as a chapter in this book, and even at time of writing Crossbasket has acquired parts of Blantyre Parish for future development, like the Greenhall Coach House for example, currently being renovated for letting out as of November 2018. Crossbasket Castle's recent renovation this decade has certainly put this area back on the map.

The cover photo above, exclusively pictured here for the first time is a Blantyre delivery driver standing at General's Bridge on Stoneymeadow Road. His poor horse looks as cold as him. Although the exact date is lost, David Ritchie likely took this photo sometime between 1900 and 1915.

ALDERS OR ALLERS FARM

People in Blantyre may be aware of an old, detached stone built property called Aller's Farm, located just off Stoneymeadow Road. The name Alders appeared on old maps, but Alders and Allers are essentially the same name, and both signify the Alder tree, which grows at the Lee Burn nearby. During the 1800's both Allers, and the aptly named "Doghillock" names were used intermittently so there appears to have been no preference.

The name Doghillock and its connections with Dogs relates to the fact that the building used to be used as kennels for the Maxwell's Calderwood Estate, of which Allers/Doghillock was part of. The farm sits on a large mound of earth, hence the name hillock. Today, the farm buildings are used as a modern home and a kennels business belonging to Alan Reardon. Alan told me that animal bones were found in the gardens after he moved in.

Chris Ladds, EK history enthusiast added, *"Doghillock aka Allers or Alders came into being sometime between 1725 and 1750. It is not mentioned on any of the Teinds, legal disputes, rentals, or correspondence for the entire lands of Calderwood, but ALL the other farms/crofts that were there are, because these are detailed itineraries. Even the 80-page decree I found makes no mention.*

Figure 156 Aller's Farm, situated on the hill above Stoneymeadow Road

The land it is on was within the Blantyre Parish boundary founded as late as the 1500's, but probably earlier. Those lands were not part of Kilbride Barony, and if they were a 'Bonnet Lairdship' there would at least be mention in testaments, marriage documents, births, Sasines (Glasgow & Edinburgh), all of which I have checked and there is no mention. 1725-1750 makes a lot of sense as the replacement trade road should date to about that time which passes the old farm. The older road was the ancient Peddlar's Way further west. The names Doghillock, and Allers are both Scots/English origin and not Brythonic/Old English like many of the older areas around here, so it's a newer name(s). There is a mention in the old rentals of a place called Hillmaleel, also spelt Hilmaline, Kilmaline, Hillmilne, etc... I believe it derives from Hill Mailing, but this place name could easily relate to several different areas on the old estate, and so we can't conclude it relates to Doghillock.

The layout of the buildings and the older stonework are all 18th century local vernacular with little hint of 1600's unless they replaced an older building. The draining of the lands didn't begin here until the mid 1700's, around which time Renfrewshire and Kilbride hunts became popular. It was too boggy and Moorish before that. I would say that all the facts point to Doghillock being 1725-1750, and indeed the facts seem to exclude the place as having existed prior to then. The later 1750 end of the range is because this area was surveyed c. 1750 by Roy and Paul Sandby and Crew for the Military Map."

Today, the Kennels business offers far more than just boarding. Hydrotherapy for dogs helps animals through recovery processes, and is a great way to keep dogs fit, lose weight and stay healthy.

On social media, **Christine McClenaghan** said, *"Family on my mothers side lived and worked at Allers Farm for many years. The farmer was Robert Chalmers. He was like an honorary uncle. We would always visit in the school holidays and my great auntie, who was housekeeper, would always make me a clootie dumpling complete with coins for my birthday, which is in the October holidays. I have a lot of happy memories. If the bones in the garden were from dogs I may even be able to put a name to two of them...."*

Alan Reardon the current owner, added, *"An interesting article Paul but while I agree the house at the Allers is from around the 1700's the original building that now forms the office is from much earlier it consisted of a small house with a building attached for the animals. There have been buildings added later including what was a byre where the hydro pool and grooming parlour now are and a small building that was used at one time as a place to cool the milk when it was farmed that had slate shelving for the cooling pans. As methods changed other buildings were added that when I bought the Allers were in a fair state of disrepair and demolished these were attached to the front of the original building and comprised of a dairy building and a single room workers bothy. Bob Chalmers and Chrissie his house keeper and Christine's great aunt added a building to the front of the 1700's house to form a bathroom and kitchen probably some time in the 1940's but when we bought it they had still retained the long drop in the midden for the workers. I have a copy of the deeds and I am sure an old map that I will look out. The animal bones were from a horse more than likely a Clydesdale."*

STONEYMEADOW FARM

By 1793, applications were approved for a Tollhouse to be created on the Turnpike road at the Dalton Junction of Stoneymeadow Road, High Blantyre. There were no other buildings there at the time, so it is likely that the first building dates from the mid to late 1790's. Built in stone and perhaps once originally with a thatched roof, the Stoneymeadow Toll was constructed to tax travellers with horse and carts going up and down the road. The building was twofold, one part for the Tollbooth, and another to house the person working there.

We know the tollbooth was still operating by 1849 when a murder was reported in some detail occurring nearby on the adjacent road. The newspaper reports of September 1849 make a clear reference to the toll point still being used.

However, by the early Victorian period, tollbooths were perceived as an impediment to free trade. During the early 1830's tolls on turnpike roads were abolished in Scotland (although some continued to operate quite illegally for some years after). During the 1830's, the Turnpike Trust operating Stoneymeadow Toll, ceased to exist and the building became available for another purpose.

It was to be bought by Cambuslang woman Mary Paterson (nee Shearer) and was to be used as a farm building. Mary was born in 1770 and didn't buy the farm until she was 60 years old. She had 10 children with her husband, who passed away in 1848.

The 1859 maps show this little building was renamed as "Stoneymeadow Farm". Outbuildings were created, presumably to house cattle and other farm animals. In 1861, Stevenson and Margaret Boyd (nee Dean) lived in one of the cottages, a labourer and his wife. A busy house though, as they also had 10 children and it would appear that they were farming this land for Mary Paterson in her old age. Mary Paterson was a remarkable woman who lived until she was 3 months short of being 105 years old! On her death on Sunday 7th February 1875, it was noted she had been a remarkable woman of intellect and had retained possession of all her faculties up until a few months before her death. She had spent the greater part of her life in the area of Stoneymeadow and gifted with rare conversational powers, she was well known with people coming from afar to see her. Upon her death she had over 100 grandchildren, 60 great grandchildren and 2 great, great grandchildren!

Figure 157 Stoneymeadow Farm pictured around 1911 at junction of Dalton Road

In 1875, the Stoneymeadow Farm went up for sale, forcing some of the Boyd family to move too. Indeed, splitting up some of the family, the Boyd grandmother moved about as far as she could get, to East Gore, New Zealand that same year along with her 7-year old grandson, William Boyd. The other Boyd members continued to stay at Stoneymeadow Farm, presumably acquiring the property from the Shearers.

The property later became a shop, which you see pictured around 1911. Today, the building is no longer there.

CALDERWOODGLEN HALT

We're ever so slightly out of Blantyre Parish with this article, but it's worth sharing, for this was the railway station above and near Crossbasket, at the opposite end of the Greenhall Viaduct and should not be confused with High Blantyre Station which was further east.

Calderwoodglen Halt was a small platform built at the edge of the railway, directly opposite on the elevated position across from Allers Farm, near Stoneymeadow.

Figure 158 Former Station, "Calderwoodglen Halt" high above Crossbasket, 1907

It was requested and constructed with the intervention of the SCWS (Co-op) in 1907, for their specific use of taking tourists down to Stoneymeadow and up to Calderwood Castle. SCWS built a small ticket office in 1907, which doubled as a small rain shelter. The sign on the platform, located on the south side of the railway line (which ran east to west) simply said "Calderwoodglen". The line was suspended to passengers during WW1 and WW2 and both the line and platform are now no longer there. Behind the camera, the line ran in the opposite direction over the Greenhall Railway Viaduct Pillars and on towards the junction at Hunthill, High Blantyre.

Beyond the little building and person standing in this photo, was an immediate path to the left, which ran steeply down the hill coming out at a point between Allers and the Dalton Junction, on Stoneymeadow Road.

Out the picture to the left about 20m away down the steep hill, is the former site of the fabled Crossbasket stone cross, which is alleged to have given rise to the name "Basket" and thus the naming of nearby Crossbasket.

CROSSBASKET, 1915

This next photo dates from WW1. Whilst that terrible conflict ravaged European battlefields, this photo was taken around 1915 at High Blantyre. More specifically at Crossbasket Estate, then home to George Neilson. The photographer was David Ritchie, whom I'm beginning to suspect provided photos to be made into postcards.

Figure 159 Crossbasket House, now Crossbasket Castle, pictured in 1915

During this time owner George Neilson, who owned Summerlee Iron Foundry and Spittal Colliery was mostly absent on business in London. Norah Mary Neilson (nee Addie) and Thomas Paterson Neilson, one of George Neilson's sons had been living at Crossbasket from 1904 until 1912. The couple had married in Uddingston on 17th August 1904 living at Crossbasket with George immediately after.

As you can see, the fashionable tennis courts were located out front where now the formal gardens and fountains are. Even then, this grand house was well looked after, tended by many domestic servants. The stonework still looks new, perhaps from modernisation and extensions, which took place in the years recent to the picture.

Given this was 113 years ago, the whole scene does actually look fairly unchanged, with the exception of tall conifers now towering above on the opposite northern embankments. Crossbasket is of course now a 5 star luxury hotel and restaurant enjoying monumental success and popularity, especially as a wedding venue. The recent additions of a ballroom and ceremony room, only making the property a National treasure, right here on our doorstep. Wonder what George Neilson would have made of it all?!

FATAL IMPALING

About ten o'clock on Wednesday 19th July 1933, just as the light was dipping, a terrible accident occurred at the junction of Stoneymeadow Road and Dalton, which left one person dead.

Richard Dale, residing at 48 Park Street, Cambuslang was running his Blantyre sweetheart back to High Blantyre, when tragedy struck. He was riding a motorcycle with the young woman as pillion passenger towards Blantyre when through some unexplained cause; he skidded severely across the road at the junction of Stoneymeadow and crashed heavily into the kerb. The bike was thrown up into the air, at speed and the woman was thrown over a five feet high iron fence into the field. Richard Dale was also thrown from the bike, but was not thrown over the fence. Instead, he was thrown on to the metal fence, which had spikes upon it. He was caught on the spikes and impaled. When a doctor arrived it was found that Dale was dead. The young women, left shocked, was uninjured and had been left alone to raise the alarm.

FATAL CRASH

Continuing the above theme and in a nearby location. A spectacular crash by a bicycle into an oncoming Motor Car occurred on the Stoneymeadow Road on Saturday 27th July 1935. The fatal road accident occurred in the vicinity of Stoneymeadow, midway between High Blantyre and East Kilbride, on that Saturday night.

James Dyet (49), 02 Sempic Road. Burnbank, Hamilton, who was riding a push cycle towards his home, came into collision with a motorcar travelling in the opposite direction. The accident occurred at a curve on the road. The cyclist crashed into the side of the car, the mirror of which and the side pane of glass were broken. The police at High Blantyre and a doctor were notified, and were quickly on the scene. They found that Dyet had sustained severe head and body injuries, and he was rushed to Glasgow Victoria Infirmary in the ambulance waggon. His condition was critical, and he died on the morning of Sunday 28th July, leaving a widow and family.

CHIEFTAIN BUSES

Laurie of Hamilton, the proprietors of the Chieftain Buses, ran a bus service from Hamilton, along High Blantyre Road, Burnbank, Main Street, High Blantyre and up to Stoneymeadow Road, up to East Kilbride Village and Hairmyres during the mid to third quarter of the 20th Century.

Avril Laurie messaged me saying, *"Thanks so much for your post of the chieftains. My husband's grandfather owned the chieftains and the family of brothers drove the chieftains and his dad. Brings back good memories for the family."*

Helen Lawson Taylor said, *"I travelled on the buses going to work in 1960 they were freezing old buses!"* **Stuart MacRae** added, *"The Laurie depot was to the right of where Robertson Cars is now and the shops just before the old bridge over the railway that was Burnbank station.*

STONEYMEADOW JUNCTION

Here's another great photo of Stoneymeadow Junction. With view beyond up to the "Lady Nancy" fields, this is the junction at Stoneymeadow as if coming from Dechmont. On the right, the former Boyd's Farm by this era had given itself over to a being a little shop. The shop on the right is now demolished, the land having several uses since. It is currently vacant. The little shop on the left of the photo also prompted much discussion and nostalgic references.

Figure 160 Stoneymeadow Junction pictured in the early 1960's

Elizabeth Weaver said on social media, *"Many's the walk we had up this road as children. We sometimes went up that way to roll our boiled eggs on Easter Sunday (further back down the road from the shop) but occasionally on hot summer days, we'd be allowed a drink or an ice cream from the shop before setting off back home. I remember sitting on the bench outside. Happy days!"*

Jack Bethel said, *"To the right, there was a new filling station on the corner, late 60's or early 70's. It became a used car showroom for a while then lay empty for years. The building was demolished a couple of years ago."*

Alan Baird replied, *"aye a mind of it Jack. It was a Texaco garage. When we were out on the push bikes for a run wee would stop in there for wee bottles of ginger and crisps."*

Jean McIntosh also commented, *"I remember the garage across the road from it. Mrs Birch was the woman in there early 70s. You could get 4 galls for £1. No Asda in those days. Long before the* *expressway. I don't remember the shop across the road just the outbuildings. Lovely cottages still there today."*

Margaret Elma Griffin said, *"I used to walk to Stoneymeadow with my friends. We always visited the shop."*

Isobel Hollis added, *"Blast from the past! I used to walk that road with my father! He told me constantly to push my shoulders back; I was growing very tall and tried to mask it! I think ice cream was the reward!"*

Ann Brown said, *"Remember the wee shop well. Went with my dad. We stayed in Crossbasket at the time and we used to walk there for Old English spangles."*

Archie Peat added at the end, *"To true Blantyronians this was known as "Sleenemeedie!"*

GENERAL'S BRIDGE CRASH, 1967

On Monday 16th January 1967, the first phase of the EK Expressway was still being constructed and as normal, traffic coming from East Kilbride could only get into Blantyre by the Stoneymeadow Road, the quickest route at the time.

That day, a lorry driver sped down the Stoneymeadow Road heading towards Blantyre and his lorry in icy conditions lost its grip with the road, swerving to the side and right through the stone wall on the west side of the General's Bridge.

The lorry tumbled through the five foot high stonework and overturned falling a full 40 feet down to the river Calder below on the Crossbasket side, eventually coming to a rest upside down in the water!

Figure 161 General's Bridge in 1920's with no 'traffic'

The driver had a remarkable escape for during the accident, he was thrown clear of the vehicle landing on the river embankment and incredibly only suffered minor cuts and bruises.

The vehicle was salvaged from the river later that week and the county council repaired the wall at once to make the area "safe". Today, the western parapet on Stoneymeadow Road still bears the mark of that accident by a short section on the approach to the bridge being visibly different from the rest of the older walls. The repaired section has a flat cope and is made of more modern stonework, by comparison to the round copes of the remaining three parapets.

CROSSBASKET FETE, 1967

Figure 162 Opening Crossbasket Fete in 1967 smiles as rain comes down

The Rev Dr Donald Caskie opened a May fete at Crossbasket House, High Blantyre in 1967. He was better known as "the Tartan Pimpernel" for his exploits in helping servicemen escape from France in the war. It was all smiles despite the weather.

He opened the fete at the James Little Training College in the grounds of Crossbasket in aid of the Roosevelt Memorial Polio Fund. The heavens opened though and as can be seen when the minister and friends attempted a shot at the darts stall, he had to take cover under an umbrella.

FOVERAN

"Foveran" is a sizeable field in High Blantyre adjacent to Crossbasket. Indeed, it once belonged to Crossbasket Estate but was sold to private ownership in the early 20th Century. The field, bordered by the River Calder on the north side and Crossbow Estate to the east was used by horses for some time and was recently screened off by Crossbasket when they renovated the Castle. The origin of the place-name is from the Gaelic word 'fuaran' indicating a place with a little spring. Crossbasket Estate has recently acquired Foveran again. It pieces back together land that was under the original ownership of Crossbasket, something to celebrate. The acquisition, meant the end of all talk of private houses being built there, which was confirmed in September 2017, as something that WONT be happening. Crossbasket have expansion plans for this land in 2019.

FORMER WOODEN BRIDGES

In 1891, when George Neilson acquired Crossbasket, there were four wooden footbridges crossing the River Calder, two of them leading to woodland trails in the woods to the North of the house. Today, none remain, removed for safety reasons when Crossbasket was renovated in 2015. A circular path once ran around the entire estate, with thick woodland adjacent to the General's Bridge and along the boundary wall with Stoneymeadow Road.

Figure 163 Crossbasket Wooden Footbridges over the Calder, 2005

Blantyre man Alex Rochead, a decade prior to the removal of the wooden bridges, took this photo at the rear of Crossbasket Castle around 2005. The former wooden footbridge spanned the River Calder.

MONKEY PUZZLE TREES

There are several Monkey Puzzle Trees in and around Blantyre, which people agree are very beautiful to look at. There are now thought to be around a dozen or so in Blantyre. Robert Stewart sent the photo of this monkey-puzzle tree he took at Crossbasket Estate.

Robert noted there were several younger trees nearby and added, *"do you know that the semi-precious stone 'Jet' is fossilised monkey puzzle!"*

Figure 164 Crossbasket Monkey Puzzle 2014

I can't help but think this will be a particularly impressive tree in future generations, a distinctive look already marking it out from others. Crossbasket gardens have been completely renovated in recent years with many new additions planted around the nursery and Castle itself.

On social media:

Elizabeth Weaver said, "*The one in Victoria St/Small Crescent may be smaller but it stands out for me because it always looked so exotic among the other gardens. In the 1950's, most of us only had privet hedges and traditional shrubs – the monkey puzzle was a thing of wonder!*"

Jean Gibson added, "*That was probably the same one in a garden in Victoria Street when I was a wee girl 60 years ago.*"

Gord Fotheringham said, "*I think I knew that wee girl sixty years ago. Still lovely!*"

John Mcnulty told us, "*The biggest monkey puzzle tree I ever saw was just outside the poor Clair Convent down the dandy and that was 60yrs ago! Must surely be still there.*"

Ann Sutherland, confirmed, "*I remember the one on Victoria St. 70 years ago!*"

Ashleigh Fyfe said, "*The monkey puzzle tree in the graveyard at Cemetery Road, High Blantyre is about 20 times the size of this!*"

Jane Johnstone said, "*I planted three in my present garden in memory of the one I remembered in Glasgow. It made an impression on me as a young kid.*"

Another Monkey Puzzle tree exists at Station Road planted in recent years outside the old Mill Wages Office, next to the David Livingstone Bridge. Do you know of any others?

Reference: Araucaria araucana (commonly called the monkey puzzle tree, monkey tail tree, piñonero, or Chilean pine) is an evergreen tree growing to 1–1.5 m (3–5 ft) in diameter and 30–40 m (100–130 ft) in height. It is native to central and southern Chile, western Argentina. Araucaria araucana is the hardiest species in the conifer genus Araucaria.

Because of the longevity of this species, it is described as a living fossil. It is also the national tree of Chile. Keep that in mind next time you see one in Blantyre!

CROSSBASKET PRE-RENOVATION

With Blantyre's newest renovated building now firmly on the map, it's worth a reminder just how run down Crossbasket USED to be. These photos courtesy of Urban Environments page "28 days later" show the state of the interior of the listed building, back in 2010 and into 2011. This was around the time the new owners bought it, but before any work had commenced. It was a building at risk, with dampness inside, mould and mushrooms growing in the corridors and water running down the inside of the stairs. Today, Crossbasket Castle has had a remarkable £9m transformation and is the absolute height of 5 star luxuries.

Figures 165 - 169 Crossbasket Before Renovation in 2010 and 2011

Figures 170 - 179 Crossbasket Interior and Exterior pre Renovation 2010 and 2011

The entire history of Crossbasket from it's humble beginnings 6 Centuries ago, through all ownership with 34 owners, charting the renovation and acquisitions and additions of this decade are explored in my dedicated book, *"The History of Crossbasket Castle, featuring Tales of Crossbasket"* available on Amazon.co.uk.

ALBERT ROUX AT CROSSBASKET

Monday 21st December 2015 saw a successful 'doors open day' at the newly renovated Crossbasket Castle. The general public saw the renovated Castle in High Blantyre and were also treated to a 5 star buffet, cooked by the wonderful award winning, and globally known chef, Albert Roux Everybody was surprised to see how hands on Albert was on the day with his team of chefs, very busy indeed. Albert was in the kitchen from an early hour overseeing quality and workload.

Figure 180 Albert Roux in Crossbasket Kitchens in 2015. Photo by Brenda Rochead

Albert Roux OBE, aged 80 (born 8 October 1935) is a French-born restaurateur and chef working in Britain. He and his brother Michel operated Le Gavroche, the first restaurant in the UK to gain three Michelin stars. He helped train a series of chefs, including TV personality Gordon Ramsay, and he went on to win Michelin stars. His son, Michel Roux, Jr. continues to run Le Gavroche and has had involvement at Crossbasket often.

I attended this function after work that evening and was mighty impressed by the building work and the culinary skills of all the chefs. Sampling the fine dining buffet, I have to admit in having not much clue what I was eating half the time, but concluded it was entirely 'delicious'.

<u>RENOVATED GATE LODGE</u>

The Gate Lodge is a renovated traditional two bedroomed house, located at the entrance to the Crossbasket Estate on Stoneymeadow Road. Approximately a three-minute walk from the Castle, it is perfect for families, or for those looking for a five star experience with the amenities of home. Bought over in Autumn 2017 it was stripped entirely inside and outside of its white render and renovated to luxurious standard.

Figures 181 - 185 Crossbasket Gate Lodge House Renovated in Autumn 2017

The accommodation comprises:

- Living room with gas fireplace and dining area
- Kitchen with washer/dryer, induction stove, fridge freezer, microwave and kettle.
- Main bedroom with a large king size bed, sauna, steam room and shower. The French doors lead out to a veranda, which is complete with hot tub and views over the gardens and mature woodland.
- Second bedroom with twin beds, which can also be made into a double.

- Family bathroom, which is fully equipped with separate shower and bath.
- Everything you need to make your stay with Crossbasket a memorable experience.

A full Scottish breakfast is available for you in the Castle. Unfortunately, room service is not available in the Gate Lodge.

Figures 186 - 191 Crossbasket Lodge renovated completely inside to luxurious standards

Crossbasket and its associated buildings are certainly the grandest in Blantyre, by a country mile. I'm sure you'll agree it is absolutely stunning.

However, at an eye-popping £560 per night to rent, I think I'll be saving my pennies for some time yet, before having a chance to stay here!

BY PAUL D VEVERKA

WEE YANNI'S ENGRAVING

Many people will know of local man John Dunsmore (aka Wee Yanni) and his passion for the River Calder. A favourite fishing spot, John loves nothing more than spending time near the river.

Figure 192 Wee Yanni, John Dunsmore in May 2018 at his latest engraving at Crossbasket

His skills include stonemasonry, something he's become very accomplished at, and notably renewing the plaque on the Blantyre Disaster memorial and cleaning up the park plaques too. In recent years he carved a beautiful message embedded professionally into the natural stone at the riverbank. John's latest activity however, was to celebrate the renaming of Crossbasket Castle (formerly Crossbasket House) by engraving the name "Crossbasket Castle" into the natural stone at the side of the River, below the Castle.

Beside the '4 Angels Falls' below Crossbasket Castle, the new engraving can be found. I was sworn to secrecy as his work took some time, and although not being in the best of health, he 'kept at it' with the finished beautiful result today as shown.

So, for the record, this new engraving was done in May 2018 and will be remembered here in these words and by the excellent craftsmanship of John, for generations to come.

CHAPTER 10
SPRINGWELLS & CRAIGHEAD

To the North East and North of Blantyre are the areas of Springwells and Craighead. Springwells has humble origins with a farmhouse of the same name but it took until the 1860's for a small community to manifest, with the arrival of businesses, shops and modest homes mostly in support of the nearby Greenfield Colliery over the boundary in Hamilton. Today, Springwells is largely associated with the huge housing estate and a number of businesses. Craighead to the west of Whistleberry and north of Glasgow Road is derived from the former estate of the same name, which has now been carved up into fields and industrial areas, ripe for development. The old estate house, once adjacent to William Baird's Colliery is gone, as is the railway viaduct, but those events still recent enough for the name 'Craighead' to continue an association with this area.

Our cover photo above shows William Aroll Contractor's employees in 1931 replacing the railway bridge at Whistleberry. In the background, along Glasgow Road you can see Chalmers Buildings. Little did they realise how quickly this passenger line would end in the decades after.

VICTORIAN CALENDARS FOR SALE

By 1892, a trend had formed of giving a Calendar as a Christmas gift, something that still exists today. Artistic calendars showing fine art were considered quite the perfect present and something that could be used all the following year. On Friday 23rd December 1892, Mr McCaffrie, the wine and spirit merchant of Springwell had TWO different fine calendars available for anybody looking for a last minute Christmas gift. They were available to buy from his public house (more recently known as Miller's Fireplaces).

The Calendars featured "pretty girls", socialites and actresses. One was a life like picture of Mrs Langtry and the other was Miss Ellen Terry. Both pictures were considered to have artistic merit and Mr McCaffrie considered them suitable for framing and worthy of adorning any home.

FOUR FAMILIES EVICTED

Four Blantyre families were in a pitiful plight in mid September 1923, having been evicted from their houses in Springwells, which were said to be uninhabitable, and being unable to find any accommodation as the weather turned colder.

Figure 193 Eviction had catastrophic consequences for many families

The houses were situated in Dalziel Place, just off Glasgow Road, in a location opposite the Robertson's Aerated Water Factory. In a time of mass unemployment and lack of housing, the homes had been condemned for some time, and people were warned. The householders searched high and low for houses without success, even applications for dwellings in the new housing scheme nearby being in vain. One of the families was understood to have made a request to be received into the Hamilton Combination Poorhouse, but, it was said, they could not be accommodated.

At the Police Office, too, a request for shelter was refused. The result was that four sheriff officers arrived and evicted the families and their goods into the street. The evicted tenants were: — Joseph Barr, widower, and his two daughters; Mrs Cleland and family; David McKinnon, his wife, and two children; William Smith, his wife, and five children, the youngest of whom was just two months old.

Slept in Washhouse

It was a wet, stormy night that September evening, and the Smiths and McKinnons sought shelter in a nearby outbuilding, a washhouse, The washhouse, however, was without windows, and the tenants had to use coats and wax-cloth to keep out the rain. In order that the younger children might get to sleep, Mr Smith nursed two of them on his knees ail night, while Mrs Smith and Mrs McKinnon cuddled others in their laps. The bedding of the families was stored overnight in the stables of Mr McDougall, but the furniture had to remain in the street all night soaked with rain.

These homes were demolished in 1929 and no known photos have been unearthed (yet), so I have, with guidance of old maps, drawn how Dalziel Place (formerly called Semple's Land) once looked like.

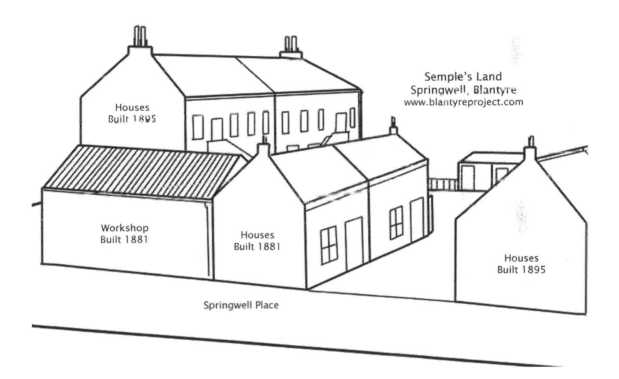

Figure 194 My Sketch of how Dalziel (Semples Land) may have looked

RETAIL PARK

The last few years seem to have forever had businesses in the news closing down on the High Street. Our area has had its fair share of casualties too, as many businesses suffer from online retail competition. Standing the test of time so far are the businesses at the corner of Whistelberry Road and Glasgow Road. In the retail park are LIDL, B&M Stores and Farmfoods. As of time of writing in November 2018, these businesses have been there a while, despite a spate of major businesses like Frankie & Bennys, Mothercare, Pizzahut, Carphone Warehouse being closed down in 2018 alone in surrounding local areas to Blantyre. It's always a concern to see businesses struggle.

HOGMANAY FATAL EXPRESS

Figure 195 Tragedy on Board the Steam Train

On Saturday 31st December 1927, during the morning, the communication emergency cord of the Glasgow to London express train was pulled abruptly by a panicked passenger, signalling that the train should come to stop.

The train was travelling at 60 miles hour through Hadley Wood in England. As the staff rushed to the carriage to see what the commotion was, a woman passenger informed the officials that a man had fallen out of her carriage as the train was passing Hadley Wood.

As the train stopped on the track, a search was instructed of the line behind and eventually they found the dead body of William Hyslop, of Mount Pleasant, Springwell, Blantyre, Scotland. William had been returning to London after having spent the Christmas holidays in Blantyre with family. According to the 1925 Valuation roll, William Hyslop (or Hislop) lived at number 40 Glasgow Road at Watson's Building, which was immediately next to a former house named Mount Pleasant, next to the row of cottages still there today (next to Dunn's Food & Drink).

An inquest was heard on Tuesday 3rd January 1928. William Hyslop jnr, the son of the dead William Hyslop, identified the body and explained that his father had been a railwayman in the employment of the London and North Eastern Railway Company and had been 65 years of age. He was always sober, good health and was not known to walk in his sleep. The mystery deepened.

Chrissie Hyslop, his fourteen-year-old daughter, said she left Scotland with her father on the previous Friday night, on the 9.45 train from Glasgow to London. The train was a corridor one, and her father was sitting facing the engine, in the corner farthest from the corridor. She sat opposite her father and there were two sailors also in the compartment.

Towards the end of the journey she left the compartment, meaning to be absent only a moment. She left her father asleep in one corner, and one the sailors sitting on the opposite side of the carriage. The other sailor had gone out. When she returned, some two minutes later, her father was not there, and the outer door was open. The sailor was asleep and she awakened him and told him the door was open and her father was gone! The sailor pulled the communication cord, and this having no effect the guard was informed and the train pulled up and stopped about 10 minutes after the communication cord was first pulled.

Dr. C. N. Scott stated that Saturday morning he was called to a spot about a mile-and-a-half north New Barnet Station, where he found the body of Hyslop lying between the tracks. His skull was fractured. There were other injuries, and Dr. Scott was of opinion that Hyslop had been dragged along for 30 or 40 yards. Death, he thought, was due to the fracture the skull, caused by the fall. The body had not been run over. Stoker Francis James Scullion, H.M.S Nelson, and Stoker Matthewson. of H.M.S. Lion Duke, the two sailors referred to by Miss Hyslop, confirmed her account of the events preceding the accident. Neither of them saw Hyslop leave the carriage. I H. Keleher, a carriage inspector at King's Cross, said he examined the door of the carriage from which Hyslop fell when the grained reached King's Cross. The locks hinges were in perfect order. There was no way of opening the door from inside the carriage, except lowering the window and reaching to the handle from the outside.

A full examination of the train revealed a small piece of flesh on the handrail of the guard's van, some distance behind the carriage in question, and another piece of flesh on a fish van at the rear of the train. Daniel Kipp, the foreman platelayer who found the body, said the marks in the snow, some 32 yards north of the body, made him think Hyslop had been dragged along by the train after falling.

Summing up, the Coroner said the evidence by the examiner of the carriage showed that he must have done something to the door, besides going to the window. He could only suppose that, waking up, Hyslop missed his daughter and perhaps being sleepy, had tried to open the wrong door. There was so little evidence that perhaps the jury's best course would be find a verdict of Death by misadventure. Mr F. H. Doubleday, a guard travelling on the train, who had given evidence, was recalled and stated that the window of the Carriage was found closed. A juryman asked how Hyslop could have closed it after opening the door, and the Coroner said it was a complete mystery and impossible to him. Nobody could tell what had caused it. The jury returned verdict of Death misadventure.

SPRINGWELLS BUS CRASH

On Friday 15th August 1938, a bus veered off road at Springwells injuring four people on board. An electric standard with which it collided saved the bus from going over embankment. The vehicle was returning to a garage at Peacock Cross, Hamilton, and when negotiating a bend on the road, across from the foundry (present Bus garage) it is believed that a tyre burst. The bus swung across the road and came to a halt after it had struck and broken the standard. Had it not been brought to a standstill then it would have crashed through fence, which guards the embankment. The driver, Samuel Hickson, Kirk Street, Wishaw, had to be dragged from the damaged cabin. It was found that he had suffered internal injuries and body bruises, and he was removed to his home in a car belonging to his employers. The conductress, Alice Austin Street, Cadlow, suffered shock and facial injuries, whilst Charles Malone, another driver, and his conductress, Jessie Brown, both of Blantyre who were inside the bus, suffered from shock.

ROSENDALE QUADS

A rather rare event was talked about for some time after when it became known that a Blantyre woman had given birth to her 4 children, all on the same day. On 9am on Sunday 6th May 1928, the young Blantyre woman, Mrs Flora McLean, wife of miner, who both resided at Rosendale Place, just off Glasgow Road, gave birth to quadruplets, to four sons in Bellshill Maternity Hospital. Unfortunately though, this story does not end happily. All four were still-born. Mrs McLean was reported by Dr. H. J. Thomson, of Uddingston, who was present, and later advised press who were keen on the story, that the heartbroken mother, was progressing favourably under the circumstances. A sensitive subject, but it got me thinking of those four poor little "lambs" and I wondered if there has been quadruplet children in Blantyre since?

ROBERTSON'S GINGER CART

This fantastic picture of Robertson's Ginger 'cairt' has Blantyre man Peter McDonald standing beside it. His great grandson, Johnny Gilluley shared the picture.

Figure 196 Robertson's Ginger Cart upgrades to rubber wheels!

The cart actually looks quite new, well certainly the wheels do and I suspect this is what the photograph was showing off. The words *"Springwell Bottling Works"* are written along the side. It's incredible to think of these horses and their drivers going out in all weather, all year round on their deliveries at a time when there was hardly a motorised vehicle on the roads. The date is unknown, but I suspect from the clothing and styles it was a pre WW2 time when great transition to motorised vehicles was taking place.

FLOODING OF BURNSIDE COTTAGES

Tom Campbell from New Zealand shared this message. *"As a boy from 1958 until they were utterly destroyed by flooding of the Park Burn ten years later, I lived at Burnside Cottages, Springwells. I recall more than one cottage (at least three) occupied in the late 1950's but by the time they were flooded only ours, which was the biggest was left.*

I remember the water rose so quickly that we just had time to grab some papers and photos before it went from lapping the doorstep to shoulder height. The fire brigade came but had nowhere to pump the water to, as the land there was the lowest lying around the area. I later emigrated to New Zealand where I still am now"

In 1898, the two cottages nearest the burn were there, but there were FOUR little homes on the site of the third cottage. This was the case until 1930's when the third cottage had been built, presumably first by knocking down the little row of four homes. So by 1936, three cottages existed, just as Tom described. Today, there is a modern small industrial estate (Parkburn) on the site, directly across from the First Bus garage. The Parkburn stream was known to cause many flooding problems. Tunnels and culverts were later built, enclosing much of the Parkburn in Low Blantyre, underground, to prevent future flooding.

BRAIDWOOD BUILDING CONTRACTORS

Figure 197 Janet Duncan at Braidwood Builders, 1968

Pictured here in 1968 in the back yard of Alexander Braidwood's Building Yard, on the right in my mother Janet Duncan. I'm unsure who the person on the left is, but a summers day was certainly being enjoyed by taking work outside.

Braidwood Builders was located at 5 Logan Street, Low Blantyre where my mother worked as a clerk.

The builders were Andrew and Alexander Braidwood and the firm employed a considerable number of local tradespeople. The yard later relocated to near Rosendale, further along Glasgow Road. My mother gave up her job to become a mother in 1971.

VANDALISM OF PLAY AREAS

In August 1978, vandals turned towards the new leisure area in Springwells. A £90,000 scheme was underway to turn the ground into a play area, with landscaped grassed areas. However, shrubs had been attacked and uprooted, as quickly as they had been planted and the project was not due to be finished until the end of that year. The expensive ash playpark had been churned up even before it was finished with motorcycles and cars driving upon it and brand new goalposts were ruined, by somebody actually stealing the crossbar!

By far the worst damage though was 90 young trees uprooted and left for dead, representing half of the total planted at the taxpayers cost. Hamilton District Council commented at the time that the trees had been taken 10 years to grow in a nursery before being planted in Blantyre, and had died in a month of being out the ground. In the end, those 90 trees were NOT replaced, hence today the play area looks fairly open, rather than having the intended wooded perimeter.

BEER CAN TOWER

Some stories I need to be careful of, as 1979, is a little "*modern*" and where high jinks end in arrest, I have no wish to embarrass anybody or dwell on things that happened 40 years ago. So, in this instance, I won't name the rather well known man in Blantyre, who once lived in Burnside Crescent that was fined for aforementioned high jinks whilst a lot younger than he is now!

Figure 198 Whistleberry Roundabout

The date was July 1979 and motorists coming from Burnbank were astonished to see a man in the centre of the mini roundabout at the Whistleberry Road junction carefully setting up a tower of beer cans, placing them in the middle and around the perimeter of the roundabout. He'd clearly brought the cans with him as 'building materials!'

Local police decided he was a traffic hazard and charged the Springwells man with a breach of the peace. In court later that week, the man somewhat regretted his actions stating he had only been celebrating getting a new job, which he was looking forward to. Justice David Hume fined him £50. Now, if he'd like to come forward and name himself, that's fine, for it was a long, long time ago! If not, don't worry, your secret's safe and perhaps this will be a story for a future historian to disclose!

BOTHWELL BRIDGE ENGRAVING

Figure 199 Bothwell Bridge, 1859

Pictured in 1859, Bothwell Bridge still looks very rural and sleepy. The large central tower than once adorned the bridge in earlier centuries is gone and the structure takes on a more familiar appearance as it looks today. Indeed much of the bridge appears to have been rebuilt in the 1820's.

In 1822, it was widened by 22 foot, modernised and the approaches levelled with the addition of massive supporting masonry abutments. In the late 1890s, footpaths were added. The completion of the Expressway and renovation of Bothwell Road gave a more level appearance. Speaking of the previous bridge, a man who wrote this died in Edinburgh on 5th June 1767. At a time before the Covenanter's Battle, the previous bridge was described, "*About a short half mile east from the Kirk stands the famous bridge called Bothwell Bridge, upon the river of Clyde consisting of four arches. Here all passengers whether on horseback or on foot as likeways all kinds of merchandize pay a small custom to the town of Hamiltoun. The bridge indeed belongs to the Government, but it is sett in tack to the toun of Hamilton who are allowed to exact custom of the leidges, for upholding the bridge.*"

BAIRD'S ROWS (CRAIGHEAD ROWS)

Baird's Rows or Raws were located in the Craighead area of Low Blantyre. The miner's homes consisted of three equal length rows of single storey terraced properties. They were tied to the nearby Colliery at Craighead. The rows were named after the Colliery and Craighead house.

In April 1878, just as Blantyre was experiencing rapid population growth, contractors Purdie Builders of Coatbridge started building the homes, on an area now Parks of Hamilton Bus depot. The land was previously vacant to this, bordered between Forrest Street and Whistleberry Road. Each home had a number for the address, but no actual street names were given, nor are any street nicknames known. The development was fairly significant at 108 houses comprising of 2 apartments and a small hall/workshop to the east side of the front row. Houses were numbered 1 to 108 inclusive starting at number 1 on Glasgow Road up to 108 at the back not far from the railway. House 35 and 36 was a store belonging to William Baird & Co.

Figure 200 Baird's Rows near Forrest Street pictured in 1955

At the front of these homes stood an isolated and detached store, a double storey property although this was not added until between 1898 and 1910. In between each of the rows, were a dozen washhouses, equally spaced with 4 in each clearing, between each row. The homes would have been noisy at the best of times being situated so close to the busy railway and nearby Craighead junction. When the rows were first built, the Craighead lodge house stood in the field between the rows and the Glasgow Road. By 1910, the vacant ground around the rows, which had previously been used for open air boxing matches, had given way to two football grounds, one being where the speedway was later to be sited. Blantyre Celtic ran the football ground to the south of the rows. Also by then, six water taps served the entire area, equally spaced out near the washhouses, and fed from pumped water from the nary Craighead colliery. A housing report of 1910, confirmed that 206 of Craighead collieries 690 miners lived at Baird's Rows. The report went on to give a good description:

- 108 Two-apartment houses Rental £5 15s to £6 4s.
- Erected about 30 years ago – Stone built, one storey – no damp-proof course – Back wall of room strapped and lathed, others plastered on solid – Wood floors, ventilated – Some front walls slightly damp – Internal surface of walls and ceilings in good condition
- About one third of these houses are occupied by Polish miners, but the majority of these are of cleanly habits
- No overcrowding – apartments large
- Garden ground available- mostly uncultivated, common wash houses, coal cellars
- Water closets recently introduced, in the proportion of one closet to every 4 tenants
- No sinks- surface channels
- Gravitation water from pillar wells in front of houses. In some cases these wells are about 200 feet distant from the dwellings
- Scavenged at owners' expense, but houses are now included in Blantyre Special Scavenging District

On 25th March 1914, a housing report was presented as evidence to the Royal Commission. Whilst researching this article, I determined that some of the information on the report is careless and approximate. For example, it talks about there being two rows, when actually there were three. It mentions they were built "nearly 40 years ago", when actually it was exactly 36 years previous. However, the rest of the words are a good indication of what the rows were like. I quote,

"These two rows of miners' houses, which are owned by William Baird & Company, are situated near to the Glasgow Road in the Parish of Blantyre. They consist of 108 houses of two apartments. They were erected nearly forty years ago, and are built with stone throughout, and have boarded floors. The rent, including all local assessments, is 2s. 9d. per week. There is a good gravitation water supply, which is served up in a niggardly fashion by means of standpipes erected at short intervals along the rows. There are no sculleries nor sinks in any of the houses, so that all the dirty water has to be emptied into an open gutter that runs along in front, of the row – a most objectionable feature, which is very common to miners' rows.

There is a washhouse to every ten families, and coal-cellar to each house. By the inclusion of this property in a special scavenging district the county authorities have greatly improved the sanitation of the place. The old common ash-pits and dry-closets have all been removed, and a flush closet has now been erected for every five families. Dust-bins are also now in vogue, with a daily collection of refuse, and a local scavenger is employed to tidy up the place."

By the 1930's, the adjacent football ground was by then Blantyre's famous greyhound track opened by Frank Doonin, which would have been popular with the miners nearby. It is rumoured that Baird's Rows officially became Craighead Rows, when the nearby colliery changed in ownership and the owners wished to disassociate themselves with the former Baird's name. According to the valuation roll of 1930, William Baird & Co Ltd owned the rows at that time. The rows were shortly after cleared to make way for new infrastructure and business redevelopment, but were known to have still been there in 1957.

SALVATION ARMY CITADEL

Figure 201 Salvation Army Citadel, 1955

Pictured here in an aerial photo from 1955 is The Salvation Army Building, nicknamed, "The Citadel". Actually, the name Citadel applied to most Salvation Army headquarters buildings. Located at the top, South East end of Forrest Street, the building stood directly opposite the gate of Blantyre Vic's Castle Park Grounds.

Its style is quite unique for Blantyre in terms of its architecture and design. Whilst researching this article, I was surprised to see it on maps as early as 1897, when I always thought the style was more art deco 1920's. The building was made of brick with architectural features common for Salvation Army buildings. At 12m x 25m the building was modelled on the Army headquarters buildings in London and Sheffield and although Blantyre's was smaller, it contained familiar parts like the towers and arched entrance. The Citadel commenced construction in summer 1886 and was officially opened at the end of November 1886.

The Salvation Army, perhaps as they represented a new movement, initially had a hard time in Blantyre. There was general non-acceptance of their beliefs, which even at times manifested in violence towards these Salvationists.

In January 1887, nine men from Blantyre were charged with breach of the peace and assaulting 4 Salvation Army officers. John Smith (cobbler), Chirstopher McKenna (coal carter), Hugh and Michael Flynn, James Daily, Matthew Carrigan, David McInally, John Ferguson and Thomas McVey (all miners) were the guilty parties. With exception of Smith at 63 years old, the ages ranged between 18 and 24. That first year since opening, it was common for the Salvation Army to be subjected to these sorts of attacks. Earlier that same month in January 1887, Mr Edward Smith was charged with continually "snowballing" the Army. In court he was admonished, but the incident was not unnoticed by Smith's friends, who then took exception to the Salvation Army. The judge noticed that the accused were all Roman Catholics, who were at the time looking for their own religious outlet to be formed. The judge determined rightly so that the Salvation Army had the same rights to be in Blantyre as Roman Catholics did. Each was fined £2. This incident I belief incited unrest amongst people in Blantyre and aggravation towards the Salvation Army. Not a month later Mr Edward Cornfield, a miner was charged with assaulting Thomas Gray of the Salvation Army. Cornfield was punch drunk at the time, quite literally, for whilst Gray was making his testimonial, Cornfield appeared and without reason, punched him to the ground. For that action, Cornfield received 60 days imprisonment. Later that year, during the infamous Blantyre riots, the rioters stopped to take time from their vandalism, to mock the Salvation Army.

As the decades rolled on and various denominations got their own religious outlets, the good work that the Salvation Army does was accepted, especially during their compassionate activities in WW1. During WW1, officers included Brigadier Orr and General Booth. On Sundays, the Salvation Army Band became a regular sight in our town, accompanying the preachers as they gave out sermons on streets.

Figure 202 Former Salvation Army Citadel on Forrest Street in the 1960's

Speaking of The Citadel, **Thomas Dunsmuir Hartman** of Chicago said, *"My little pals and I used to go down to the hall in a Sunday afternoon for our Ginger and biscuits all free, and you were encouraged to sing at the top of your voice, which I could not do in my own home, it was just great. We did not know what we were singing about but with biscuits and ginger who cared. We were all little tough guys, so girls always suffered. After we came out of the service, if you can call it that, we would immediately start making fun of the Salvation Army, like singing songs about them. One I can remember went.*

> *"The Salvation Army free from sin all went to heaven in a corned beef tin.*
> *The corned beef tin began to smell, so they jumped out and landed in hell "*

I have the greatest respect for the Salvation Army, and in my books they are the very best, in all that they do. Pictured from that era is the Citadel in 1960. Jeannie Lindsay was a sergeant there at the start of the 1990s. The Citadel was demolished in the early 1990s, a reflection of its age. The Salvation Army celebrated its 150th year Anniversary on 5th July 2015.

BLANTYRE ENGINEERING WORKS FIRE

About ten o'clock on the morning of Monday 20th August 1923, fire broke out in the pattern store at the Blantyre Engineering Company's works at Forrest Street.

Figure 203 Blantyre Engineering Works, 1922 a year before the fire

By the time the fire brigade had arrived from Cambuslang, the store and valuable patterns it contained were practically gutted. The flames rapidly spread to the pitched glass roof and the moulding shop adjoining. The firemen succeeded in confining the outbreak to this portion of the works, which still suffered considerably.

The damage was estimated between £4,000 and £5,000. The cause of the outbreak was never published, perhaps left unknown.

This amazingly clear photo from 1922 shows the Blantyre men who worked in the Engineering Works and many of them would have been there, the day of the fire a year later. I've zoomed in on the faces, just in case there are some fathers, grandfathers and great grandfathers in there. With thanks to Gordon Cook for sharing this photo.

BLOODY ESCAPE

Kaziners Skudauckan was a Lithuanian miner living at 40 Craighead Rows Blantyre during the 1920's. He went locally by the name of Charles Smith, far easier for people who knew him. Shortly after midnight on Thursday 2nd September 1926, William Cullen, a neighbour who resided next door to Kaziners, heard terrifying female screams and like others in the former miner's row in Low Blantyre, he looked out his window to see what the commotion was.

However, what William saw, gave him a fright, for there was Mrs Skudauckan attempting to leave the house by a window, her blood curdling screams suggesting something clearly was amiss. Mr Cullen, quickly called another neighbour, Mr James McGuire, and "manned up", they together rushed to the help of the woman, tried to get in via a door but found the door locked. They both then gained access to the house via another window, assisting the woman from out of the window and back into her home, shocked to find that she was bleeding profusely and fighting against them at the thought of being back into the house.

William and James then went into the kitchen for water to clean the injured woman and there observed her husband Kaziners, in a corner of the small kitchen with a nasty gash on the left side of his throat. In his hands, he was holding a razor, which they took from him. The police and a doctor were called, when it was found that the woman had been viciously stabbed in six or seven places, Kaziners, clearly her attacker. Later to police, although it was not revealed what prompted the attack, the woman, known locally as Mrs Smith, admitted that her husband had been acting strange in his manner for many weeks.

Mass unemployment and the prolonged miners strike of many months in 1926 made life in Blantyre very difficult for people, especially miners. Dozens of families left, some abroad seeking employment and opportunity elsewhere. There's no indication in the story that unemployment is behind the outburst of this man, but the timing is more than coincidental and should never have been any reason for violence of this nature.

HEARTLESS FINE

I encountered a story recently, where I felt the authorities handled the situation very strictly and un-compassionately. At Hamilton Court, on Saturday 10th May 1930, John O'Hare, a miner of 72 Forrest Street, Blantyre, pleaded guilty to a charge of attempting to commit suicide.

It was explained in Court by the Fiscal that O'Hare threw himself into the Clyde. With great difficulty some people succeeded in getting the accused to the river bank, but not before he was unconscious. John explained that what had happened was entirely due to drink. He asked for a chance, and a fine of 15s, or ten days' imprisonment, was imposed.

Fining somebody who was trying to commit suicide regardless of how he arrived in that situation seems very strict and perhaps it would be dealt with differently today, by means of monitoring or helping his situation in some way.

DOING TIME FOR SON

When 2 boys from Blantyre stole coal from the Bing at Craighead Colliery; their actions would have far reaching consequences for their families. There was a scene Hamilton J.P. Court on Saturday 25th June 1931, when those two boys from Blantyre finally admitted the theft of coal from the Bing at Craighead Colliery. Being minors, their fathers attended the hearings with them.

George Hulston, a miner living at 79 Craighead (Baird's) Rows was the father of the older boy, and ended up being questioned alongside his son. George maintained that workman at the pit had volunteered to give his lad a bag of coal. Pressed to disclose the name of the workman, Hulston refused to give further information or inform. Consequently, the Justices imposed a fine of 15 shillings on the boy Hulston or ten days' imprisonment. The penalty in the other boys case was slightly lesser at 10s or a week's imprisonment.

However, not wishing his boy to start out in life with a criminal record or prison sentence, George Hulston stunned the court, by handing a Treasury note to his son. Hulston indignantly remarked —*"Here, take that home to your mother to explain and I'll do the time for you. Nobody will be fined here!"*

The second boy's father was given time to pay the fine at his own request and seemed quite stunned that a small coal theft by boys had resulted in the imprisonment of his colleague. Hulston walked off angrily to the cells.

INJURED IN BANANA ACCIDENT

On Saturday afternoon of 11th August 1934, at the Whistleberry Bridge, Blantyre, a motor delivery lorry belonging to Messrs Elder & Fyffe, banana merchants, Motherwell, was involved in a smash, and the driver had a remarkable escape from serious injury.

The lorry swerved to avoid a collision with another car and cycle, and ran on the pavement for a considerable distance, and then glanced off an electrical standard. It was hurled right across the road, and came to a halt against the five-foot iron rails at Springwells. The lorry was loaded with boxes of bananas, and these were scattered all over the road. William Cleland, residing at 6 Gladstone Street, Burnbank, who was walking on the pavement, was caught by the falling boxes, and was injured on the head but later was able to proceed to his home. The driver, fortunately, escaped without injury.

POLICE HEARD THROUGH PHONE

Stephen Walker of 31 Forrest Street used some ingenuity one evening in August 1935, when he became tired of hearing disorderly conduct outside his Low Blantyre home. The lewd and disorderly behaviour came from a nearby neighbour a Mr James McFaul of 18 Forrest Street who took it upon himself to use foul and loud language when returning home each evening from the pub.

Stephen, a commercial traveller, desperately in need of some sleep, called upon a new device installed in his home. He used his new telephone and called the police. Holding the handset up to the window, he made sure the Blantyre Police officers on the other end of the phone could hear the language coming from McFaul on the pavement. James McFaul left before the police arrived but was apprehended shortly after. The Justice imposed a court fine of 30 shillings or 15 days imprisonment. I wonder if James even knew how he had been caught.

PLAYING AT BAIRDS ROWS

Figure 204 Pete Smith at Baird's Rows 1955

Lets go back now to 1955. Pictured out the back of Baird's Rows (Craighead Miners Rows) is little Pete Smith.

His brother Anthony Smith shared the picture and the family lived in the raws in that era.

Whilst his father took the photo, little Pete had made a slide out of crates and planks of wood, clearly enjoying himself and making his own entertainment.

I look at this and wish kids today would return to playing outside and the simple pleasures of childhood. We've become a nation obsessed with 'soft parenting', protecting our kids from learning about freedom of play outside.

Lets put down the gaming consoles for a moment for some fresh air and outside fun!

CHAPTER 11
BROOMPARK & LARKFIELD

The area of Broompark generally centres along and branches off Broompark Road, so named because of the former farm "Broompark" once farmed by the Rocheads. Broompark links Barnhill at Bardykes Road all the way to Main Street in High Blantyre and has some public buildings like St John Ogilvie Church along its route. Larkfield is the area were now High Blantyre Primary School, Carrigans, Watson Street and the shops at the top of Stonefield Road are. There is a public hall with that name at the top crossroads on Stonefield Road. It's a small area, but with a defined identity and several interesting stories and photos, it's worthy of inclusion into this book.

Pictured in the cover photo above around the turn of the 20th Century are the end homes on newly constructed Broompark Avenue. At the door stands a member of the Ritchie family. The photographer was David Ritchie, who would later move to Main Street. To the right were farm fields, this exclusive new picture being a full 20 to 25 years before Kirkton Park was laid out.

BREAKING GROUND FOR RAILWAY

The ceremony of breaking ground on the under section of the Strathaven Railway took place on Tuesday 4th May 1858 at the farm of Broompark, Blantyre, the property of John Gardiner, Esq. Under the direction of the engineer acting on the line, a number of the adjacent proprietors and landowners whom the novelty of the occurrence had attracted were also present.

The occasion was to mark the commencement of construction of the Blantyre sections of the Strathaven railway, which would connect Low to High Blantyre with the formation of a new station and good connections. Blantyre at the area of Broompark was then just fields, with one or two homes and substantial earthworks would be required to elevate the railway with ground rising gently between Low and High Blantyre.

On that day, 160 years ago, the first barrow of soil put into operation on the line was ceremoniously filled by Alexander Gardiner, Esq. of Priestfield. Alexander was an eighty two year old, 'stalwart navvy' and when he had filled the barrow, it was then manfully wheeled away to its destination by his kinsman (father of the owner of Broompark) being nearly an Octogenarian also. The efforts and courage of the two old gentlemen was applauded by all the spectators.

To good health

Mr William Johnstone, baker of High Blantyre proposed a toast to the health of the two elderly men, the oldest navvies in Blantyre and to work on this new line, and suggested they should both go and get 'enthusiastically drunk' after the opening event. Amongst other toasts, recorded, the health and success of the spirited contractors (Messrs. McDonald & Grieve) was given, and Mr McDonald responded in a very friendly, humorous way. He hoped that during the progress of the work, the greatest good feeling would exist between the contractors and the surrounding population and he assured all that he would promote peace and goodwill during the process.

He was aware that navvies, generally speaking, were not in very high repute. They were not, certainly, the most refined class of her majesty's subjects, but indomitable vigour and perseverance were necessary elements in this undertaking.

The Contractor told people to perhaps put up with or "turn a blind eye to" a little rollocking behaviour as the navvies ended their shifts each evening, as long as there were no offensive intentions! It was perhaps an indication that Mr McDonald knew his workers well already and that he was setting the scene for what he knew would happen! In conclusion, he toasted the "Prosperity of Blantyre and its inhabitants." The meeting dissolved amidst expressions of friendship and good humour.

Where did this take place? Looking at the former position of Broompark Farm and the position the railway was built on next to it, we can confidently state this ceremony took place around this area pictured at Broompark Road, (opposite side of John Ogilvie Chapel).

GIRL CYCLIST KILLED

On Wednesday 8th August 1934, Mary Brodie Paterson, the 16-year-old daughter of Mr A. Paterson, of 73 Broompark Road, High Blantyre, was fatally injured when the cycle she was riding was involved in a collision with a motorcycle ridden by a young man.

I recall quite some time ago being told about this, and that the accident allegedly happened on Main Street near Auchinraith Road junction. However, that's all the details I could find. If you know more about this tragic incident, please do get in touch.

COLE FAMILY AT LARKFIELD

Margaret Clark shared this photo saying, *"Hi, I have an old picture of Blantyre folks that I thought may be of interest. It was taken behind the Larkfield Bar in Blantyre (as the family lived above the pub). My Gran (Margaret Cole) is the youngest in the photo and was born in 1921 so I estimate the picture was taken in the late 1920's. The Cole family were all born in Blantyre and in the photo back row: John, Patrick, Ellen & James. Front Row, Philip, John Cole (my great grandfather) Margaret (my gran) and Annie (my great grandmother). My mum was actually born above the pub but her parents moved to Ashley Place and I was brought up in Ashley Place/ Birch Place. "*

Figure 205 The Cole Family during the 1920's at Larkfield, Blantyre

The Larkfield Bar was where the Doonin now is located at the bottom of Watson Street. By 1925, John Cole and his family lived at 40 Watson Street, Larkfield (beside the pub). He was renting the house from William Dixon who owned the colliery Pit 4 opposite. John is noted as being a miner in 1925 and was paying £10 and 6 shillings per year in rent for his family to live there.

This would have been a fairly grimy place to live in the 1920's. Directly opposite the colliery, the dust from coal and Bing would have landed on most steps and pavements. My grandmother who lived at the Danskin's shop at the cross opposite the road fro this location would tell me once that her family had a never ending task of continually cleaning the steps and windows, overlooking the Bing.

CAUSEYSTANES DAIRY

Hamish Dow shared this excellent photo adding, *"I attach a photo taken outside the Causeystanes Dairy, 9 Broompark Road around 1935. The photo shows my Great Grandmother M Dow (née McLauchlan) on the left with my Aunt Rosemary Scobbie (née Dow) in the centre. I'm not sure if the gentleman on the right is my Great Grandfather Malcolm Dow. If it is, he is the father of Dan Dow the butcher who had his shop on Main Street, High Blantyre.*

Figure 206 The Causeystanes Dairy, Broompark Road, 1935

My Great Aunt Lizzie Lawson (née Dow) worked in the dairy and continued working when Mary and Joe Hobson bought it) My aunt Lizzie continued with her shopping expertise when she worked for Jim Wilson in his general store on the corner of Main Street and Victoria Street. My aunt Lizzie was a character, great in body and wit. She was affectionately called Lizzie Dow all her days – a usage that didn't really upset her husband, Uncle Billy. The Lawsons lived with my Great Grandmother and Great Uncle Jock Dow in the tenement building opposite the cemetery on Cemetery Road until they moved to a council house in Muir Street.

In the 1970's, I had the privilege of being appointed the Resident Engineer for the East Kilbride Expressway construction. Not only did I help to bypass my birthplace, taking the heavy traffic off Main Street, but I also removed the last surface traces of Dixons pit where three of my family (Sneddons) died in the explosion of 1877. My parents left 1 Small Crescent (the house with the monkey puzzle tree) for Quarter in 1974. My father, Malcolm Dow still retained a presence in High Blantyre."

Wanting to add a little more, I found out that in 1935, Malcolm Dow was the tenant of the shop and the house above. The shop was the only one in that entire row of tenements. All the other parts of that property were homes on the ground and upper floors. Malcolm was renting the shop and house from Robert Stewart, the owner who lived remotely at Cambuslang, the trustee of James Aitkenhead, the previous owner. Malcolm's annual rent for the shop was £22 and 11 shillings per annum that year. Today, the dairy would have been on Broompark Road, at the entrance to the carpark, just behind Blantyre Family Dentist & William Hill.

PLANTING TREES AT LARKFIELD BING

On Friday 10th March 1978, two councillors put their backs into it along with more than a little help from dozens of local schoolchildren, to make Blantyre a more beautiful place.

Figure 207 High Blantyre and St Blanes Pupils planting trees at Larkfield Bing, 1978

This was the scene that day when local Councillor Mr George McInally (left) and Hamilton District Provost Charles Brownlie helped plant the first of many trees all around the border of the former Dixon's Bing at Larkfield. The pupils of High Blantyre Primary and St Blanes Primary rolled up their sleeves to finish the job, moving from one tree to another in holes, previously dug by the council. This was all part of the Council plan to restore the area back to beauty and provide a lasting green plan for the future. The venture was widely publicised and gained support from all the community, but did not get off to a good start. Like many things in Blantyre in 1978, the trees were immediately vandalised, almost all of them uprooted. These trees are still there and their trunks today exceed a metre in circumference. This one pictured (on Broompark Road, next to Collins Bakery with High Blantyre Primary School car park in the background) is now very sizeable!

REAR OF ROBERTSON'S BUILDING

This photo dates to the 1950's, taken at the back of Robertson's Building at the top of Stonefield Road. The houses were directly opposite the Larkfield Bing, where now the Larkfield shops are. Shared here by Bill Duncan, this is a rare, expanded view of the 3-storey tenement building viewed from the back.

Figure 208 Duncan and Savage Families at Robertson's Buildings, Stonefield Road 1950's

Bill's mother is to the left and fellow neighbours, Mrs Savage and family to the right. The buildings ran in a northeast to southwest direction and had open fields of Broompark Farm beyond and out the picture to the right. The back yards must have received a lot of sun during the day and been a lot more pleasant than looking out the front windows to the former Dixons Larkfield colliery.

CHAPTER 12
ANECDOTES & LOCAL MEMORIES

Throughout writing this book, I've been collecting local comments, memories and anecdotes from kind people who were willing to share. From sad and happy tales to witty lines and memories as always Blantyre likes to get vocal about its history. This final chapter gathers the comments people have kindly provided via email, discussion and social media, between summer 2015 and summer 2018. Pictured in the header above, for the first time seen exclusively here are the former terraced gardens surrounding the old Quoiting Green at Auchentibber. The earthworks profile is still visible today, observed from beyond the War Memorial looking west.

First up, I asked who could remember the Stonefield Public Park it is prime.

Elaine Speirs told me, *"I remember paddling in the Stonefield Public Park pool in plastic sandals. The park was beautiful back then, full of flowers and great things for the kids. I remember the rowing boats and the paddle boats you could hire on the big pond too with Punch & Judy shows in the summer."*

Elaine Hutchison added, *"I mind the swings they were so high. The chute was super slippy as we used the wrapper from a mother's pride plain loaf to make it so!"*

Michelle Nicholson said, *"Loved the park when I was younger, remember the gala days? It was mobbed, sun was always shining and the park was great with the boating pond. Such a shame to see the changes from then till now."*

John Cornfield commented, *"I played down the paddling pool every summer. As a wean I don't remember much broken glass in the paddling pool, occasionally a cut foot. We'd walk down from Camelon Crescent with just swimming trunks budgie smugglers! Most of the times with no shoes* *on! Seems hard to believe now but we there was water drinking fountains all over the park, a piece on jam or if Mam was flush it was butter and jam and that was us all day. In the summer holidays no sun tan lotion, nothing. Oor James, the Allan's, the Murrays, Steff Brownlie, Mick Lennon all the boys from Camelon. The park then in the 60's and 70's was in its heyday as well as paddling pool boating pond putting green. Beautiful flower beds all over it, the big draughts / chess board up at the Cowan / Wilson arch and two sets of swings and chutes and roundabouts. The top Park also had a horse that I split my head on and was taken over to Doctor Cassidy's house in Station Road to get stitches without an anaesthetic. Happy days."*

Attention turned next to some funny stories and recollections.

Paul McBain shared, *"My family are from the old village and I always loved this story. A shopkeeper used to be known locally as 'Heid First' as his real name above his shop was 'R. Slater'. That's just pure Blantyre humour at its best!"*

Angela McGuigan told us, *"The Stones Hotel was very much a large part of my childhood from first holy communions to Christmas dinners. The owners at the time Ian and his wife (can't recall her name unfortunately) used to give me all the records out the jukebox when they changed them and let me wash the glasses behind the bar. I always left with pockets full of change from the punters and also learned how to play pool and dominoes great memories!!"*

Keith Black said, *"My grandfather owned the Black Baker Blantyre shop and bakery. I used to visit the shop with my Mum and then go to the bakery where I was interested in the cats that lived amongst the bags of flour. They had one job and that was to keep the mice and rats away. Not very health and safety by today's standards but they did the job. I wanted to play with them but they were feral so all you could see was the little eyes hiding amongst the darkness of the store area. The smell of fresh bread still brings back many memories of that bakery."*

Gord Fotheringham recalls, *"I remember having loved ones come to visit Friday to Sunday. We were not a very big family but the fun we all had was to last a lifetime! After WW2 we took oor big gramophone record player oot oan the street. The Village Bar emptied oot to a glabor dance. Oh it wiz gratifying! Ah wiz only a wee boy...now I'm an elder to most people. The memories of the village I grew up in will be with me forever. Mick 'Snowy' Rouse, Jim Brankin, Mick Milligan, John Coby McGuire tagie Mullin, Jimmy Rooney. The priory where we as children played and then worked in the tottie pickin. All jist memories now. The roarin fire when anyone came was a welcome to all who entered. Never a dull moment. We were family back then. Now we are jist distant relatives. Shame on us.*

In the village where my parents settled down no one could pronounce our family name, so everyone who knew us referred to us as the furnIngram's. Ma da's nickname was "big furnie" so my big brother was called "wee furnie". My grandmother's name was Mcgrorty, but in the village it was Mcgourty. In the village you could call out someone's name and you would get them to answer. My mother who's married name was Fotheringham, was still called Cathy Mcgourty."

A person who wishes to remain **anonymous** said, *"Roughly around 1985 when 'Nightmare on Elm Street' film first hit the Cinema, a resident of the aforementioned Elm Street dressed up as scary, 'Freddy Kruger' for Halloween. He waited for some poor soul coming home from the 599 club which was formerly known as the Masonic hall (The Cobblers Club). The poor soul cut across from Elm Street over the back doors into Auchinraith Road. However, Freddy was there waiting to give him a fright, but it was all to go horribly wrong. Freddy jumped out on to the poor unsuspecting soul and instead of giving him a proper scare, Freddy had jumped into a garden* *washing line, nearly strangling himself. It was pitch black and as the poor soul was screaming in fright, Freddy was frantically trying to untangle himself. Elm Street and Auchinraith Road was in fits of laughter with this story and as such, to this day 'Freddy Kruger' has never revealed himself. Haha!"*

Senga Arbuckle had a good story. She said, *"The old cemetery at High Blantyre kirk has an archway on the wall across from the Cornerstone pub. Above the arch there's an inscription. My mum was born just around the corner in 1937 and she would ask her gran what it said. Her version of it was that it said, "Don't eat chewing gum, dirty, dirty chewing gum. That's what brings you here (cemetery)" From then on, my mum wouldn't put a piece of gum in her mouth"*

Sadie Crawford (nee Ennis) added her story. *"Around the mid 1950's, the first houses were completed in Coatshill Avenue. Such excitement! We were moving in from the prefabs across from the industrial estate. So excited because we had an upstairs. I was 6 years old. Poor mum and dad struggled to carry the tallboy upstairs and it was so heavy they nearly dropped it. The got it eventually to the top landing and the door of it swung open and out popped my older, eight year old sister Delia. A few choice words were said!!!! Hilarious!"*

And last and *very much the least,* here are a couple of my own little anecdotes....

During the mid 1980's a new men's product came out in local shops. The "Just for Men", or "Grecian 2000", hair dye as it was then. Of course as a teenager I didn't need to bother about such things back then, but I did take great delight with friends in sometimes swapping the blonde dye packs with pure black packs whilst in Boots! The dye was usually the same colour, despite the outcome so nobody would have realised until it was too late! A silly thing to do on reflection but causing some mischief to middle aged men seemed like a good idea at the time!

*One winter's evening in 1987, I was walking along Calder Street as a sixteen year old, with my friend (one of the Leggate twins), when we heard an almighty roar from just around the corner. To our absolute horror, a huge gang of similar aged males came running over to us, carrying batons, sticks, baseball bats and the like. This is it, I thought. We're dead. One of the guys approached us, with hate and aggression all over his face screaming loudly a foot from our faces, "Are you from Blantyre or Burnbank?" I looked at my friend. This was a 50/50 outcome. We were in Blantyre at the time of course, and near the junction of Boswell Drive, were pretty far into Blantyre, far from any Burnbank boundary, so we simply said, "Blantyre". There was a pause and the guy the screamed, "Right! Great, Let's go get those Burbank B*****ds!" We didn't join their mob, but left quickly knowing how that could have gone very, very differently.*

During the late 1980's, I used to own an old black Ford Escort Van. It was a cheap first vehicle for me and like typical young man, I spent much time repairing the bodywork, usually with fibreglass and repairing compound. Things "got serious" for my safety when one day I could see the road whizzing by in the passenger floor below the seat. It was time to get scrap it quick. I headed to Mount Vernon to a scrapyard and whilst sitting at the lights, a vehicle smacked into the back of me, causing the rusted bumper to fall off. Remember, I was actually on my way to scrap the car and had just 35p on me to get the bus back home. The girl driving the car behind burst into tears when she saw the bumper. I told her not to worry, we exchanged details and I turned round and drove home. Three weeks later, I receive a cheque for £300 from(now defunct) insurers. It was a legitimate claim, if not unexpected. I remember clearly, the very next day, I promptly headed back to Mount Vernon, where I got just £25 for scrapping the entire redundant van! When I retold this story, my brother said, "Doesn't surprise me. You're so jammy! You could fall into the river and come back up with two massive Salmon in your hands!"

AND FINALLY

Website: You can read more history about Blantyre at www.blantyreproject.com where there are over 5,000 individual stories and articles and approximately 12,000 old photos of Blantyre's past, being added to daily. The website is proving popular and as far as I'm aware, continues to be the largest factual and free collection of Blantyre's history online. Thousands of people have contributed to the website, which is receiving record daily visitors.

Facebook: Currently in 2018, Paul Veverka is also on social media with frequent daily posts at www.facebook.com/TheBlantyreProject

Please do keep sending in photos and stories. There's so much more history to tell and remarkable events and stories being uncovered on a daily basis. Anything at all Blantyre related 'peaks my interest!' Your enthusiasm for reading more, your time and efforts in scanning and sending in items and of course my on-going motivation will drive me further in ensuring each new book is of the utmost quality.

Once again, I've thoroughly enjoyed my latest delve into Blantyre's history, met some fabulous people and seen further kindness I never imagined could exist. I leave you with the same message as previous Volumes:

"Without the warm stories of Blantyre's history and heritage, without unconditional kindness to neighbours and creating a sense of community pride and understanding that this is where we are from, we would truly have nothing of any real, lasting value to pass to our children".

Paul Veverka, November 2018

ABOUT THE AUTHOR

Paul D Veverka is a local Blantyre businessman with an active & growing widespread interest in all aspects of History & Community life in the South Lanarkshire town.

Born in 1971, Paul is the eldest of four children of Josef and Janet Veverka (both dec) from whom he inherited his growing interest in the history of Blantyre.

Married, with a young daughter, he is a former Chairperson of Blantyre Community Committee and employed in the Construction Industry on a full time basis as a Commercial Manager working on such major projects as the Queensferry Crossing and Aberdeen Bypass. He is also owner and author of the monthly Blantyre Newspaper, "The Blantyre Telegraph", a non-profit organisation that is voluntary run for local Blantyre good causes, to date raising over £20,000 for Blantyre. Paul is also sole organiser of the annual charity event, "Blantyre Oscars."

"The Blantyre Project – A Journey in Time Volume 4" is his long awaited fourth book in this particular series about the town and also represents the 9th book he's written to date.

Paul writes, "*This latest book in the popular series has been 3 years in the making. Taking care to promote accuracy, spelling and grammar, I hope readers can see the effort and dedication put into it, with a more mature and deliberate style of writing. With over 5,000 articles now on the Blantyre Project website exclusively researched, I was truly spoiled for choice with choosing what stories go into this latest publication. I'd like to thank each and every person who has bought a Blantyre Project book for his or her support, loyalty and interest, which only serves to drive me further. Rest assured, I'm nowhere near done with 'A Journey in Time'.* "

Paul Veverka, November 2018

REFERENCES

Research for this book was made possible not only with the assistance of the kind hearted people and businesses listed in the aforementioned Acknowledgments section, but also due to the excellent historical reference publications and organisations, namely as follows

"Blantyre – An historical Dictionary" by Neil Gordon 2004

"The Hamilton Advertiser" c/o Scottish & Universal Newspaper Group

"The Annals of Blantyre" by Rev A Stewart 1885

"High Blantyre Auld Kirk & Graveyard" by Blantyre Heritage Group

"Images of Scotland (Hamilton & Blantyre)" by Peter Stewart

"The Scotsman" Archives, The East Kilbride News Archives, The London Daily News Archives

The Mitchell Library, Glasgow

The Hamilton Town Hall Library, Hamilton

"Strother's Christmas & New Year Annual" 1910/1911

"A Blast from the Past" by Andrew Paterson

The Sunday Post Archives, The Daily Record Archives

The Paisley Herald & Renfrewshire Advertiser Archives

Edinburgh Evening News Archives

The Dundee Courier Archives, The Evening Post Archives

The Westminster Gazette Archives, The Caledonian Mercury Archives

The Evening Telegraph Archives, The Falkirk Advertiser Archives,

The Blantyre Gazette Archives

The Blantyre Telegraph (Facebook page), The Blantyre Project (Facebook page)

Old Ordnance Survey Maps – Stonefield, Bothwell & Blantyre. The 1897 Godfrey Editions.

Blantyre Old Parish Magazines

The Auchentibber School Register

"The History of Crossbasket Castle", by Paul Veverka

Historic Hamilton website by Garry Lee

The British Newspaper Archives

National Trust for Scotland & The David Livingstone Centre

New Calderglen Care Home

Gilmour's – Promotional Brochure 1904

Ancestry.co.uk, scotlandspeople.co.uk

Scotlandsplaces.co.uk, Livingstone Online

Geni.com ancestry website

Printed in Great Britain
by Amazon